JOURNEY INTO WHOLENESS

JOURNEY INTO WHOLENESS

PRAYER FOR INNER HEALING— AN ESSENTIAL MINISTRY OF THE CHURCH

Alan Guile

GRACEWING

First published in England in 2013
by
Gracewing
2 Southern Avenue
Leominster
Herefordshire HR6 0QF
United Kingdom
www.gracewing.co.uk

ISBN 978 085244 806 9

Typeset by Gracewing

Cover design by Bernardita Peña Hurtado

DEDICATION

I dedicate this book to my very dear wife Betty, who in 58 years of marriage played a great part in God changing me, and to all my wonderful four children and ten grandchildren.

CONTENTS

CHAPTER 8: MINISTRY TO PRIESTS AND RELIGIOUS...175

CHAPTER 9: THE CHALLENGE FOR THE CHURCH.....187

APPENDICES..215

Contents

PREFACE

My wife and I began to be asked to pray with people for healing in 1973, but we did not imagine that this would lead to my giving up my job eleven years later, so that we became available full-time for hundreds of people to come to our home for inner healing prayer. Nor did we expect to be asked to give teaching weekends and courses.

As the years went by we became grieved that some people came long distances because they could not find anyone available in their own locality. We could not understand why what we were doing was not also being done in every deanery if not every parish; because it seemed to us that it should be a normal part of being church.

In 2011, whilst preparing for a weekend course I had been asked to lead in another diocese, I began to examine what we had learnt about inner healing from too many others to thank them by name, in the light of the teaching of the Catholic Church. This led to writing a short paper in the hope that it might contribute to some in the Church taking this ministry more seriously and extending it. This was read by Fr Jim McManus, who suggested enlarging it into a small book in which testimonies were included. Since we had learnt so much from him over the nearly forty years that he has been ministering, teaching and publishing books in inner healing, it was clear that his advice must be followed. Until the moment I received his comments I had absolutely no thought of being able to write a book, but I began the next day.

After a few days I looked at the growing pile of manuscript and realised that as I did not have a computer I would need someone not only to type the book but also to check the clarity of writing. I prayed, 'Lord, please send me someone to help with the presentation'. That evening I attended intercessory prayer led by a lady who had read the short paper. She made exactly the same suggestions as Fr Jim and then said, 'My husband would like to help you with the presentation'. It is to him, Mike Webster, that I and anyone who reads the book owe a great deal of gratitude for his hard work, patience, good humour and kindness. In the final stages, Stephen Hornsey's technical expertise was very welcome in helping to meet the publisher's guidelines. I am also grateful to Dr Petroc Willey and to Rev Robin Fletcher for reading the manuscript and for helpful comments, and of course to the many people whose testimonies are included.

Most significantly though, I wish to give heartfelt thanks for the patience, wisdom and love of my late wife, to whom I owe more than words can ever express. Our experiences together inform every page.

Ultimately, this book has only been made possible by the power of God Himself. I hope and pray that people will be blessed by reading it, and that it may play a part in more and more suffering people being able to receive Christ's powerful ministry, as the Church discovers afresh the depths of the mission given to it by the Lord, and actively seeks to make them real and available in the local community.

FOREWORD

Professor Alan Guile tells us that 28 years ago he and his wife Betty were commissioned for their ministry of healing by their parish priest and confirmed in it by their bishop. They were probably the only couple in England to receive such a call to this ministry by a bishop. Alan and Betty faithfully, prayerfully and zealously carried on their ministry in their home for almost thirty years.

This book by Professor Guile, unlike his many scientific papers and text books in Electrical Engineering, was the fruit, not of long hours of academic study and research, but of over '10,000 hours of listening' to those who came to his home or his retreats and conferences for help. He learned this new art in his retirement from being a Professor at Leeds University, namely, the art of listening to the pain and the trouble that can rob a human heart of peace and joy. He comments encouragingly for the rest of us, 'I would never have picked myself as a possible candidate for something which involves a great deal of listening… Truly, God picks the most unlikely people, in human eyes, because He puts his treasure in earthen vessels (2 Co 4:7) in order to show that it must be His power which is at work.' Indeed he tells us how 'at one of the lowest points in my life when I felt completely useless,' God worked a great miracle of transformation in the person who had almost run away from him.

In this book you will hear many voices, the voices of the hundreds of men and women who received deep inner healing through the power of the Holy Spirit as Alan and Betty listened prayerfully to their stories and prayed with them. Alan gives them centre stage to share their own story with us. You will be deeply moved as you read how they came from a state of brokenness to wholeness, from painful self-rejection and self-condemnation to grateful self-acceptance, from the prison of negativity to the freedom of true love for self and others. One voice recalls, 'As God gives me the grace to accept my loss over and over, I find not emptiness but fullness'.

The Holy Spirit gifted Alan and Betty with the wisdom they needed for their ministry. This is highlighted in the testimony of one lady: 'Alan and Betty have taught me that we need to be real before God—He is big enough to take our anger, lack of faith, admitting our pain and uncertainty, our jealousy and resentment. None of us can move from human frailty and sin to trust and acceptance on our own—it is purely grace, God given.'

There is something in this book for everyone. If you are picking up a book on Christian healing for the first time you will be amazed and delighted by what you will read here; if you have already experienced the ministry of healing in your life, your faith and trust in God's promise will be renewed; if you are a priest or minister or lay pastoral leader, you will be inspired to open your ministry in new ways to the power of the Holy Spirit. This book is rich in pastoral wisdom and good pastoral theology.

Professor Guile's book appears at a providential moment in the Church's history. Pope Benedict XVI has called for the Celebration of a Year of Faith in thanksgiving for the 50th anniversary of the beginning of the Second Vatican Council. He has also put the New Evangelisation at the very forefront of the Church's awareness as it reads the signs of the times. This book will give us all greater courage to speak about the Good News that Jesus brings to us, especially when He describes His own mission as 'binding up the broken heart' (Lk 4:16). That is precisely what this book is about, about how the Lord shares his ministry of binding up the broken heart with us.

Fr Jim McManus CSsR
St Mary's
Clapham Common
London
SW4 7AP

INTRODUCTION

'Blessed be the God and Father of our Lord Jesus Christ, who has blessed us in Christ with every spiritual blessing in the heavenly places.' (Ep 1:3)

We have in the Catholic Church all that Christ needs to give us. Above all, the constant presence and power of the Holy Spirit, and the power available through all the sacraments, particularly the real presence of Christ in the Holy Eucharist. This makes present the one sacrifice of Christ, by which through God's infinite and utterly unfathomable love for each one of us, His beloved children, we are saved and offered healing of all our sin and wounds. We have the clear mission and authority given by Christ in the Scriptures to give the Good News and to heal. We have written evidence—Tertullian, Origen, St Eugenia, for example—that up to about 325 AD the Church carried on the mission of Jesus in healing and deliverance. We have the present day teaching of Vatican II, of the Catechism, of the most recent popes, including the statement of our present Holy Father, that 'Healing is an essential dimension of the apostolic mission'.[1]

Yet, in this country today, and perhaps in many others, particularly in the West, it is difficult for someone, realising that they need prayer ministry for healing, to find people within reasonable range who are called by God into this ministry of God's love. Even worse, most of those in the Church have never been told what Christ longs to do to release them from their agonies, and the necessary expectant faith that He can do so has not been sufficiently fostered. It is no wonder that Francis MacNutt published a book in 2005 entitled, 'The Nearly Perfect Crime—How the Church Almost Killed the Ministry of Healing'.

There can be no suitable analogy for such a sad and complex situation. Suppose, however, it became known to the general public that in dealing with a particularly widespread and virulent disease, the hands of their GPs and hospital doctors were tied, because crucial parts of the treatment which would cure it were never taught in the medical schools, although the information was there in published research. There would be an immediate outcry leading to the swiftest possible action. We are dealing here with the worst possible disease known to man—sin!

Two big obstacles to effective action are unawareness and fear. A deep-seated need to be in control (which is in virtually all of us to a greater or lesser degree), is also involved, but the root of this is fear. We find it very difficult to let go of control to God and to trust Him more and more totally. Many times, priests have said they were taught nothing about healing and deliverance in the seminary. Some have thanked me for involving them and helping them to learn more. A number of others, when asked to deal with or help with a deliverance, have said, 'I'm afraid to do it—you do it'. Priests need help to prepare for this important part of their mission. It can help to lighten their heavy burdens, as the Lord shows them those lay people whom He has chosen to work with them for souls, and then equips and empowers them all to work in partnership.

Many years ago I wrote to the then bishop of another diocese, saying that a lady from his diocese had come to us for help, and we felt that she needed deliverance and that it would be wise for a priest to deal with her particular case. We advised her to go to the main exorcist of our diocese, and she did go, though it involved her in a very long journey. I asked the bishop, 'The next time someone from your diocese is in this position, to which priest do you advise me to send them?' I never had a reply, though two priests of that diocese told me that the bishop spoke to them about my letter. Years later, when I checked, that diocese still did not have a single appointed exorcist.

In 2000, the Congregation for the Doctrine of the Faith issued the *Instruction on Prayers for Healing*,[2] signed by Cardinal Ratzinger and approved by Pope John Paul II. In 2001, the Pontifical Council for the Laity, together with the International Catholic Charismatic Renewal Services, convened a meeting in Rome of eighty-seven invited partici-pants, presided over by Cardinal Stafford, in order to discuss the healing guidelines set out in the Instruction. When the proceedings were published in 2003, the 320-page book of invited papers included some which connected with inner healing e.g. psychological healing; false spirituality and 'alternative healers'; and exorcism and deliverance. However there was only one paper, of just seven pages, dealing entirely with inner healing. In this paper,[3] Fr Raniero Cantalamessa, Preacher to the Papal Household, began:

> Spiritual healing means, first of all, healing from sin. The term inner or spiritual healing usually signifies the healing of something that, though in itself it is not a sin, has a link with sin either as its result or as its cause or as an incentive to sin; or it signifies healing of a state or situation which has nothing to do with sin, but which

prevents, nevertheless, the full flowering of the life of grace. This kind of healing is presented by Jesus as an integral part of His messianic message when He says: 'The Spirit of the Lord is upon me because He has anointed me to bring the Good News to the poor. He has sent me to announce release to the captives, and recovering of sight to the blind, to set at liberty those who have been bruised, to proclaim a year of favour from the Lord'. (Lk 4:18–19)

As this book will show from thirty-nine years of personal experience with many people, the process of praying for inner healing is nothing less than allowing the Holy Spirit to sanctify us by leading us through deepening relationship with Jesus Christ, towards our becoming more and more holy, as He heals us of sin and its effects. It will be shown that this ministry is an essential complement to the sacraments.

More and more people are coming forward in search of healing. As I write this, aged 87, in the year following the death of my wife, the number of sessions in my home for listening and praying for inner healing, each of about two hours, has risen by 50% above the yearly average of just over two hundred, which it had been for the previous twenty years. More will come from the New Evangelisation—the Church's mission, at the call of Pope Benedict XVI, to re-evangelise the West, including—in the words of Archbishop Eterovic, when he gave a press conference in the Vatican to present the *Lineamenta*, 'those who have moved away from the Church, and those who have been baptised but not sufficiently evangelised'.

Sometimes people in the Church are not only in great need of being called into a much deeper personal relationship with Jesus, and new openness to the Holy Spirit, but are actually looking in wrong and dangerous directions, as I will discuss in Chapter 1. The Church needs to empower the clergy and the laity to meet these needs—always bearing in mind that priests, nuns, brothers and laity may well need healing of their own, as evidenced by the number who have asked us for prayer in our home or at our retreats, days of recollection and teaching weekends over the years. The more free we become from our own damage, the more use we are to other people, as we are led by God's Spirit to fulfil His work of love (Ep 2:4–10; 2 Co 1:3–5).

The purpose of this book, then, is:

- to highlight the significance of inner healing and deliverance ministry

- to show it is part of evangelisation, and therefore an essential ministry of the Church

- to encourage joint united ministry between priests and laity

- to raise consciousness of the need for urgent action by people at all levels in the Church

- to provide examples and testimonies of prayer working to help address the needs of suffering people

- to show that prayer for inner healing is directly connected to the call of Pope Benedict XVI for the New Evangelisation

The approach involves:

- describing how God, through my background and experiences, led me to healing

- exploring the underlying roots of damage leading people to seek healing

- showing how praying with others can be a potent tool, working with the sacraments, particularly the sacrament of Reconciliation, to free people from deep-rooted damage that they are suffering from the effects of sin—their own, or that of others.

- drawing upon extensive experience of cleansing people from all the effects of sin

- using case testimonies to illustrate the underlying causes of damage, and how they may be remedied by Christ, through loving prayer for the whole person—body, soul (mind, will and emotions) and spirit

- emphasizing the need of people for protection from evil

- discussing needs of the clergy in all these matters

- encouraging lay people to ask for God's love for their priests and to pray for them

Some may see this book as a handbook on healing, or a framework for action. Others may simply wish to consider their own lives in the light of the insights shared, and to seek healing for themselves. Some may realise that they themselves have the capacity and calling to become involved in the ministry of healing. Others may be in a position to institute change at a higher level.

It is my hope and prayer that all will find deep joy and wonder at the infinite love and mercy of God our Father for each one of His beloved children. If you should be called by Him to this wonderful privilege of praying with others for inner healing, then you will have the added joy of witnessing wonderful people emerging from their past hurts and limitations, and gradually becoming their real selves, under the awesome power of God's love. This book includes many testimonies, all written by people who were suffering in a variety of ways.

It is vital always to remember Christ's words: 'Without me, you can do nothing' (Jn 15:5). We have a Saviour, made present and real through the indwelling of the Holy Spirit, not a method or procedure. He can work most powerfully when we acknowledge our weakness and total dependence on Him.

Notes

1   Pope Benedict XVI, *Jesus of Nazareth—Part 1* (London: Bloomsbury Publishing, 2007), p. 176.

2   Congregation for the Doctrine of the Faith, *Instruction on Prayers for Healing* (2000).

3   P. R. Cantalamessa, 'Spiritual Healing' in *Prayer for Healing* (International Colloquium, Rome: International Catholic Charismatic Renewal Services, 2003), pp. 221–225.

1

A BRIEF OVERVIEW OF THE PRESENT SITUATION

Many Years of Past Experience

For thirty-nine years I have been praying with suffering and troubled but very wonderful people for their inner healing. For thirty-six of these years it was in partnership with my wife. Since her death, I have mostly been on my own. We have been available during the last twenty-eight years, for them to come to our home at any time of the week. This has led to learning more and more, and reflecting deeply about the nature of this ministry. In that time, over five hundred people have come for sessions which last for two hours (more when necessary), because they needed God's help in a vast variety of ways and situations (see Appendix 1). Most of them had been receiving the sacraments for many years.

Some have made journeys of several hundred miles in their need. They have included many priests and religious and some doctors, psychologists and a psychiatrist, and many have come from a variety of churches. Our parish priests and several bishops have given us invaluable support.

The insights gained by my wife and myself over this time have led to my present attempt to look at the needs of people, and how the Church could and should help them more. It will be shown that this ministry is an essential and inescapable part of the mission of the Church given by Jesus Christ, because it is part of evangelisation, leading towards complete conversion of heart and mind to Christ, and sanctification through the Holy Spirit.

Over the last forty years or so there have been various opportunities in the Catholic Church throughout the UK for people to ask for prayer ministry for healing. Those have been mostly at conferences, retreats, days of renewal, healing services, or after a Mass which has been celebrated with a particular emphasis on healing.

Various limitations on such occasions have generally meant that such ministry has only lasted from a very few minutes up to perhaps twenty minutes. We have ourselves taken part in all these ways for nearly four decades. We have witnessed some physical healings which occurred at the time or very soon afterwards. It is more difficult to be sure about the nature and extent of inner healings because these need to be assessed by knowledge of changes in the person's behaviour over months or indeed years, following any prayer.

Generally, those praying and those asking to be prayed with may live miles apart, so that follow-up was difficult and unlikely. As far as we could tell from the small number of people with whom we could have real long-term contact, we were only aware of a small number of clear, lasting inner healings following a single session of prayer. Many of those who had brief prayer ministry may well have needed further continuing help over a considerable period, after they returned home. That help has not generally been readily available in their own parishes or anywhere within reasonable reach. This unmet need has been confirmed by very many who have come to our home.

It was only after the bulk of this book had been written, that I learnt that Pope Benedict XVI, in his book *Jesus of Nazareth*, had written: 'Healing is an essential dimension of the apostolic mission and of Christian faith in general.'

This is exactly the conclusion to which I had come, after reflecting on my many years of involvement in the inner healing of the deepest roots of all manner of human hurts brought about by sin, in the light of the teaching of the Church in *Evangelii Nuntiandi* written by Pope Paul VI, the Catechism and the documents of Vatican II. This will be discussed in more detail in Chapter 9.

As always, the truth is there in the Catholic Church, because Christ Himself, the Truth, is the root and source of the life of the vine. However, for very many people in the Church, it is as though the life-giving power has become blocked, and is not flowing out freely and completely to every furthest branch, in order to bring about the wonderful fruit in people's lives, for which Christ suffered and died. The poor are not always receiving the good news; the captives are not always being set free; the spiritually blind are not always being given sight; the oppressed are not always being released and unbound. In fact, too often, and in too many places, these things are hardly being experienced at all by suffering people. The difference between the theory in the teaching documents of the

Church, often couched in unfamiliar language and terminology, and the 'practice' out in the parishes is very often vast.

Only One Healer—Jesus Christ

Healing comes from God through the suffering of Christ on the Cross, 'through His wounds we are healed' (Is 53:5), and Chapters 6 and 7 develop this in relation to inner healing. Many of the members of the various health care professions are unaware of the part played by God as they use knowledge, skills and experience (Si 38:1–14). Others, outside these professions, can only say that God may choose to involve them occasionally, or in some cases in a more regular way, in the healing ministry through the gifts and power of the Holy Spirit. There is only one healer – Jesus Christ.

If we hear of anyone calling themselves or being styled as a 'healer' by others, then we should check very carefully indeed. Healings of physical conditions can occur through the power of Satan, using people involved in such things as spiritualism or Reiki or a number of new-age practices.

This was first brought home to me in the 1970s. Two priests of the Anglican Community of the Resurrection at Mirfield invited me spend a day with them. They needed to talk to me about their distress at the recent abrupt resignation of their Superior. Then, after lunch, they asked if I would drive them to the rectory at Emley Moor. They had been invited there for Christmas Day lunch by the rector, John Baker, who exercised a ministry of healing and deliverance. Because they were not free that day, but were free on Boxing Day, they had telephoned several times that morning, but had got the engaged tone. When we arrived at the rectory, we were told that the telephone had not been used that day, and I realised that I was being given the opportunity to meet John Baker, and to ask his advice about someone in our prayer group who might need deliverance. I also asked him by what power Harry Edwards healed. The latter was very well-known as a 'healer', and appeared on television to be a very kindly and well-intentioned man. I learnt later that he himself claimed to heal through the departed spirits of Pasteur and Lister when he spoke to the Anglican Archbishops Commission. John Baker replied that Harry Edwards healed by the power of Satan, and told me about one of his parishioners who had gone to Harry Edwards and received some physical healing. John said to her, 'I hope to heaven you or your family have not been affected by evil'. He asked her to come with her small son to his church, where they knelt at the altar rail. He told me that there was no outward sign when he laid hands on the mother and prayed with her. When he did this with the son, the small boy went down on the floor, threshing about, and he said to me, 'I had to deliver him of an evil spirit'.

Sadly, there are many who style themselves as healers or faith healers or spiritual healers. Many may genuinely believe that they are helping others. They may be deceived, or choosing not to become aware of the source of the power which they seem to exercise, or of consequent damage to their clients. I have met a number of Christians, including some Catholics, who have become deceived, for example into using Reiki healing. One such couple, when I spoke to them after Mass about this, defended their becoming Reiki masters by telling me that they had been taught in a Commonwealth country by a nun who was supported by the local bishop.

Two studies which examined these matters[1] reveal that, although people may receive an almost immediate healing of some infirmity, after a little while the apparent healing can be gone, and they are now worse off than before. They may now have added burdens of mental and spiritual distress, which can include depression and suicidal tendencies. One study states: 'In many respects, the Church's ministry of healing is the very antithesis of the popular view of 'spiritual healing', which sees it as a specialist's public activity to relieve physical suffering by miraculous or semi-magical means'.[2]

Slow Progress

I had talked to Francis MacNutt in Rome in 1975 about the conference on healing in Manchester, which those of us on the National Service Committee for Catholic Charismatic Renewal in England and Wales had asked him to lead later that summer. I said that I felt it was not meant to be solely about the people whom the Lord would heal through his prayer at the conference, but about its leading to a growing establishment of what would become a widespread healing ministry in the Church in the UK. I have been praying and longing for this ever since. I am still waiting in hope thirty-seven years later.

Things can move very slowly in the Church. For example, many years ago, a friend in another diocese felt, after very much prayer, that the Lord wanted her and others to set up a centre where people could come and stay for some days to receive prayer for healing. A number of others sharing her vision began to provide substantial amounts of money. A convent in her locality eventually came up for sale. When she saw it she burst into tears. She recognised it as the building which the Lord had revealed to her by a picture in her mind. This picture and discernment was then confirmed by several others. She consulted her bishop, who encouraged her to go ahead. She made a bid, of the amount which had been discerned in prayer, only to be overbid—by the diocese. The money donated was given back to the donors or, in some cases, they asked for it to be given to their chosen charity.

There is still today no Catholic centre in the UK, wholly and exclusively devoted to providing accommodation and ongoing prayer ministry, for inner healing of the whole range of human ills, provided by a united community. By contrast, there are a substantial number of such centres, with a residential community supported by others in the local area, scattered around the country, run by people, some ordained, belonging to Anglican and other churches. In 2000, the Anglican Church published a wide review of the ministry of healing, written by a group led by a bishop, but including also a psychiatrist, a psychologist and a psychotherapist.[3] It gave many recommendations. Every Anglican diocese has been encouraged to have a healing team, which may include advisers on healing and deliverance, as well as chaplains, psychiatrist and GPs. In the Catholic Church in the UK, there is no such structure or connection, either diocesan or national, by means of which someone needing healing can make contact with those who can help. We now look at what is available to them.

Need for Ongoing Prayer Ministry

A number of times I have been telephoned by someone, asking if I know of anyone in or near a particular town who has been called into a ministry of prayer like the one the Lord has so unexpectedly given to my late wife and myself. There may well be someone, but I have generally not been able to suggest anyone. If they can't find such ministry near them, then people may consider a retreat, course or conference at which prayer for healing is offered. However, many of those who come to our home would not be able to afford the cost involved, or would be unable to go away for several days because of family commitments.

God may manifest great power at any time He chooses, and it may be particularly evident when a substantial number of people gather to praise

Him at such retreats, courses and conferences, or at a Mass celebrated with the specific intention of healing. Often at these occasions, because of the numbers, the prayer ministry time with each individual may have to be quite limited. People may not have the opportunity to speak at any length about what is troubling them. It is true that the Lord has all knowledge and understanding and may, and often does, act powerfully through a brief prayer, perhaps in tongues or the use of a word of knowledge. Our experience has been, however, that because inner healing is generally a gradual process over a long period (for reasons discussed later in this book), people most often need ongoing ministry, preferably in their local area, available at any time and at no cost. What is important is not how people feel after attending some session of prayer ministry, but whether, over the following months and years, the fruits of the Spirit are growing in them and that they are experiencing blessings in their everyday lives and relationships, as they grow in faith in God and in inner peace. We ourselves have frequently led or taken part in a large number of residential retreats, conferences etc., and many people are greatly blessed by the Lord at these. Often, however, they realise—perhaps some time later—that ongoing ministry is also needed. Hence these two kinds of ministry are to be seen as complementary for those able to attend them. 'How might people obtain help and ministry in their local area?' is the question which is now addressed in the following sections.

Help through Small Groups

In their journey towards wholeness (holiness), people can receive love, help and support through coming together in small groups, where there is no pressure to share, but confidences are kept if they do choose to speak. It is so easy, particularly in the Catholic Church, to come to church regularly, perhaps even to daily Mass, and yet be unknown to others in the church.

We need the support and the prayers of others in the body of Christ. Most of us need to learn more about how we may be guided by the Holy Spirit in our prayers. It is only too easy, for example, to have become stuck unconsciously in an attitude of 'Please God bless me, and change this other person (or number of people) who make(s) my life difficult or seemingly impossible to bear'. God wants us to realise that the only person I have the right to want to change is myself, so that the prayer should become, 'Please God change me and bless this other person'. We can help one another to learn that those who make our life uncomfortable can be the means by which God is offering us an opportunity to bring our painful emotions to die with Christ on the Cross, and to receive from Him both the grace to forgive and experience more of His love for these others. These things, and much else about how the Lord wants to lead us further and further on the path leading to holiness, can be learnt with others in a group, particularly when the Scriptures play a significant role.

There are many varieties of small groups available where one can pray and learn about God's ways in different churches. They vary in how far they help people to grow in personal wholeness, so as to be able to reach out in loving service to others. It is vital, however, that confidences are not broken. Much damage can otherwise be done. Before going on to look at some ways in which people may find such support within their parish, we look first at help which can come from others in a similar situation, and from healthcare professionals.

The Importance of Mothers' Prayers

A high proportion of those who have come for help were women, with not only their own personal hurts and problems, but also with great distress and sadness about things which had happened, or were still happening, to their children or grandchildren. The variety of situations and pain and damage in families is vast. These women were more deeply wounded or affected by the hurts inflicted on their children and grand-children than they were about those which they themselves suffered in their own childhood or later life. Whilst writing this section, I have had a telephone call from a mother, some 200 miles away, with long-standing suffering over a child, who had hoped for more help from the Church, and who has arranged to travel to Norton for prayer ministry.

Testimony 1A (p. 25), written by a lady from another diocese, speaks of the great distress of a mother on learning that her two sons had sexually abused their own sister, and that she hadn't been able to discover it at the time so as to protect her daughter. This is followed in 1B (p. 26) by another mother expressing her pain at a rift in her family, and how important it was that she shared this in a small group and asked others to pray.

For twenty-seven years, we have given to many others and have ourselves prayed the following prayers each day for our own children, their spouses and our grand-children: 'In the name of Jesus Christ, I claim each one free from all the powers of the world and the powers of darkness, and in the name of Jesus Christ I put each one into the kingdom of God. I pray that Christ may be reborn in each one of them, that each may repent of their sins, may come to know Christ as their Saviour and Lord, and may experience the power of the Holy Spirit working in their lives. In the name of Jesus Christ and with the sword of the Spirit, I cut all the emotional bonds and soul ties between * and * Amen.'

Much of that prayer comes from our going to a FIRE (faith, intercession, repentance and evangelism) rally in Manchester in 1984. Four talks were given by four people, two of whom were priests from the USA. Ann Shields told the following story. She had received a phone call from a detention centre 2000 miles away in America. A 13-year-old girl had been arrested for drink, drugs and sex offences. She would not speak to any of the staff, but she had one of Ann's tapes, which she played under the bedclothes. She was overheard to say, 'Could God ever forgive someone like me?' They offered to pay for a monthly telephone call if both Ann and the girl were willing. The calls began and Ann asked a number of her women friends to join her in praying for this girl.

Some time went by, and Ann returned home one day to find the girl there, with two others. 'How did you leave the centre?' she asked, to be told that the girl had 'sprung' herself and the others out of detention. 'How did you travel?' 'We stole a car,' she was told. 'How did you pay for petrol?' 'When we ran short, we stopped the car, made signs to lorry drivers, had sex with them and got money from them.'

Ann was furious, and said something like she did not want to hear from her again until she had got herself right with God. Ann went into prayer, devastated that after so much intercession for the girl things had become far worse. She asked the Lord what had gone wrong. 'You never asked me how I was praying for her,' came the reply. 'How are you praying for her?' she asked, and the answer came: 'That she repents of her sins, comes to know me as her Saviour and Lord, and experiences the power of the Holy Spirit in her life'. Ann and the others then began to pray that way for the girl.

There were no more phone calls; no communication of any kind.

Some years later, Ann was a speaker at a conference. Several people wanted a word with her afterwards. Among them was a well-dressed young woman, who said, 'You don't remember me, do you?' Before Ann could reply, the girl said, 'I have repented of my sins [she even told her what they were], I have come to know Jesus as my Saviour and Lord, and I have experienced the Holy Spirit working in my life.'

Jesus is praying at the right hand of the Father for every one of their beloved children (Rm 8:34), and He loves them even more than mothers do. It seems likely that His prayer will always include these three vital parts: repentance, coming to know Him as Saviour and Lord, and experiencing the power of the Holy Spirit. We have strongly recommended this to many people, particularly mothers and grandmothers, giving them a laminated prayer card. This prayer can of course be prayed for anyone. The more deeply we allow the Holy Spirit to transform us towards union with Christ, the more likely we are to discern how He is interceding with the Father for that particular person or situation, and the greater the likelihood of our prayers being answered. Praying in the name of Jesus Christ is not a mere formula of words. We are meant by God to be coming into an ever-deepening relationship with Christ so that there is an increase in the likelihood of our prayers conforming with His prayers.

It can help people concerned for a child, and undergoing great suffering in this, if they know another mother or grandmother with whom they feel able to share deep concerns. They can agree to pray for one another's children. This is much easier than praying for one's own child, because we have no emotional bonds or soul ties with someone we may not even have met.

This is a wonderfully important ministry for mothers. In 1995, 'Mothers Prayers' was launched in England by two grandmothers who felt led by Jesus to pray in a special way for their children. Through prayer they learned that Jesus wishes all mothers to surrender their children into His care, so that He can take away pain from mothers and pour blessings on their children. 'Mothers Prayers' has spread throughout the world and is already in over 200 countries. There have been many wonderful answers to prayer. There are prayer groups of mothers of between 2 and 8 members, usually meeting weekly. There is confidentiality and trust as they share together and their burdens become lighter. They have produced a booklet of prayers. More recently, fathers and grandfathers have begun to meet as Fathers Prayers to pray for their families.

Medical Treatment and Counselling

We have always stressed that people should seek proper medical treatment, as well as prayer for healing. We have met people, some of whom came to us because harm was done by some Christian group, where they advised people to stop their medication and rely on God alone. These groups may have been unaware that one of the Apochryphal books devotes fifteen verses to the importance of doctors and pharmacists, and to their roles in God's plans (Si 38:1–15). Only a doctor should decide when to stop prescribed medication.

In the USA there has been growing awareness among many doctors that prayer for healing is important. One survey of 1100 physicians reported in December 2011 that 85% of them believed that spirituality and prayer aid in the recovery and wellbeing of those who are sick. 75% said that religion and spirituality, including prayer, help individuals to cope and maintain a positive outlook. Such awareness and evidence has been building up for years. In 1999, Dr Larry Dossey wrote, 'Courses on the role of religious devotion and prayer are currently being taught in approximately fifty US medical schools'.[4] Dr Elizabeth McSherry predicted, 'Hospitals nationwide could save as much as 4000 dollars per patient stay if they made better use of their pastoral care program'. She added that the cost per patient of salaried chaplains averaged only one hundred dollars.[5]

Other writers have made similar points:

> Research shows that rates of drug abuse, alcoholism, divorce, and suicide are much lower among religious individuals than among the population at large. People who practice religion are much less likely to suffer from depression and anxiety than the population at large, and that they recover more quickly when they do. Spiritual practices such as meditation, prayer, or participation in devotional services, have been shown to reduce feelings of anxiety and depression significantly, boost self-esteem, improve the quality of interpersonal relationships, and generate a more positive outlook on life.[6]

One doctor friend of ours advised a number of patients to travel twenty-five miles to us for prayer ministry alongside the medical treatment. A number came, and the doctor advised them to regard any prayer or scripture which we gave them in the same way as they would regard the drugs which she prescribed. Use them every day, not just when you feel like it or think of it. Two testimonies, 1C (p. 27) and 1D (p. 28), the first written by her and the other by a fellow-parishioner, give examples of God working both through the care and skill of doctors and through prayer at the same time.

Very many of those coming to us have simultaneously been going to a counsellor or psychologist. Particularly if they have been suffering with severe depression, they have frequently been under the care of a psychiatrist. We have asked them to check if their health care professional is entirely happy that they also want to go for Christian prayer. No one has ever raised any objection. The only difficulty which ever arose was when a couple asked us to have sessions with them both together and alone. When we began we did not know that they had gone to a counsellor of what was then the Catholic Marriage Advisory Council (now Marriage Care). When the latter discovered this, she was very angry with us, and accused us of unprofessional conduct because we saw someone who was coming to her. What the man had, at his first session, told us was that he had always found it difficult to get in touch with his emotions. Through CMAC counselling the emotions did come out, but he said he didn't know what to do with all this pain, and he felt that he had been left, in his words, 'raw and bleeding'. If one does not help people to bring their pain to Jesus on the Cross and ask Him in prayer to take it into His suffering, and receive His power to forgive, then their suffering can go on or seem to get worse.

It was particularly wonderful to see the change in one man who had for a long time been under a number of psychiatrists and psychologists. On his first visit he arrived in tears. For a number of sessions he would drop into a chair, saying 'Oh, I'm in a bad way; I'm in a bad way'. At his last few sessions we heard him whistling as he walked up the drive. We have seen many who have come out of depressions which had not been lifted by medication alone, despite care from many professionals. Often they kept seeing different psychiatrists, as the latter moved on to another post or were replaced by an assistant or locum, and these changes of carer did not help. Testimony 1E (p. 29), by a lady from another city, illustrates how both psychotherapy and prayer ministry can complement each other. Testimony 1F (p. 31) from a wonderful Christian lady who has done amazing work for others but who, later in life, needed herself to come to us for ministry, is an example of prayer and counselling working together.

There are many groups and organisations which use counselling therapy to try to bring healing to a particular area of need: marriage difficulties, drug and alcohol abuse, pre- and post-abortion, etc. Some indeed offer long-term residential rehabilitation. Where they are based upon faith in Christ, there is much greater opportunity to address the needs of the whole person, including spiritual, so that there is more likelihood of lasting wholeness and peace.

The personal accounts just given bear out the wisdom and need to seek professional medical help as well as prayer, rather than following the 'fundamentalist' approach of some Christians who tend to rely on prayer alone as a true test of faith. There is, however, great need to check carefully before going to practitioners of various alternative therapies, as illustrated in the section on protecting people from evil later in this chapter. Whilst seeking medical help for our body, and sometimes our mind, we would hope to find help for our soul and spirit in the Church, particularly in the first instance within our own parish, as we will now consider.

Prayer Ministry within the Parish

Some years ago, our newly appointed bishop was told of our ministry and asked us to see him. Our parish priest drove us to his house, and the bishop, having studied all our correspondence with his predecessor, had no questions or reservations and expressed his wish to see this ministry grow. At his request, we arranged meetings with those priests in the diocese who had been showing interest. As we drove back, our priest asked us if our teaching tapes (now CDs) could be used to begin a group in the parish. Interestingly, that very morning a lady from the parish in our home for ministry had made the same suggestion. And when I mentioned the idea to friend with whom I go walking each week, he said he had suggested it six months earlier. I had completely forgotten.

Our priest suggested that the group should meet in the Blessed Sacrament Chapel. It has now been in existence for several years, meeting on two evenings a week to give people a better chance to be free to attend. People have come from other places and churches and stayed for as long as they felt they needed to learn and share. Some have continued to come. The more that people meet in groups to share experiences, learn about the Lord's ways, and receive loving ministry for their own family concerns, the more help becomes available to them. As one lady put it: 'I have never known love in my whole life until I came into this group: I feel we are one.'

This group spends some evenings in intercessory prayer for such needs as the care of the elderly, those involved in police, social services and probation, those affected by addiction, and many other groups of people.

It also prays for individuals and families when asked to do so. Some years ago the members of the Guild of St Raphael in another city, who meet to pray for others, attended the group for a year to learn about praying for inner healing. Recently one member wrote to resign on leaving to live in another part of the country. In her letter she expressed her thanks to the group in Norton:

> They prayed that my daughter-in-law might locate and be reconciled with her brother whom she had not seen for some twenty years since her parents had divorced. About ten days later a few men from the council were standing in her road. She opened the door to see what was happening. One of them came up to explain—it was her brother. My grandsons now have another uncle, her mother a son and my daughter-in-law a brother. Thanks be to God and the group in Norton.

Three testimonies, 1G (p. 32), 1H (p. 32) and 1I (p. 34) all illustrate how vitally important such a group can be.

The Vatican II decree on the apostolate of lay people told us:

> The parish offers an outstanding example of community apostolate. The laity should develop the habit of working in the parish in close union with their priests, of bringing before the ecclesial community their own problems, world problems and questions regarding man's salvation, to examine them together and solve them by general discussion.[7]

The last three testimonies given at the end of this chapter all illustrate that people are far more likely to be affirmed, blessed and healed if they come together in small groups in their parish for prayer for God's help, rather than through discussion alone. It should also be within our own parish that we can learn about the protection which God gives us from evil, and this is discussed next.

Protecting People from Evil

As well as it being difficult for Catholics to find someone accessible who will pray with them for the healing of deep inner hurts, we haven't sufficiently proclaimed the good news of the victory of Jesus over evil, and we haven't always warned people sufficiently, or shown them enough love and care. Sadly, many—some Catholics among them—are turning to wrong and very dangerous people, places and practices in their search for help. Among these are Reiki healing, spiritualism, Ouija boards, fortune telling, horoscopes, Tarot or other card reading, clairvoyance, psychic healing and fairs. Some years ago we went with two priests and others on a pilgrimage to shrines in Ireland. Parishioners were passing horoscopes to one another on the coach. For many Catholics who simply attend Mass once a week, the opportunities for the priest to give teaching become restricted, perhaps only to the homily, or bulletin, so it is difficult for him, even if he is fully aware of these things. Sadly, many are not.

Years ago, at the request of one of our priests, we called on a young lady living almost opposite the church. We said that we were from St Joseph's. She said, 'I used to go there but now I go to the spiritualist church'. We said, 'It is against God's will, and very dangerous'. 'Yes,' she said, 'I know, because Fr ... told me, but they make me so welcome.' What an indictment of us. Thus people may, in their need and searching, run into grave danger because the Church and the individuals in it have not met their needs for love and help through Christ, and have therefore not brought them to a real understanding and experience of Christian faith and hope, and the experience of growing relationship with, and dependence upon, Christ.

An example of the very real dangers of going to spiritualist meetings occurred about this same time. When we first came to the parish in 1984, there was a weekly prayer group led by the parish priest. One evening, my wife suggested we should pray about, and actually go round the area containing the spiritualist church, situated about 100 metres away. Our parish priest said that, immediately after the prayer meeting, he would go out with holy water to pray, and all were welcome to join him. My wife and I went a day or two later, when they were holding a service. We walked on roads and paths right round it, praying all the while and using holy water.

Two days later, the priest called after us as we were leaving the church after Mass. He asked us to join him in the presbytery that afternoon to meet a lady. The night before, an Irish couple visiting this lady and her husband witnessed lights going on and off in the house without anyone touching the switches. Realising that there was something evil or wrong, the Irish man took this lady to the nearest Catholic church. The deacon there phoned our parish priest. The lady told us that she had been going to the spiritualist church near St Joseph's for eight years. It was only in the previous five weeks that she had begun to realise that something was wrong. One day, she had brought her grandson shopping and then came on to Norton by bus, to sit and pray in this spiritualist church. He went rigid and white and cold, and they had to leave. She said, 'I am now afraid to have any of my grandchildren in my own home'. She did not seem to have any Christian background, but we asked her if she would tell God she was sorry, ask for His forgiveness, renounce spiritualism, and invite Jesus to come into her life and take charge of it. She agreed and we prayed. We stressed the importance of never going back to the spiritualists.

She did not want us to contact her—she had an elderly husband whom she said she did not want disturbed. She asked for our phone number, and we also gave her (with their permission) the phone number of a couple living nearer to her. She made no contact with any of us.

A few years later, we were waiting for Mass to begin, when our curate came over to us. He said, 'At 3am this morning the phone rang. It was a lady who said that she was in trouble because of the spiritualist church. She said she saw a priest and two people. Are you the people?' We said that it sounded as though we were, and he asked us to come to the presbytery that afternoon. It was the same lady. She said, 'I had a great peace for some weeks after you prayed with me; then I went back to the spiritualist church'. Every few minutes she would say, 'Please stop talking. I have to listen to these spirits in my head. They are telling me that unless I kill myself, they will attack my grandchildren'. We prayed with her and repeated our advice, but sadly we never heard any more of her.

Several attempts were made by our priest, now retired, to warn people about the dangers and harm which can come to them and their families, through straying away from the commands of God, and from the all-sufficiency of the sacrifice and Resurrection of Christ. Two examples are now given of warnings which our parish priest asked my wife and I to write in the 1990s. One was on the front sheet of the bulletin; the other was enclosed in the bulletin. Yet there is some evidence today that some in the area have forgotten, or never taken full heed. Key questions spring to mind:

- How many parishes up and down the country have warned their people of the dangers into which they or their families may go?
- How many priests are unaware of these things because nothing was said about them in seminary?

- We hear at Mass the warnings of Ezekiel 3:16–21, repeated in Ezekiel 33:7–9, but do we understand our responsibilities for the souls of others around us?

Bulletin of St Joseph's, Norton. 30 November 1997

Are Horoscopes just a bit of fun?

Jesus would say 'no', because He said we must depend totally on Him, trusting in Him with what may happen in the future.

We find it hard to live our everyday lives in total dependency on God. When all is going well we easily forget Him, perhaps saying a quick prayer when we meet anxieties and difficulties.

Many people around us read horoscopes, or go to fortune-tellers, so-called faith healers or psychic fairs, use tarot cards or play with Ouija boards.

Most people in the Church realise that scripture and the teaching of the Church tell us that these occult practices and spiritualism are to be rejected. They are dangerous, and some will know people who have been harmed by them.

If anyone is in the habit of looking at horoscopes, however light-heartedly, it would be better to say a prayer:

'Jesus, show me your way'.
Jesus Christ is the Lamb of God.
Redeemer of humanity, Lord of history.

Attachment to bulletin of St Joseph's, Norton

Do I need to ask Jesus for more trust in Him?

Psalm 23 tells us, 'The Lord is my shepherd, I have everything that I need'. This means that I should be living every moment of my life and in each new situation, in total trust and dependence upon God. As Jesus told us in John 15, 'Without Me, you can do nothing.'

Am I living my life in a way which shows that I really believe that Jesus will give me all that I need? We find it hard to be willing to let go of our need to be in control and to live our everyday life in total dependency upon God: to surrender more and more completely to Him.

Many people around us, and even more sadly, some Christians, are not only failing to trust God, but they are disobeying Him e.g. by reading horoscopes; going to a fortune teller; to a psychic fair; to a medium or to a spiritualist church or meeting; 'playing' with a Ouija board; using tarot cards; going to a Reiki 'healer' or some so-called 'faith-healer'.

Sometimes the latter appear to bring about some kind of healing, but the person is being opened up to the power of Satan, and can suffer in other and worse ways later on.

In the same way, anyone suffering bereavement who turns to some psychic or medium to seek comfort for themselves, or communication with, or assurance of the state of the one who has died, is in very grave danger of the power of evil affecting them, and through this affecting others in their family, even into later generations. The Scriptures have at least nine warnings that this is against the will of God.

These are not just abstract ideas. Many priests, doctors, psychiatrists and others have to deal with severe ill effects on people who were unaware of these warnings, or who chose to ignore them.

We have everything we will ever need in Jesus Christ. He can comfort us: through Him in prayer we can express anything we would like to have conveyed by Him to our dead loved ones. He can give us the grace to live in each present moment, rather than seeking to know the future. He is the only true healer who brings a peace beyond anything the world can bring.

'Everything you do or say, then, should be done in the name of the Lord Jesus, as you give thanks through Him to God the Father.' (Col 3:17).

This book does not set out to discuss deliverance from evil at any depth. There are other sources of information available, but it is necessary for the Church to point people towards them. This book only aims to set this area briefly in relation to the various aspects of inner healing which will be discussed. However much we focus on Christ and our growth towards wholeness in deepening union with Him, we must be on our guard. As I write, there is a place in our locality advertising Satanic practices, with such notices as the United Kingdom Church of Rational Satanism, and many are going there. Our inner healing prayer group and other Christians in the area are entering into the spiritual battle against this. Are Catholics in other places being mobilised to take up their call to be involved in this battle? They should be, because in 1972 Pope Paul VI posed this question at a General Audience: 'What are the greatest needs of the Church today?' His own answer was:

> Do not let our answer surprise you as being over-simple, or even superstitious and unreal: one of the greatest needs is defence from that evil which is called the devil. It is contrary to the teaching of the Bible and of the Church to refuse to recognise the existence of such a reality—or to explain it as a pseudo-reality, a conceptual and fanciful personification of the unknown causes of our misfortunes.[8]

Yet it appears that it is still rare to find any teaching on deliverance in seminaries, and many dioceses do not have any exorcist appointed by the bishop, despite there being further guidance from Rome since Pope Paul VI spoke. In fact Fr Rufus Pereira, a founder of the International Association of Exorcists, wrote: 'Nevertheless there is not a single exorcist appointed in most countries, and even in most dioceses in many of the other countries, and so our people in their need have no alternative but to go either to spiritists or to neo-Pentecostal healers'.[9]

The dangers can sometimes be more subtle. Some twenty-five years ago, we were approached for help by a Monsignor in another diocese, and also, separately, by a priest in our own diocese, about great damage to a family with members in both dioceses who were suffering. Three ladies in a Catholic family decided to seek hypnotherapy. They had heard of a Catholic lady in another town who was a qualified hypnotherapist. They were cautious and asked their parish priest to check with the parish priest of the hypnotherapist whether or not he thought that it would be all right to go to her. That priest confirmed that the hypnotherapist was indeed qualified and that she was receiving Holy Communion each week, and he felt it was perfectly safe.

As a direct result of the sessions with the therapist, these three ladies became convinced that they had each been sexually abused many years before within the family, and that several men were responsible. They named names. One marriage broke as a direct result, and the husband travelled a considerable distance a number of times to our home for ministry. Gradually he received deep peace and acceptance and the power to forgive, and he still keeps in touch after all these years. However, the deep rift which affected many family members has still not been fully healed today.

When I wrote to the psychology department of an Australian university which was researching hypnotism, they sent me papers confirming that everything which can emerge under hypnosis is not necessarily true. In this particular case, one might suspect that somewhere some spirit of evil was involved. This is not to decry hypnosis used by the right people. One of our friends, the brother of Cardinal Hume, used hypnosis when necessary in his medical practice.

Protecting People from Sects or New Religious Movements

In 1983, the Secretariat for Promoting Christian Unity, the Secretariat for Non-Christians, the Secretariat for Non-Believers and the Pontifical Council for Culture undertook a joint study of the phenomena of sects, 'new religious movements', or cults. A questionnaire was sent to all Episcopal Conferences, Synods of the Catholic Eastern Patriarchates and to the International Episcopal Conferences. This stimulated numerous responses, pastoral letters, articles and other publications. This was synthesised and a progress report entitled 'Sects or New Religious Movements: A Pastoral Challenge' was published in *L'Osservatore Romano* in May 1986.

Its recommendations included:

> People must be helped to know themselves as unique, loved by a personal God, and with a personal history from birth through death to resurrection. Special attention should be paid to the experiential dimension i.e. discovering Christ personally through prayer and dedication, (e.g. the charismatic and 'born-again' movements). Many Christians live as if they have never been born

> at all! Special attention must be given to the healing ministry
> through prayers, reconciliation, fellowship and care.

This is another example of the Church Magisterium giving leadership and guidance, but where even twenty-five years later there is very little result in the parishes, where young people are particularly vulnerable.

There are other ways besides evil influences and sects in which people can be constrained by influences outside themselves. One of these, common to all of us, lies within the patterns of behaviour which have been developing down the generations of our own family. This point needs to be mentioned briefly here, but will be discussed more fully later in the book.

Prayer for Past, Present and Future Family

Information has now been available for thirty years about the importance for the physical, mental, emotional health of present members of our family, and for the sake of those yet to be born, that we pray for past family at a Eucharist held with the special intention of intergenerational healing. Yet when people all over the country learn about this, they may find it difficult to locate a Mass being celebrated for this healing, within an easy journey. In the last twenty or more years, dozens of Masses with this intention have been celebrated by several priests in this area, mainly at first for people coming to our home for prayer for inner healing. In recent years they have been a regular feature, three times a year, at the usual Tuesday evening Mass in our parish, celebrated by three successive parish priests.

I am writing a few days before the next one. Last night I was told that several people are coming from York. A priest has just told me that a lady in the Midlands has arranged to come here for this next Mass. Another lady has written to me from London and is also making a special journey north, and she, too, has arranged accommodation. Others come from different areas of the north-east over forty miles away. Not long ago, man drove 400 miles from and back to Cambridge for one of these Masses. Another person came from Harrogate.

Our usual congregation for the Tuesday evening Mass is about thirty. It rose to about seventy when intergenerational healing was the intention, and for the last two Masses it has been over a hundred. We had to learn how important this is for inner healing, and that people felt that God was blessing them and their families in new ways when they came and prayed at such a Mass. This is discussed in a little more detail later in Chapter 5, but it is very sad that awareness of the importance of intergenerational Masses is very patchy. Fewer people might be drawn to seek such comfort for themselves and for their departed loved ones from spiritualism, if they were more aware of the riches which we have within the Church, particularly in the Mass. It is likely that most Catholics in the UK would say that they have never heard any teaching on this or other aspects of the healing ministry which awakened new and deeper faith in God's power and desire to heal them, either in homilies or on any other occasions within their own parish. There is urgent need to remedy this lack of sound and inspiring teaching.

The Need for More Teaching

Jesus said, 'I was hungry and you fed me, thirsty and you gave me a drink; I was a stranger and you received me in your homes, naked and you clothed me; I was sick and you took care of me, in prison and you visited me'. The righteous will then answer Him: 'When, Lord, did we ever see you hungry and feed you, or thirsty and give you a drink? When did we ever see you a stranger and welcome you in our homes, or naked and clothe you? When did we ever see you sick or in prison, and visit you? 'The King will reply, 'I tell you, whenever you did this for one of the least important of these brothers of mine, you did it for me' (Mt 25:35–40).

Often we do not perceive the depth of meaning in Our Lord's teaching. For example, there are different kinds of hunger. Today a priest called to see me, and told me of an experience recounted by another priest. He was visiting his family and a small niece came running into the house, saying 'I'm hungry'. He was going to get some food, but the child's mother was wiser, and asked, 'Why are you hungry?' 'Because I have no one to play with,' replied the child. So our hunger can be for companionship, acceptance, belonging, love. We may be thirsty for more than a drink; many of us feel strangers to our true self, and can feel alone and unwanted by others; we may feel naked in being aware of being vulnerable, unprotected. Our retired priest often said, 'We all need some healing'. We are all sick in some way, lacking total wholeness. We are many of us imprisoned by damage from early life which has left us gripped by being shut in on ourselves and bound up with many painful feelings and damaged reactions.

Many Catholics have assumed that most of these things, as well as illness or any physical suffering, were part of the Cross, to be offered up. However, the Church teaches:

> It is part of the plan laid down by God's providence that we should fight strenuously against all sickness and carefully seek the blessings of good health, so that we can fulfil our role in human society and the Church.[10]

This teaching appears at the beginning of the 'General Introduction to the Pastoral care of the Sick', of which every priest has a copy, and it was included by Cardinal Ratzinger in reference 2 of the Introduction to this book.

We need to 'let God be God' by praying to be healed so that He, not we, decides what constitutes our cross. If we are not healed and we have carefully investigated whether or not there are obstacles (see Appendix 1), and prayer and the sacraments have not led to further changes, then perhaps we may be called to some redemptive suffering for the sake of Christ's plan to help others. If it is redemptive suffering, people will be drawn to deeper faith by a sense of God's peace in our presence.

If, on the other hand, our condition is not leading to deep peace, but instead makes it difficult for us to pray and to have loving relationships with those around us, then it seems unlikely to be redemptive suffering, and we go on praying for healing and asking God's help to be free of obstacles. While we are waiting for healing, we can offer up our suffering in union with Christ on the Cross, so that grace goes out to others in whatever way God chooses.

This problem of assuming that everything 'has to be offered up', and borne as stoically as possible, has been exacerbated for many Catholics by their having a distorted 'image' of God. Through what they heard others say and because of their perception of their own father, many have 'seen' God as stern, remote, angry, keeping detailed records of misdeeds with which to confront us; more like a policeman or judge than the loving Abba Father presented by Jesus. I have known some gaze at me in amazement that they have to let go of deeply ingrained ideas and attitudes which they learned as small children. God will be grieved at how He has sometimes been misrepresented.

When requested to do so, my wife and I have tried to help people with all these matters by giving teaching on very many aspects of praying for inner healing at weekend retreats and during courses. Much of this teaching is available on tapes and CDs (see Appendix 4).

Yet however much teaching may be available, we have constantly stressed that it is not right to attempt to teach and learn a method, a routine or a technique. The Lord wants to reveal more about his ways of healing, but since only he knows the hurts and the needs, and the pace at which each unique individual can proceed, then we have to be completely dependent on the guidance of the Holy Spirit.

As soon as someone telephones for an appointment, I begin to pray for them. Then I pray just before they arrive, for an anointing of the Holy Spirit. When they come, I pray silently for protection and guidance. As soon as they have gone, I pray for the Holy Spirit to cleanse and free me and to come afresh for whatever happens next. I keep no records, and often forget some of what they told me at our last meeting, having seen a number of others in between, so that I can't rely on a human plan or procedure.

It is also important to have a good deal of back-up prayer, partly from those who have previously been ministered to; from the Norton prayer group; and from others, both alive and dead. We know that several bishops and other priests, now dead, to whom we became close, will be going on praying for us. One of those, Bishop Langton Fox, wrote us a letter just three days before he died, in which the last line was, 'I pray for the healing ministry'. There was a girl of about 21 who visited us for the first time one day, and as she left just after lunch with us, she called out, 'I'll be praying for you'. That night she died in a fire. Two contemplative communities, one Carmelite and the other Poor Clares, after ordering a number of our recorded teachings, have promised to pray for the ministry.

Those who are called by God to this ministry need to have that discernment confirmed, and be under the authority of priests. There is great potential for harm and hurt if people become involved out of their own needs or desires without being in submission and accountable to Church authority.

Vision for the Future

It has become more and more clear that inner healing ministry in depth, and over whatever time scale that particular individual requires, is a need which more and more people are experiencing. In this book, the main aspects of this ministry are discussed in order to demonstrate that it is part of the process of involving God's grace coming from the sacraments and the charisms, by which the Holy Spirit calls each person to deeper conversion to Christ, i.e. towards sanctification. This is part of the purpose for which the Church exists, viz. to bring about evangelisation, as evidenced by Pope Paul VI and the Catechism, and confirmed by Pope Benedict XVI: it is part of the mission given by Christ to the Church to give the Good News and to heal. Thus it will be shown in this book that this ministry is of the very essence of the Church, and should therefore be made available to people in their local church area. This is a great challenge for bishops, for priests and for those lay people whom the Lord will call and equip, once they have been called forth and encouraged.

Significant Points

- Pope Benedict XVI has written that healing is an essential dimension of the Apostolic mission.

- People are travelling hundreds of miles for inner healing prayer ministry.

- There has only been very slow and patchy growth in this ministry in the UK.

- Prayer ministry may be needed over months or years.

- There is insufficient warning given in most parishes about activities which are wrong and expose people to evil influences.

- Many people are unaware of how prayers at Mass celebrated for intergenerational healing, can bring healing and freedom to the living.

- One should not attempt to learn a method of praying for inner healing, but instead learn to rely entirely on the Holy Spirit at every stage.

Scripture for Meditation

The Spirit of the Lord is upon me. He has anointed me to preach the Good News to the poor. He has sent me to proclaim liberty to the captives, and recovery of sight to the blind, to set free the oppressed, to announce the year when the Lord will save His people (Lk 4:18–19).

Jesus said to them, 'There is a large harvest, but few workers to gather it in. Pray to the owner of the harvest that he will send out workers to gather in His harvest. Go! I am sending you…heal the sick in that town, and say to the people there, 'The Kingdom of God has come near you'. (Lk 10:2, 3a, 9)

Testimonies

Testimony 1A

'I was absolutely devastated by the sudden disclosure by my daughter in her late 20s, that for a number of years between the ages of 11 and 16, she had been sexually abused by her two brothers.

I had always been aware of a profound antagonism between Jennifer (not her real name) and Brian (not his real name). Neither of them seemed happy as children and teenagers. In many ways we were a family who loved each other, but there was a lot of tension around, especially as a result of Brian's anti-social behaviour. Jennifer had quite a deep depression when she was 18.

I feel I should mention the circumstances of the disclosure of the abuse. I had attended a weekend retreat where a couple were speaking about inner healing. I noticed, but only in passing, that among the books on display were some about sexual abuse. I happened to sit near the couple at our last meal there. Also at the table was a friend who was showing us a computerised address book she had just received as a Christmas gift. She took the address and the telephone number of the couple to show us how it worked.

On the very Sunday I returned from the retreat, I went to visit my daughter and out of the blue she told me about the abuse. Later she told me that she had had no intention to do so, and in fact thought she would never be able to mention it to me. I can't describe the pain and shock I felt, but I did not regret she had had the courage to speak. When I got home, the thought of the couple came to my mind, but I did not know how to contact them. Into my memory came my friend's little computer, so I rang her. Though I had no intention of telling her why I wanted this number, I suddenly found myself telling her in my very great distress. She told me that she, too, had been abused as a child. From being so ashamed to divulge what had happened in our family, I found great comfort in sharing it with this friend. I then rang the couple. I remember clearly, hardly being able to speak for tears. I could scarcely believe when I was assured that God could and would heal Jennifer, her brothers and us as a family, and might even have in His plans to use Jennifer's dreadful hurts to enable her to help others who were similarly hurt. I found this beyond what I could really take in at this point.

I have travelled to the home of this couple and received ministry three times now. Some remarkable changes are occurring in Brian as a person. He is a new person in many ways and the relationship between him and Jennifer has also undergone a most remarkable improvement. Jennifer has not felt it right yet to confront him with his abuse of her. However, she did so with her other brother, who had been less involved. This had a very positive outcome.

Jennifer suffered a nasty period of depression prior to the disclosure of the abuse. She went for counselling, which she found very helpful. Until just a few weeks ago she was coping very well and feeling much better. She has recently become depressed again. This may have been triggered by the job she now has which involves looking after people, some of whom have suffered sexual abuse in the past. I pray that God will continue her healing and will prompt her to ask for ministry herself.

As for me, I continue to pray for the healing of memories, and of the feeling of guilt and failure as a parent. I feel confident that God will go back into our family and into previous generations where the roots may lie, so as to bring us all to healing and to peace.'

Testimony 1B

'There had been a big split in the family for many months and as the mother I could not bear the hurt they were causing each other. At first I could see both sides of the dispute but as time went on it became really bad. I just prayed that they would make peace. They did not fall out with me but if one was visiting and another one called, one would walk out. So sad. Christmas wasn't good and birthdays caused more problems.

I belong to an evening healing group where we pray for various situations, and sometimes go into groups of two or three when we pray for each other. I asked if the others would pray for my family, and briefly explained. They prayed that my family would forgive each other and come to peace. They also prayed for me.

Next day I felt so different. I felt a peace so lovely it was great. I thanked God for this as all the anxiety had left me. A few days later one family member rang to tell me that she had arranged for them all to meet and talk. This was a miracle in itself, but they did meet and they did talk, and while they talked I prayed. I have no idea what was said…all I know if that my lovely family is at peace again.'

Testimony 1C

'One day, many years ago, a young woman came into the surgery asking for referral to an abortion clinic. She was quite distressed as she wanted the baby, but it would have meant great difficulty for them all as they lived in a very small flat which went with the job; and also because it was required that this woman should work part time in the shop too.

We talked about her situation, they already had two children and a third child, a new baby, at this stage or ever, would cause great anxiety, a fact, so that to them at that time there seemed only one answer—abortion. I felt great compassion for her, but did not feel at all judgemental.

(I had told her that I had friends who believed in prayer, and that we would pray that she would be helped to make the right decision for her family).

It was agreed that she would think things over for the next week.

When she returned, she requested a referral to the ante-natal clinic: she had changed her mind as she felt that in some way things would work out.

When I was thinking on my own about her situation, I realised that it is easy to applaud difficult decisions by other people, and do nothing to help in a practical way. (As it says in St James' letter, 'go home and keep yourself warm'!) So when I prayed about it, I had an idea that some of my friends might be willing to offer to assist, for example, with her current one year old, who did not always allow her mother a good night's rest. So we offered to take the child out in the afternoon, while her mother rested. The young mother accepted our offer in principle, but never needed to take it up. As the weeks passed, I did see her periodically and the pregnancy progressed, until a beautiful baby boy was born. Shortly after his birth, the father of the family was able to change jobs, which meant better living conditions, and there was then no need for this woman to work and she would be able to bring up the three quite young children.

I had assured her that this would be a very special child. I felt sure of that because in effect she had said 'yes' to God in accepting this baby, trusting that with His help all would be well.

Although they moved out of the area, for a few years I would get a letter from them at Christmas, often with a photograph of the children:

the little boy in question was said to have a beautiful nature, he was bright, mischievous and a delight to his parents and brother and sister.'

Testimony 1D

'Many years ago, when we were a newly married Catholic couple, life was wonderful. We were buying our first house and were hoping to have a happy family life with the children that God would send us. Our children were born in quick succession and life became chaotic to say the least. Money was short and my husband had to go away to work. Suddenly, there seemed to be no time for Mass or for our prayers, which we had always said together since the early days of our marriage. The children were all baptised in the Church, but we had moved to a new parish where we knew no one and so the years went by with church only at Christmas and Easter. When the children were growing up and the youngest had just started primary school, I was struck down with a mystery viral illness that kept me in hospital for seven weeks, while my poor husband struggled to work and look after the children as well as visiting me. I was moved into a single room and he was told that he could visit at any time, as the virus was attacking my system and the picture was bleak. One night after visiting, I watched him walk from the ward and realised that it may be the last time I would see him. A priest was visiting someone else on the main ward that night and I beckoned him to come into my room. I told him how desperately concerned I was about my little family and I asked him to hear my confession. Afterwards I prayed and inwardly I cried out to God to heal me and spare me for the sake of my children and my lovely husband.

Unknown to me after my husband had left the ward that night he had asked to speak to my consultant and suggested to him a treatment that might help. The consultant at first thought that my husband had some medical knowledge, but he listened to him and assured him that he would try everything he could to help me. That night I was woken in the early hours surrounded by nurses and doctors and saw that two drip stands were being set up by my bedside and needles were being put in my veins.

Two days later I was up out of bed and pushing the tea trolley round the ward, serving those who were bed-bound.

God had answered my prayers and those of my husband, who was never really sure of what he suggested that night when he spoke to the consultant. I used to tell people that my husband had saved my life, but we both knew, without question, that it was God who had healed me through the skills of the doctors and nurses. Now that I had been given another chance at life, we both began to practice our faith and say our prayers together again.

I used to question sometimes why I had been spared. What was God's plan for me in the years ahead? Our children grew up and were successful at their chosen careers and life was wonderful again. The children were all married in the church and our grandchildren started to arrive.

After a few more years I was shocked and saddened when my husband was diagnosed with an incurable disease and I was under pressure to hospitalise him, but by then I was beginning to see clearly God's plan for me and I was convinced that I would stay well and healthy so that, with help, I could nurse him at home until the end.

We still prayed daily together and towards the end when he was unable to pray, I prayed for both of us.

So be prepared to wait sometimes to see what God plans for you. Remember that God's time is not our time and sometimes the answer to our prayers is not the answer that we would have chosen, but be assured that when you need God and ask for His help, He is always ready to answer your prayer.'

Testimony 1E

'In writing this I hesitate to speak of my history of depression or my history of healing. Both have always run parallel and I realise more clearly that I have come to know the love of God more intimately through His healing power thanks to a history of depression.

I am not deeply depressed, I have not attempted suicide, nor do my colleagues at work realise I have a problem unless I tell them. I am rarely off work. On the other hand, I am very good at denying the pain until tears start to flow uncontrollably and embarrassingly. This uncontrollable crying along with permanent fatigue are the main symptoms.

At first, I sought healing only through spiritual sources. Now I am also helped by anti-depressants and psychotherapy. The anti-depressants help me to relax, to sleep well, but also, by reducing the level of emotional turmoil and pain, they help me to face more squarely the root causes of the depression. The psychotherapy has hardly started but the one or two sessions I have attended have given me some pointers and directions in the uncovering process of these root causes.

As I have told the therapist and the psychiatrist, the Christian and spiritual inner healing process has given me the confidence to seek help, has pointed me in the right direction. I think I am a 'good' subject or patient for therapy because I know now that God's love has always been in every part of my life and nothing so dreadful will be uncovered that His love won't be able to heal. I say this in faith because I am still frightened to look into my infancy and early childhood. I know also that the Lord, in His goodness, will only reveal the areas which He knows I can cope with.

I was hesitant at first to engage in psychotherapy whilst I was being helped by some people in St Joseph's parish, Norton, feeling that the therapy would double with the healing process and be—in a way—superfluous. I now find that they can complement each other. The therapist is trained and skilled to interpret any immediate reactions when past issues are raised. Whilst mostly listening, she can make me work in understanding my past more systematically than the inner healing prayer ministers who see me irregularly. On the other hand, seeing where the roots of the pain and hurts lie does not automatically heal them.

The inner healing prayers have:

- shown me that the love of God kept me safe around the time of my birth and early infancy, a time of total insecurity for me, for my parents, for France and for the whole of Europe (World War II) knowing that God was present in this period from which I had totally detached myself gave me courage to face it

- led me to forgive my parents for their neglect of me

- in turn, this made me see that they had loved me all along, and led me to be reconciled with them in spirit, as they have died

- gradually, the healing prayers are putting a more positive light on these earlier years as I see how the whole family was protected from harm and came out safe from the war years

- I have stopped regretting that I was born at all and am able to praise God for my being

The healing prayers I have received from the people in Norton and from my own parish prayer group have started the therapy process thanks to insights which some people in the groups received, or insights which were given to me directly during or outside the time of prayer. One particularly significant insight was the word FEAR which one prayer group member received. This was about eight years ago. At the time I was not conscious of being full of fear. Now it is becoming more and more evident that it is an important key to my problem. During the same session of prayers, the figure 3 came strongly to my mind. I interpreted it as meaning that I was to look back at the events which happened when I was three. This proved to be fruitful and was a good starting point in the healing process of memories.

Insights of this kind, as well as those given through mental pictures in private meditations and dreams, can bypass the therapy process or be short cuts. On the other hand, systematic counselling shows me how much my present behaviour or reflex reactions to questions is conditioned by my early fears, anguish and habit to withdraw and deny pain. Both inner healing and therapy are leading me towards mental and emotional stability, which I can see turning into well-being, and one day will be wholeness. But I know that total wholeness can be achieved only after death.'

Testimony 1F

'Many years ago I was involved in bereavement counselling. One evening I met a lady who was suffering a double bereavement. Some while before, her son had been killed in a road accident. She suffered depression and was prescribed drugs which, after a while, were found to make her unduly high. She was then given other drugs which had the opposite effect. This led to swings in her mood rather than to a balance and she was eventually admitted to hospital for treatment including ECT. One evening, after he had been visiting her, her husband suffered a fatal heart attack in the hospital car park.

After I had met her, following her discharge from hospital, I became increasingly concerned at her state of mind, and that evening prayed a great deal for her at home, and then again the next morning. I had her name, but no address or telephone number and did not have any means of contacting her.

Later that next day, I was driving towards the roundabout at the A19, on my way to Billingham. As I reached the roundabout, it was as though the car was taken without my being able to do anything else, right round and back along the ring road, the way I had come, and then through Norton High Street, and from there to another road in Norton. Suddenly it stopped. I got out of the car and knocked on the nearest door. The woman about whom I was so concerned, opened the door in tears. She came straight into my arms. For another ten years we remained in contact as God gradually strengthened her.'

Testimony 1G

'I imagine we have all suffered bereavement. Even though we know our loved ones go to Heaven, the pain of loss is still very acute. I still remember the physical pain which lasted for many weeks after my father died, even though my prayers from childhood that he would return to church, were answered because he came to a mission just hours before he died. It was some years later that I came to a real awareness of God being my loving, forgiving Father.

All grief is different and there are many stages to go through as I realised after my husband died 2 years ago: the awful shock, numbness, fear, longing, loneliness and guilt—if only—. My family helped me so much as did the love, support and hugs from people in the parish. I needed Jesus more than ever and began to go to Mass daily whenever possible, as well as to the prayer group and healing group. Each Mass tears would flow. I now know that they are healing. With the help of another lady not long widowed, there is now a friendship group of 18 at present. We hope to visit the bereaved and invite them to join us. I thank God for my family and also for my faith and the prayerful support of others without which I could not have coped.'

Testimony 1H

'Twenty years ago I contracted ME. After eighteen years of relapses, depression and prayer, I amassed so much good and bad experience by alternative practitioners that I could have written a book on the subject. All the therapists I had gone to had made me feel bad, because they said I should be able to let go of the past. If they could have told me how, I would have done so because I was so desperate.

The best decision I ever made in my life was to follow my instinct and prayer, and come to St Joseph's for prayer for healing. I was informed, through the bishop of my Anglican diocese, that ministry was available there from a couple. I was listened to non-judgementally through my worst secrets and problems and I was told reassuringly that it was possible to let go of the past through the grace of God.

I have never before met such profound love that made me feel so precious, and slowly I have realised that I am a beloved child of God, and that He is helping me overcome my fears and insecurities from the past. I am laying down my guilt and my old ways of protecting myself, and I am becoming free to love myself. By giving everything into the hands of Christ, things are working out in more amazing ways than I ever thought possible. I am sure my path to full health will be challenging, but exciting.'

Several years after this was written, this same lady has brought the testimony up to date:

'One of the central features of my journey to health has been the inner healing prayer group that I attend at St Joseph's. The first time I went I was very vulnerable, and anxious about what would happen. However, they have proved to be a great source of love, encouragement and unconditional understanding.

I felt humble in their presence, due to the wisdom gathered over years from the teaching of the couple who ran the group.

The group became the high point of the week, as I knew I could take all my concerns to them, and would leave with a previously unknown feeling of warm peace, full of courage and hope for the future. Through the week, I longed for Monday evening, and for the chance to meet these people from whom shone out the love of Jesus, and who lived true Christian lives. However ill I felt, I always went, so I could feel the grace and peace of God flowing out of them, and into me.

Another great aspect was the teaching, which covered all aspects of healing and faith, which improved my knowledge and provided me with clues to questions I had asked. It also gave me an insight into other people's religions, and different ways to pray and praise God.

However, the best gift I was given was that of speaking in tongues. Through prayer I was encouraged to explore and use this most precious gift, and it has transformed my life since then. Now I can properly sing my praises to God, humbly pray with someone, or just talk to God as I walk along. The sense of joy, companionship and peace it gives me is beyond expression, and I am still amazed that I could receive this, as I presumed I had to be very holy before it could happen.

I am so grateful to have found the group, as I had found it very difficult to find anyone who knew about the healing ministry, either within the Church or outside it. Considering that Jesus came to heal and help people, it strikes me as incomprehensible that it is so difficult to find some help.

I can't imagine how I would have been able to cope without the healing ministry, and pray that all churches will have the courage and compassion to start healing services and groups, so that others can experience the grace of God, that can transform their lives.'

Testimony 1I

'At fifteen I left school and began work as a clerk, and soon met a young man. Having gone to an all-girls' school and coming from a very reserved family, I was very naïve and knew nothing of relationships. At sixteen I became pregnant, although I didn't know what pregnancy was about. My father was broken-hearted but my mother wouldn't speak to me. There was never a single conversation between us about it. Instead she arranged for my sister to take me to a doctor, when I was six months pregnant. My mother would have favoured an abortion, but of course it was too late when she first learned about it.

My mother, without consulting me, made arrangements for me to go up north to a mother and baby home. I was to have no contact with the father. I had to look after the baby for two weeks, and then she was taken away from me and given to adoptive parents.

Eighteen months later, I met my husband-to-be and told him the whole story. He wanted to begin to form a relationship which led to our marrying in a registry office, when I was nineteen. Eventually we had four children, the last when I was forty-two.

As a baby I had been baptised in the Catholic Church, but was not brought up in the Catholic faith. My mother-in-law, who had great faith, encouraged us eventually to get married again in the Catholic Church, but I still did not attend Mass. Then my mother-in-law, to whom I had become very close, died. I felt a great longing to be received into full communion with the Church. For the first time, at about thirty-nine, I was beginning to have a relationship with my Creator, and to realise how much He loved me, and all that had happened in the past was forgiven.

That is when things began to go very wrong. My husband accused me of having an affair with the priest. My eldest daughter got into bad relationships and drugs, and this greatly affected the whole family. A number of times I wandered the streets at night, just to get away from it all. Then the priest called and told me not to let all this stop me from being received into the Church, so I went ahead. It was wonderful and I felt full of God's presence, but my husband hated it. Although he still went to Mass each week, he did not want to share what I was experiencing. He kept saying, 'You're crazy'.

Then my last daughter was born and she was a delight. She was always at my side. I never went anywhere without her. But the relationship between my husband and myself was not right. He went his way and I went mine. When this youngest daughter was eleven, my husband walked out, after numerous arguments. For four years, he came and went. My daughter was becoming a rebellious teenager. Everything was getting out of control. I had stopped attending Mass, so as to placate my daughter, by taking her to activities in which she was involved. My husband left for good.

One night, at the age of fifteen, she had been out till the early hours. I finally found her and said, 'That's enough!' I took her to her brother, thinking that she might listen to him and take notice. I left her with him, assuming she would come back next day. Instead, all hell let loose. She phoned to say she would not be coming home. That was four years ago, and she has never come back. I have only seen her briefly once or twice. She accused me of hurting her. To this day, I don't know what was in her mind when she said that. It left me broken-hearted.

Then came what I have described as a tsunami. My husband filed for divorce. My children didn't want to know me. I had no money. The house was to go up for sale, so that my husband got his share. There was so much going on in my family, including deaths, drugs, alcoholism, freemasonry, broken relationships. I was constantly being battered by new situations in which family members turned to me for support. I opened the church door in desperation, and literally fell into the arms of a startled parishioner. I said, 'I am in despair'. The priest came to see me and blessed the house.

It was then that the turning point in my life occurred. I went on a Tuesday evening to Mass at St Joseph's. Afterwards, I was sitting at the back of church. A husband and wife were coming towards me. I had met them eighteen years earlier at a bible study session. They did not recognise me. I told them, 'I think I am in the wrong place at the wrong time'. They put their arms round me to comfort me and asked if I would like to join in their inner healing prayer group, which was about to begin in the Blessed Sacrament Chapel.

Saying, 'Yes' was the beginning of a long journey, and I am still travelling today. Over the following months was to come a deep sense of loss, great heartache and complete turmoil. I tried never to miss the

Tuesday evenings, where I found a wonderful sense of belonging, love and healing. Just knowing that you are not alone while you are going through very difficult and painful times, and that there are people who are willing to share in confidence, and to pray for you daily, has helped me to become stronger day by day. Alongside all I was gaining from being a member of the group, I was also going for one-to-one ministry. During this ministry, I went through many painful stages, sometimes thinking, 'I'm not going back there again'. This was because I was reluctant to face the past. But it is necessary to let Jesus come into the painful experiences in order to receive healing, and His power to forgive others and ourselves. I have attended all the intergenerational healing Masses, and have taken the opportunity for personal ministry from one of the many pairs who are available after the Mass finishes. I believe this has been very important for my family.

I still sometimes have bad days, but now I look forward to every day. I thank God for the people He has placed in my life, and for His healing among the many tears. In an amazing, unexpected way, the Lord made it possible for me to stay in my home of forty years.

I can see something of how the Lord is at work in my family, gradually and unevenly repairing relationships. One son is now in close contact with me. Through my own painful experiences, I can understand how difficult it is for them, with all the pressures of their own lives and of society today, to come to terms with what has happened. There will be many emotions in them, including anger at the marriage breakdown, and ways in which that affected their own relationships with another. I just go on with daily prayer for their protection and for God's blessings, and have great confidence that eventually He will bring about complete reconciliation.

The last few years, I have tried to spend at least a couple of hours each day before the Blessed Sacrament. The only way to have a deeper relationship with the Lord is to spend time with Him; to get to know Him; to listen to Him; to love Him. At Christmas last year, I was called to spend the whole of Christmas Day, after the morning Mass, in the Blessed Sacrament Chapel. After asking permission from the priest, I took my music into the chapel to praise and worship the Lord. I interceded for our parish, for our new priest, and for all those who had asked me for prayers. To my surprise, the Lord asked me to come back each day for as long as possible to be with Him, to continue to intercede on a daily basis.

For four years now, I have decided to honour the Lord by turning off the television and radio altogether, and by listening to worship songs. I never buy newspapers or magazines, so I only know what goes on in the outside world by what friends relay to me. I am given great joy and peace as I spend as much time as I can before the Blessed Sacrament, praising and worshipping God, and interceding for family and for others.'

At a meeting in 2012 of the inner healing prayer group in our Blessed Sacrament Chapel, it emerged that the lady who wrote this testimony had been praying every day for just over four years, the prayer in Appendix 6, which we had given to her when she first came to our home for prayer ministry. She spoke very movingly of how she was sure that this prayer for the Holy Spirit had been vital in the amazing changes in her life, and the deep peace which she has and brings to others. It was profoundly moving and humbling to witness her faithfulness and commitment to praying this prayer every day. God has most certainly answered her prayers in wonderful ways, as He always does when someone genuinely surrenders themselves and cries out for help with humility, faith and persistence.

Notes

[1]   J. Richards, *But Deliver Us From Evil* (New York: Seebury Press, 1974), p. 7; P. Horrobin, *Healing Through Deliverance—The Practical Ministry* (Tonbridge: Sovereign World, 1995).

[2]   Richards, *But Deliver Us From Evil*, p. 7.

[3]   House of Bishops of the General Synod of the Church of England, *A Time To Heal—A Contribution Towards The Ministry Of Healing* (London: Church House Publishing, 2000).

[4]   L. Dossey, *Reinventing Medicine: Beyond Mind —Body to a New Era of Healing* (San Francisco: Harper & Row, 1999), p. 199.

[5]   E. McSherry, quoted in H. Koenig, *The Healing Power of Faith: Science Explores Medicine's Last Great Frontier* (New York: Simon & Schuster, 1999), p. 246.

[6]   A. Newberg and E. D'Aquili, *Brain Science and the Biology of Belief: Why God Won't Go Away* (New York: Ballantine Books, 2001), p. 13.

[7]   Vatican II, *Apostolicam Actuositatem*, 10.

[8]   Pope Paul VI, General Audience 15 November 1972.

[9]   R. Pereira, 'Exorcism and Deliverance, Reconciliation and New Life' in *Prayer for Healing* (2003) International Colloquium, Rome, International Catholic Charismatic Renewal Services, pp. 237–251.

[10] *Pastoral Care of the Sick—Rites of Anointing and Viaticum* (1983), p. 10.

2

OUR EARLY EXPERIENCES

Background

At eleven I won a scholarship to a well-known public school from an elementary school. My unemployed father found a job just in time to accept it, despite the extra expense. At seventeen I left school abruptly in the middle of the first term of the second year of a sixth-form languages course in order to take a job in a bank, because I felt such need of financial security. Less than nine years later, through totally unforeseen events, I found myself appointed as Assistant Lecturer in Electrical Engineering in London University, despite never having been a student in a university.

I had sometimes gone to an Anglican church in my early youth, and then to services on board a naval cruiser. However, I had no Christian teaching at home or school and I knew nothing of prayer or faith. After I was demobilised from the Navy at the end of 1946, I did not attend any church until we married in December 1951.

My wife Betty, who had become a Catholic at age twelve, trained as a nurse in a Catholic hospital and became a sister in Queen Alexandra's Imperial Military Nursing Service. She served in Africa and the Middle East where she nursed casualties when bombs were exploded among British soldiers in Palestine.

By December 1955, I had become a Catholic but could never quite understand how it had happened. I felt that I was one of the most ignorant Catholics, having read no books, had had no real discussions and certainly did not know how to pray. I suffered depression and frequently became angry, had very little sense of any self-worth, and I avoided meeting people because of my own feelings of inadequacy. I spent too much of my time writing research papers and textbooks.

In the early 1970s I felt that something was missing from my life and struggled to keep going. I sought the advice of the university chaplain, who asked if I could change my job, and how old my children were. After my replies he told me I had no choice but to go on.

A Turning Point

In August 1973 we attended a weekend retreat where my depression increased as I felt utterly unworthy to be with these people who had a faith which I felt I could never have. Words kept going through my mind: 'You don't belong'. 'Somebody made a mistake in inviting you to come'. 'You are an interloper'. By the Sunday morning I made a firm decision that when I returned home, I was finished with prayer, perhaps with God, and I would not go on meeting with other Christians. I would bury myself again in my work.

That morning a priest told us to go and pray on our own for one hour. I felt desperate, never having tried to pray for even five minutes. I had the Bible with me because I suspected everyone else would bring one, and I did not want to look different. I had never opened the Bible to read anything. I had taken it out of the bookcase and put it on the bedside table some months before, but could not bring myself to open it. After thirty minutes of struggling and failing to know how to pray, I cried out for help, and felt that I was being told to open my Bible.

Because I thought that God could not speak through the Old Testament, I opened the Bible near the end. I found that I was looking straight at 'Awake, O sleeper, and arise from the dead, and Christ shall give you light'. (Ep 5:14). I read on to the end of that chapter, how we should meet to praise God and how Jesus spoke of His love for the Church and the love between husband and wife. I didn't know what to do next, but I had been told that praying in tongues was a real surrender of some control to God, and I wanted to surrender because I felt in such need of help. For a few moments I made strange noises which probably was no more than my own efforts.

However, the moment I stopped, words came into my mind: 'Be not afraid, I the Lord your God am with you and my strength is sufficient for you.' I knew at once it was not a mistake that I was there. Later that day, the first reading at Mass proved to be from Ephesians 5 about Christ's love for the Church, and husbands and wives. Then during a long prayer meeting, only one passage from the Scriptures was read out. It was from Ephesians 5, about our meeting to praise God together.

It suddenly hit me that God was calling me to surrender. I dared not ignore this after my growing awareness of unease and my need for help. At that moment, the group began praying with a sister for healing of a back injury (more about that in Chapter 3). As soon as they finished praying with the sister, I asked them to pray with me. All I can remember is weeping for my sins and praying in tongues. I knew from that day that I was deeply loved by God and that I was beginning a relationship with Him through Jesus Christ. That same year my wife experienced a marked deepening in her faith, though her experience was less sudden and dramatic than mine, because she had a long, prayerful relationship with God going back to childhood.

Early Beginnings in Ministry

We were immediately asked by others to join in praying with people at conferences, days of renewal and retreats, as well as in less formal situations. Then a few people began to come to our house to ask us to pray with them.

One of these was a man who after one or two sessions disclosed that he was homosexual and had been dismissed from his teaching job. Then at 8:15 one morning, our telephone rang. It was his mother. We had never spoken to her though we had seen her at Mass. She was clearly distressed and said, 'I have to come to see you.' I replied that I was about to go to work but she could come at 7pm that evening. When she came we were surprised to see her son with her. She began to tell us that she and her husband couldn't take any more, and that they had just asked their son to leave home. At that, he burst out in anger, 'When I was a little child you rejected me. Now you are rejecting me again!' He knew full well that his mother had had a breakdown when he was very small and he was looked after temporarily by an aunt. It was an example of something which we only began to learn more about some years later, of how the knowledge of the truth possessed by an adult is not always sufficient to enable them to control the fear, anger and rejection, or other strong emotion which the child within them still has, based upon perceptions in very early years, even when their adult knowledge conflicts which these perceptions.

Confronted by the tearful mother and the very angry man, I was silently crying out to the Lord for help as to what to do or say. I didn't know whether to tell him to go home or to sit in our kitchen so we could try to help his mother. Then without planning I began to tell them of one crisis in my life caused by me damaging a relationship. The Lord helped me through the sacrament of Reconciliation, and very gradually the relationship was healed and became stronger than ever.

I almost stopped my story, thinking 'what am I doing, telling them of my own crisis when they have such troubles of their own?' Then I looked carefully at their faces and realised that they were really listening, so I carried on. Then I said, 'If you like we will pray a simple prayer to cut all the unhelpful emotional bonds between you'. They were so desperate that they would probably have agreed to almost anything. That simple prayer was all we ever had to do. His mother spoke to us twice after Mass. With a peaceful smile she said, 'He can come home any time he likes, and he and his father and I can even pray together'. The man contacted us years later, first when one parent died, then at the death of the second, and finally to tell us that he had been reinstated in teaching.

Another man, not a member of any church, was brought to our home by his wife, who belonged to our parish. He was unable to work with depression, which had not responded to treatment. He talked freely but we did not discover anything which might have played a part in his illness. My wife, however, received the word 'ridicule' as she listened to him and prayed. She asked if this conveyed any significance but he was unable to identify anything. We prayed the best way we felt able and they went home. Next day they telephoned us. As they drove home, he had to stop the car to clean frost off the windscreen. As he did so, he remembered a girl ridiculing him, and her name came back to him. A day or two later they returned. We invited Jesus in prayer to come into that memory to take his discomfort and to help him forgive the girl, and to free him from the effects of the incident. His depression soon left him and he was able to return to work. A while later he came into the Church.

In the course of my visiting people as a member of the St Vincent de Paul Society, I learnt of another man, not a Christian, whose depression was so bad that he had not been able to work for some time. He had had a great deal of treatment by psychiatrists, but each day, after his wife and daughter went to work, he just sat all day. He did not want to wash up, read the newspaper, watch television or anything else. I began to visit him a number of times and just let him talk when he wanted to do so. At first nothing was said that gave any clue to his condition. Then one day he spoke of being ill and in his mother's bed as a very young child. He said, 'There was a mirror on the wall at the foot of the bed and one day I saw my grandmother's face in it'. She was dead, but he recognised her from a photograph. I consulted friends in London and was advised to ask if there was any spiritualism in the family. When I put the question, he said

'Oh yes, my aunt was much involved and she took my mother and me as a young child to meetings.' A very prayerful sister was coming to our house one evening a week for over two years, where, with our curate, we prayed for our parish. She offered to accompany me to the home of the man, where we prayed deliverance prayers. Meanwhile, my wife prayed at home in support. Some while later, without further treatment, he was able to resume work, and was still well when we left Leeds a few years later.

A lady, devastated by her husband leaving her and their children, wrote to an organisation in Bristol asking for help. They referred her to the Vicar of a large Anglican church in Leeds. He advised her to come to us. She turned out to be a Catholic in our parish, but because of the large number of weekend Masses we had never met. For the first few visits she asked repeatedly, 'What are you going to do to get my husband to come home?' I replied, 'There is nothing we can do as he has free will.' After a while she stopped asking that question. Then she telephoned to ask, 'What are you going to do to get my husband to come to your home?' I replied, 'Why should we even try?' She said, 'Because he has never been in a home in which there is such peace.' She was still coming, but now much more at peace, when we left Leeds, but we wondered how she was and still prayed for her. Then, a few months later, a Mass in our old parish in Leeds was being televised. There she was in the front row of the choir with a lovely smile on her face. We thanked God that she appeared to have accepted the situation, and had found fellowship in the Body of Christ.

Healing of Memories

In the 1970s and early 1980s, we had learnt, mostly from books by priests, how Jesus could be invited in prayer into all the painful memories, particularly in early childhood. He can enable the child within us to get in touch with every painful experience and emotion, including those buried or partially buried through our natural defensive reactions, and He can help us to give him permission to begin to dismantle the defensive walls which we built up very early in our life. Instead of the child feeling alone and hopeless, with no one to talk to, understand or help, Jesus can enable the child to become aware of His loving presence and to depend only on God's protection. Jesus is longing to touch the wounds of the child with His wounds, and, through His precious blood, enable the child to let him draw out all the pain into His suffering on the Cross.

When the person acknowledges that as a child they made damaging judgements of parents, family members and others such as teachers, who hurt them or failed to give them the unconditional love and nurture which they needed, then they can quietly ask for God to forgive them. They may even have hated a parent or wished that a sibling had never been born, and we can pray for the Lord to set them all free, and begin to bond them afresh with His love. We are never sitting in judgement on parents or others who knowingly or unknowingly hurt the child. As discussed in Chapter 6, there is no need for any of these people to ask for the child's forgiveness, or to be visualised as doing so. The adult and child within can choose to ask God for the grace with which to forgive those who hurt them, so that this person ceases to be a victim of whatever others did or failed to do.

While we are praying for the child to give all their pain to Christ, and asking Him to give them the power to forgive the offender(s) and themselves (because children frequently take on guilt and blame), they do sometimes receive the gift of visualising how Jesus is transforming the painful memories. Very often, however, they do not visualise anything, but we go by faith and wait for the fruits of changes in attitudes and behaviours and growing peace in the adult over the following years and months.

God is sovereign and, although He keeps teaching us more, He is not constrained to work within the ways He has already revealed. A case in point is the man who came with his mother, as described in the previous section. We were prepared to have a second session to pray for healing of memories, but did not need to do so. In the great majority of cases, however, further prayer for healing is needed, and may need to be repeated, because there are many aspects and stages in the inner healing process. Only Jesus knows when and at what pace the person is ready to work through them and to be ready to cooperate. Jesus never puts any kind of pressure on and we must avoid ever doing so. If we were to impose any kind of method or timetable we would be risking doing damage.

In Chapter 5, we look particularly at the commandment to honour our parents; in Chapter 6, at the child within being freed and healed from the very earliest roots, so as to be given the grace to forgive themselves and others; and in Chapter 7 at freeing ourselves and others of strongholds and other binding. All of that is needed, so that when we think back to all our past memories, we no longer flinch or hold onto negative feelings and attitudes. Instead, we have memories for which we can be grateful that God has been transforming us with His love, through all the past sufferings and difficulties, and we can say with the Psalmist, 'Praise the Lord, my soul. All my being, praise his Holy name'. (Ps 103:1).

Personal Experience of Healing

We also had our own personal experience of God's power to heal. Whilst we were in Burma between 1958 and 1960, my wife injured her back and needed immediate treatment. After further treatment in the UK, a laminectomy was performed in 1969. Within a year the pain was extremely severe and she had examinations and treatment from a neurologist, and orthopaedic surgeon and a long stay in a hospital specialising in arthritic conditions under another consultant. Nothing alleviated the pain which prevented her from sitting for long so she frequently spent evenings lying on the floor.

In 1975, at a conference in Manchester, Francis MacNutt asked if anyone had had a laminectomy. Betty was the only one and was invited onto the platform. A lady who followed her, at the invitation of Francis, walked slowly up on crutches with severe scoliosis. As she approached the platform I had a sudden feeling that she would end up dancing. Francis asked me to join him as he prayed with the two. He showed people that there was a difference in Betty's legs of one and a half to two inches. I have the only tape in existence of this session, and after prayer lasting less than ten seconds, he told the three hundred people that the difference had gone. He said, however, that it might take much longer for the pain to go, so he advised that I pray regular 'soaking' prayer with Betty.

For the following two-and-a-quarter years I prayed each day for Betty's back pain to be healed. After some time, she asked me to change the prayer from asking to thanking and praising God that it would be healed, but the pain continued. Then we attended a service at an Anglican church in Leeds, where Jean Darnell had travelled from London to give a talk. After a time of worship she stood up to begin, but remained silent. Then she said, 'I don't think the Lord wants me to give a talk at all — will you all please pray.' She then said, 'There is a Catholic woman here with back trouble and the Lord wants to heal her; who is she?' Betty stood up and the people around her began to pray. Jean then spoke of the Lord wanting to heal other conditions.

Later that evening, when Betty spoke to Jean, the latter said, 'There is some resentment in you that needs healing before the pain can go.' Betty realised she hadn't fully forgiven me for being too strict with our children.

About two months later Betty was suddenly taken into hospital with what at first appeared to be some stomach blockage. It took over three weeks for the hospital to diagnose the rare condition of a non-malignant growth in one of the parathyroid glands. This was removed and she became very ill and was put on a calcium drip for about four weeks. When she was eventually discharged she had to learn gradually to walk again. Some three weeks later, whilst sitting praying the Office of the Church, she suddenly realised that she had no more back pain. Shortly after, she dug away deep snow to get the car out, and she had no more back pain right up to her death thirty-three years later. This operation should not logically have led to a cessation of back pain. It was an example of how inner healing and physical healing can interact. Physical conditions may sometimes improve as God does more inner healing within us, particularly by giving us the grace to forgive.

To return to the lady on crutches who was with Betty on the platform and was crippled with scoliosis. After an extended time of prayer with her, Francis MacNutt had to leave, to be driven to the airport for his return flight to the USA. When he had gone, I was still kneeling beside this lady. Without planning to do so, I found myself saying to her, 'I believe you could dance now'. She got up with the support of a priest, and, in front of over three hundred people, she danced.

A few weeks later, we in the national committee who had organised the conference, received a letter from her. She had been examined by her doctor, who said, 'You now have a perfectly normal spine.' She was asking for advice as to whether or not to seek publicity, perhaps through newspapers. Rightly or wrongly, we advised against publicity. These two healings, of this lady and of my wife, highlight the variety of ways God may answer our prayers.

In two of the books by Francis MacNutt, he writes about the healing which Fr Benedict Heron OSB received at the same conference. He had approached Francis at the beginning to explain the severity of his depression which had lasted for years, despite psychiatric help. With so many people needing ministry, Francis prayed briefly in tongues with him. Betty and I kept moving past him as we went to pray with others during the two hours and twenty minutes that he 'rested in the Spirit'. Fr Benedict told me the next day that the Lord had taken him on a wonderful journey, and he has since written about the Lord teaching him so much, particularly about forgiveness. He was shown that nearly forgotten incidents had left a deeper imprint than other events which proved to be relatively unimportant. He was at once restored to the active priesthood, and has ministered directly to many people as well as helping them with his books on healing.

The only time we ever met him again, was over ten years later in Medjugorje, where we found him praying with a long queue of people from all over the world. He greeted us warmly and gave us half the queue to pray with. His immediate release from overwhelming depression, and other experiences, like the mother and son described above, played a part in our being slow to learn that, for many, indeed most people, the road to inner healing takes a long time of ongoing, persistent, patient prayer.

At the previous conference, one year earlier, we met a lady who had physical and psychological problems stemming from her mother's attempt to abort her. She would travel anywhere in the country to anyone with some reputation in the healing ministry to ask for healing. In 1975 I saw her apparently 'resting in the Spirit' and sensed that it was not entirely of the Holy Spirit, and that she did not really want to be healed. When she got up from the floor, I told her this; gently, I hope. She was furious. Within three weeks she telephoned us and said, 'You are right'. She could not really face what life would be like if she received no 'strokes', got much less attention and faced the unknown demands and challenges which could follow if she became really well. She stayed in close touch with us for over thirty years, with many phone calls, and having travelled several hundred miles to stay a weekend in our home for further prayer. When we last heard from her she was still struggling with her fears and her reluctance to let go.

These encounters and our praying with people at conferences, retreats, and meetings were only occasional, being spread out over a number of years. We never had any real thought that we would be called more frequently or deeply into the healing ministry, although my wife had been commissioned in the healing ministry by Francis MacNutt in Hawkstone Hall in 1975. I was obliged to be in the University that week because of examiners' meetings. In other ways, however, God was enlarging our horizons in several directions.

There is No Limit to God's Power

We even had direct evidence that when God chooses, He can make changes in inanimate objects, and involve men and women by guiding them to pray with expectant faith.

When a renewal conference in Manchester ended in the summer of 1976, I asked if I could take away two cine films, in order to make them available at the first charismatic renewal conference at Ampleforth, which Betty and I and Eileen Jackson had organised, to take place two weeks later. We had to register 400 people on the Monday afternoon, and then show the 240 who were not camping where they would be sleeping in one of the many houses of the School, so that they could leave their belongings. To occupy them from that time until the first meal or session, we wanted to have these films available. One was on priesthood; the other, made by Francis MacNutt and others, was on healing.

When the films were handed to me, I was told that the one on healing was faulty and that I would need to take it to a film laboratory. Betty had gone into the hall when it was on, and she confirmed that the soundtrack was so bad that no one could hear it properly.

The day after I arrived home from Manchester, the telephone rang. It was the curate at St George's Church in Leeds. He was asking, on behalf of Radio Leeds, if I would do a 45-minute broadcast on my life and faith. I agreed to do this. Just before he rang off I felt prompted to ask, 'Do you happen to know anyone who knows anything about cine films?' 'Yes,' he said, 'Jack Appleyard, a member of our congregation; I'll give you his phone number.'

I rang Jack that Saturday or Sunday afternoon and he told me to come straight down with the film. When I arrived at his house, he was in the front garden, talking to his next door neighbour. The latter immediately began to tell us about the spire of his own Anglican church, in that part of Leeds. Because it was thought it needed to be inspected, men went up inside it. When they came down they reported there were a number of sizeable holes in it, through which they could see right across the city. 'It is unsafe,' they said. 'It will have to come down and be re-built.'

When a diocesan official came to the Vicar to talk about how this might be paid for, the Vicar told him that they didn't have a problem — they didn't need any money, and he quoted some Old Testament passage to him. Confronted with this 'mad' Vicar, the official went away and sent back the diocesan architect with a steeplejack. They went up into the spire. When they came down, they reported that there were no holes at all — it was structurally sound. Later that day, being of a sceptical nature, I phoned the Vicar, whom I happened to know well personally. He entirely verified the story, but said that he wanted to avoid publicity.

When Jack and I went into his house, he examined the film carefully. He said, 'The soundtrack appears to be scratched and nothing can be done about it, but if you care to come to the Taylor teaching centre where I work on Monday morning, we'll check what it sounds like.'

I went home to Betty, telephoned the Vicar, and said to Betty, 'If the Lord can 'heal' a spire, he can certainly 'heal' a cine film'. So together we touched the film and prayed in tongues.

On the Monday morning I said to Jack, 'let's put the good film on the projector for a few moments to judge the sound level, and then we'll put the other film on.' When we listened to the sound of the healing film it now sounded better than the film about priesthood. For years it went all over the country and was watched and listened to by large numbers of people.

Background to this Experience

How had the curate and I met? A year or two earlier, I had been invited to give a talk one Sunday evening in a third Anglican church in Leeds. Afterwards, the Vicar said to me, 'Do you have any contact with the clergy at St George's?' 'No,' I said. He replied, 'Well, I think you should.' Two days later I was on the train to London to attend a meeting at the Electrical Engineers Institution, to which I belonged. Sitting opposite was a professor from another department. After we had spent most of the journey reading the papers for our respective meetings, we began a conversation. He spoke about all the troubles in the world. 'There's only one answer', I said. 'What's that?' he asked. I answered, 'Jesus Christ'. He did not want to know, saying that mankind was capable of sorting out its problems.

'I'm so glad to hear you say that about Jesus,' suddenly said a young man on the other side of the gangway, whom I had not previously noticed. 'Come and sit over here,' I said. When he introduced himself, he told me that he was the curate at St George's Church. A day or two later his Vicar said to him, 'I wish I knew some Roman Catholic in Leeds who has been baptised in the Holy Spirit.' 'I've just met one,' replied the curate. The Vicar, Canon Michael Botting, a well-known Evangelical, came to our home, and told us he was chairman of a committee which was organising an eight-day evangelising campaign in Leeds Town Hall, led by Rev. David Watson. He asked if I would find Catholics who would attend a counselling course. If they passed the examination they would be available at the end of each of the eight evenings, so that those who came forward to give their lives to the Lord could talk to them and be given information. He asked if Betty and I would host and lead one of the follow-up groups, and he invited me to be the only non-clergy adviser, to any of whom a counsellor could turn for help if needed. David Watson wrote to me to say that he was thankful that some Catholics were playing some part, though he was grieved to be told that, officially, Catholics could not be involved, because of anti-Catholic feelings of a number on the organising committee. Michael Botting had told me that if he were to involve Catholics officially, he would lose one third of his organising committee.

A few years later, Michael contacted me again to ask if I and Betty would play a similar role in a ten-day evangelising campaign by Luis Palau, to be held in a 3000-seater marquee on Woodhouse Moor, near the centre of Leeds. I replied that there was a problem, and he asked me what it was. I said that his committee had already distributed, to tens of thousands of homes, a leaflet in which Luis Palau gave just one example of a person giving their life to Christ in one of his campaigns. It was someone who was a Catholic. It made clear his views that one would need to leave the Church to have a real personal encounter with Christ. I said that I had been told of his rejoicing at other similar cases in a book which he had published about his work, particularly in South America.

Michael then read me two resolutions of his organising committee: (1) no Roman Catholic shall be permitted to be a member of this organising committee, (2) no Roman Catholic who answers the call will be allowed to be referred to a Catholic follow-up group. I told Michael that I could not accept his invitation to be an adviser, and that he was setting back ecumenism in Leeds by many years.

The next day, a Baptist minister friend rang me to ask if Betty and I would host and lead one of the follow-up groups. He didn't seem to know about resolution (2). I told him of the problems and he said, 'Oh dear, I'll have to talk to the Chairman.'

I realised that I was the only Catholic in Leeds who knew what was going on, so I rang the Bishop and spoke to his Secretary, who quickly arranged for me to see the Vicar-General on the Friday. The night before, however, Michael turned up and solved all the problems. He said that he had written to Luis Palau to tell him that he must say nothing anti-Catholic whilst in Leeds. He said, 'I'll put my tongue in my cheek and tell my committee that I haven't had any Catholic who comes forward referred to the Catholic Church for a follow-up group. I will refer each one of them to you personally. I asked if we could ignore his booklet for follow-up groups, and he agreed. I said that we would base the follow-up on the Life in the Spirit seminars, and he was happy about that.

I was out late each night of the campaign on Woodhouse Moor and fifty-four Catholic names and addresses were given to me. I met each one of them subsequently and offered them a group where and when it was convenient for them to attend. Two of the groups were in our Cathedral House, led by priests, one of whom was the Vicar-General. One of the fifty-four went on to become a priest.

Whilst at the official reception for Luis Palau held in Leeds Civic Hall, I spoke to Canon Michael Botting about another matter. Some years earlier, I had been appointed by Bishop William Gordon Wheeler to represent the diocese on the Ecumenical Commission for England and Wales. There I had heard from a bishop that in some parts of the country they were meeting with other Christians at Pentecost, feeling that the week for Christian Unity in January had lost a lot of impetus, and they needed fresh help from the Holy Spirit. I had taken the idea to the bishop, who said it was a good idea, and asked me to pursue it with the Anglican priest who served both our dioceses as an adviser.

The adviser and I had been invited to a meeting of the Leeds Council of Churches in the home of the Bishop of Knaresborough. When they reached our item on the agenda, we were invited in. We said we hoped for a great gathering of Christians from all churches praising God together in Roundhay Park, and praying for help to become more deeply united. They looked at us and asked, 'How many portaloos do you want?' 'We've no idea,' we replied. 'In that case, we can't possibly get involved,' and we were shown out.

This is what I told Michael at the Civic Reception. He said, 'As soon as we have finished with Luis Palau, you and I will get together and do something about this'. We began meeting with a Baptist minister, and after prayer and discussion felt we should consider the Leeds Parish Church, if the Vicar of Leeds would agree. I realised that we needed some official Catholic participation and our Vicar-General agreed to join us.

We put out posters, invited a speaker and went ahead with the arrangements. At the last moment the speaker could not come and I was suddenly asked to fill in. On the Sunday afternoon, when we had gone to the Parish Church to check microphone arrangements etc., the Vicar of Leeds said,' I doubt if you'll get 200 people tonight.' That night 2,000 people turned up — the church hadn't been filled in living memory. Later that evening, a little boy said to the Vicar, 'Can we do that again next week?'

It was soon after that that we had to move to Norton in answer to God's call, and I did not check whether any similar gatherings were held in later years.

Significant Points

- The Lord may choose the most unlikely and apparently completely unsuitable and ill-qualified people for this prayer ministry.

- The Lord needs to awaken us to the reality of His love for us and of our dependence upon the Holy Spirit, not on ourselves.

- God chooses those people to whom to give particular gifts and to share in some ministry in the Church, and it will not be a burden, but a privilege.

- This is likely to evolve and develop out of the ordinary events in our life.

- God is sovereign and may heal immediately or over a long period.

- Even inanimate objects are not beyond God's power.

Scripture for Meditation

At that time Jesus said, 'Father, Lord of heaven and earth. I thank you because you have shown to the unlearned what you have hidden from the wise and learned. Yes, Father, this was how you wanted it to happen. Come to me, all of you who are tired from carrying heavy burdens, and I will give you rest. Take my yoke and put it on you, and learn from me, because I am gentle and humble in spirit; and you will find rest. For the yoke I will give you is easy, and the load I will put on you is light.' (Mt 11:25–26, 28–30)

3

THE BEGINNINGS OF FULL-TIME MINISTRY

An Unexpected Call

In April 1983, the parish priest of St Joseph's, Norton, Stockton-on-Tees, invited us to be present at a parish renewal weekend which he was conducting in his parish. On the Saturday morning my wife and I, having been in different groups, spoke over coffee and discovered to our complete surprise that during the previous session we had both sensed that the Lord was asking us to move to that parish. If only one of us had sensed this we would have ignored it, but we felt that this was a real call which we needed to obey. We asked the priest to pray that we did discern correctly.

How had we come into contact with that particular priest? We had met him briefly in about 1974 at a day of renewal in Harrogate. Then Betty had gone on a pilgrimage to the Holy Land with him and a large group. One Friday in the later 1970s I had to go to Teesside, where I was a consultant to a very large chemical engineering company. Betty decided she would like to come to see the area, and also meet up with this priest. We wrote, and had no reply. The Thursday night I rang the presbytery. The housekeeper said, 'Father is on holiday, coming back on Saturday, but I'll put the curate on the phone.' He suggested that I drop Betty at the presbytery in the morning and return there when I had finished work.

When I came back at the end of the afternoon, the curate told me he needed to talk to me. I hadn't realised who he was. A few weeks earlier, at one of the Ampleforth renewal conferences which we had organised, I was walking along a corridor late one night with one of the monks. We heard strange noises and traced them to a room. We opened the door and found two priests trying to deliver a lady from evil spirits. The monk fled and I was about to go when the priests asked me to join in the prayer. The curate turned out to be one of these priests, and he was continuing to try to help this lady, who lived a few miles away. He wanted to talk to me and get my advice. He also said that the parish priest would return the next day, and that they would like us to stay in the presbytery that night, so that we could meet him again. Betty had packed night things, having had a feeling that the Lord wanted us to go on from Teesside to Scarborough for the weekend.

Next day the parish priest asked us to stay another night. At nearly 11pm, we were talking to the housekeeper in the kitchen when the curate came in. Earlier in the evening he had seen a lady weeping in the church. Later he decided to go to her house. There, in great distress, she spoke of something she hadn't been able to reveal before. He said, 'We have two people staying in the presbytery who would pray with you. If I go and fetch them, would you like them to listen to you and then pray with you?' She agreed. We were there till about 1am.

We had been invited for the weekend in 1983, to stay with a widow in her bungalow on the edge of the Catholic school field. She had already told us that she had put her name down for a flat in a block that had a long waiting list, but that she would be moving when the flat became available. As we walked back over the field that evening, we said, 'If we have to move to Norton, may we buy your bungalow?' The name 'Shalom' was already on it, in olive wood from the Holy Land.

I immediately asked the University if I could be allowed to retire early because I could not live in Norton and work in Leeds. It was some months before it was agreed that I could retire from my post of Professor of Electrical Engineering, with the title of Emeritus Professor. For the sake of undergraduate teaching and of research commitments, I would need to wait till the end of an academic session. The six months' notice in my appointment terms ruled out retirement in 1983. The next year our friend wrote to tell us that the flat was empty but needed extensive work. We put our home on the market and for weeks nothing happened until suddenly new people came one day. They wanted us out as soon as possible. When we moved, our friend had only removed the last of her belongings two weeks earlier.

After retirement, I did no further professional work, apart from external examining. One day, I had a telephone call from the University of Wales in Cardiff, asking if I would be an external examiner for four years. I was about to refuse, not relishing the journey a number of times, when it occurred to me that the Lord might have a purpose in this, so I accepted.

A month or so later, a man wrote to me from Cardiff. He had gone into a church and had bought the CTS pamphlet 'The Healing Power of Christ', which I had written based upon the University of Leeds Sermon I had given just before I retired. He was asking if there was any way in which we might meet.

I wrote back that I would be in Cardiff very soon. Each year I met him, and I stayed once or twice for a night after the meetings in the University, to listen and to pray with him. The fourth year, Betty and I drove to South Wales, booked ourselves and him into a farmhouse. We picked him up and took him there, and over several days, as we visited beauty spots, we did more ministry. He continues to keep in touch.

A similar appointment, as external examiner in Nottingham, enabled me to meet a man who had contacted me earlier, after he had bought a tape of a talk which I had given near Leicester.

A Bewildering Time

We thought the parish priest might know what use we would be in the parish. He did ask us to begin and to lead the RCIA programme, and I became chairman of Governors of the school to ease his load. It was very bewildering not knowing why else we were there and we even began to wonder if we had been mistaken in the call. Because the Lord had involved us in so many ways in the Church and in ecumenical activities during the previous eleven years, our encounters with healing described above did not lead us to have any expectation that it was for further involvement in healing that we were needed. Our previous experiences had been amazing and completely surprising but mostly in other ways and directions.

One very rewarding encounter came very soon after our move to Norton. The Bishop of Leeds, to whom we had grown very close over a number of years, wrote to ask us to request permission of the psychiatrist at a nearby Regional Secure Unit, to visit a man known to the bishop. Permission was given and we began visiting. He was a wonderful man, very devoted to God, and we learned from some of his spiritual reading. He very soon asked us to pray with him that he might be baptised in the Holy Spirit. The time came when we were able to bring him home for a meal, and to arrange for him to have some ministry from a priest who was visiting the area. We were also liaising with the priest, whose duties included visiting people in this unit. Then the Home Office decided he could be released if he lived with his parents. His father refused, so that his mother faced the choice of remaining with her husband, while her son remained locked up, or leaving her husband to give her son freedom. With sadness she chose the latter, and he became free again. We heard encouraging news after his release.

Within a few months of coming to Norton, we attended a parishioner empowerment weekend at Burn Hall with others from our parish, and groups from other parishes. At the end of the weekend of prayer and sharing and teaching, the discernment of those from our parish was that we were meant to be available for the ministry of praying for healing.

Our parish priest agreed with this discernment and commissioned us in it.

By June 1986, we were members of a group asked by Bishop Harris of Middlesbrough to work towards building up the healing ministry in his diocese. We were among a small number asked to undertake this work, and we were given blessed oil to use in it by Bishop Harris, during the special Mass in his cathedral when he commissioned us for this work.

Gradually the telephone would ring and we would be told that someone had been recommended by a friend, a priest or a doctor, to ask if they could come to our home for prayer for healing. We listened and we prayed and we offered further appointments. Because of some of the earlier experiences described above, we became more and more surprised and disconcerted as the months went by. There was no sudden or even rapid progress in this small but increasing number of people who were coming.

Correction or Encouragement?

We began to wonder if something had gone wrong. Did God want us to try to help these people? Had sin or other obstacles in us prevented Him from healing them? Did we just not know enough or understand enough for Him to use us? Or, were we on the right track, and were meant to plod on doing the best we could? In that case we needed encouragement. We felt we either needed that, or else some correction or re-direction. So we just prayed and carried on waiting to see what would happen.

Then, within a three-week period, we received letters from three of the people who had been or were still coming. That was remarkable. In the whole twenty-eight years which have followed, we have only ever received a very small handful of letters. These three letters did not report spectacular progress, but they told of growing faith in God and in an inner peace, so we took this as encouragement and continued to wait.

Then two things happened. Friends in London, who knew far more about inner healing than we did, recommended us to read the books of John and Paula Sandford. Later we were able to learn from John and Paula in person when they gave a course of teaching in Durham. We also went on a twelve-day residential course at Kinnoull on 'Personal Coun-selling & Spiritual Direction in the Context of the Prayer for Inner Healing', taught mainly by Fr Jim Mc Manus C.Ss.R., whom we had already known for over ten years.

Both of these taught us a great deal and had a great influence on us. We gained much information, but we were beginning to learn that transformation is always a higher priority than information. With the benefit of hindsight, one can see how many of our experiences were pointing to something far more important than learning more. They were pointing to the sovereignty of Jesus Christ; to our goal of deeper and deeper relationship with Him leading towards union with Him, rather than a goal of some healing. They were emphasising that Jesus said, 'Without Me, you can do nothing'. He did not ask us to learn all we can and to rely on that and our experience, and if we got stuck somewhere later on to turn to Him and ask Him to help.

In later years, whenever we have given teaching, we have stressed that however much we may be allowed to learn about God's ways of healing, we can never suppose that we are equipped now; that we have learnt a method or a technique or a way of going about it. Jesus is the only way and we can only do what He wants by deepening surrender and utter dependence upon His Holy Spirit, and He continues to surprise us.

Among those surprises was that people began to come to us from outside the local area, and this has continued to happen. Later in this book, mainly in Chapter 9 and in Appendix 7, the case will be made for the Church to recognise that it has a duty to make this ministry available in local areas as quickly as possible, so as to avoid the pressure on people to have to travel a long way.

Why Should People Have to Travel Long Distances?

The first person who came from far away was the lady already mentioned in the previous chapter whom I had told 'You don't really want to be healed'. She came to Leeds from near the South Coast to stay a weekend for prayer. We were telling her the truth: that her problem was deeper than asking the Lord for physical healing, for which she had been prayed with by others all over the country. Another lady came to us in Norton from Leeds, because she was searching to discover who she really was, and whether she had a vocation to the religious life.

Soon after we came to Norton, a lady came from Sheffield, quite unable to sleep at nights, despite the best medical and other attempts to help. The root of the problem emerged: when she was a little child her mother was a sick woman, who went to bed early each evening. The child was left to face her father who would come home drunk, and sometimes very violent, late each night. The child not only had too much responsibility and burden placed on her in this and other ways by the mother, but was deeply fearful and anxious. After we had prayed for Jesus to heal these memories, take into His suffering all her stored-up emotions, and help her forgive, she was able to sleep again.

Early on, a man came many times from West Yorkshire. He had homosexual tendencies but was determined not to give in to them, and avoided involvement with any man. He knew that there were Christian organisations which helped people in his situation. He wanted to find out if there was also a Catholic organisation which would support him in his resolution to live in obedience to the teaching of the Church. After a few visits he told us that he had written to Cardinal Hume to put this question. The Cardinal had written back, offering him the name of a well-known organisation. Because he was doubtful and suspicious, he was not willing to give his address or telephone number to the group. He had given them the number of a callbox opposite his house, and a time to contact him. When he spoke to their representative in London, he said all he wanted was support to lead a chaste life. He said that the representative didn't want to hear that, and seemed only interested in giving him information as though similar to a dating agency. He had written to the Cardinal about this and had been given an afternoon appointment to see the Cardinal.

On the day of his appointment, a week or two ahead, we already knew where we would be going to Mass—in Westminster Cathedral. We were booked to go to London the day before, to visit an aunt of mine that evening, and travel via Victoria next day to visit Betty's brother, who was dying of cancer. We met the man at Mass and went into the Blessed Sacrament Chapel afterwards to pray for him and the Cardinal. When he next came to Leeds, he said that the Cardinal said, 'Well, if that organisation isn't right for you, I don't know who can help you'. He continued to come to our home when he needed and he obeyed the teaching of the Church, but without contact or support from others who were struggling in the same way.

An Anglican lady came from near Shrewsbury on two occasions to stay in the neighbourhood with a retired vicar and his wife. Each time they brought her on two different days. She had very deep hurts and we did some further ministry by telephone, but she made great progress. Very recently she has telephoned for further prayer ministry.

One Sunday, I received a phone call from a lady in Durham who said that a man in Cambridge wanted to come the next day. Next day he drove the 400 miles journey, and he did this three times. Then when there was a Mass for intergenerational healing in our church, he (an Anglican) drove the 400 miles to be there. How had he heard of us? The lady in Durham has a sister in the North West who, thirty years before, had been in college with a lady in the North, who knows the man in Cambridge. Subsequently, this latter lady made a number of journeys of over 100 miles to our house for ministry for herself.

Some years ago, we stayed in the Bar Convent in York for several nights, and saw a notice about a prayer meeting in the pastoral centre next door. The first person to greet us was a man who said, 'You came here, years ago, and prayed with me, and I remember what you said'. When the time of prayer ended and there was a cup of tea, he told the other eight or so people that we prayed with people. We spoke briefly and gave them some information.

Two weeks later, one lady wrote to order ten of our teaching tapes for a friend (who had been at the meeting) and for herself. Two further weeks on she asked if she could come to Norton for ministry, and she came several times. Now, ten or more years later, she has resumed coming again, because the Lord is revealing the need for deeper healing.

About three months after our visit to York, the other lady telephoned to tell us that a man in Gloucester wanted to come to Norton for prayer. I replied, 'It's too far for him to have to travel. There is an Anglican healing centre at Harnhill Manor, some fifteen miles from Gloucester'. Some days later, the man himself telephoned. I gave him the same answer. Then the lady in York phoned to say he couldn't get to Harnhill Manor and still wanted to come to Norton. At that I gave in. I thought, 'This is so odd that it must be what the Lord wants'. His father drove him to

Cheltenham station (not much nearer than Harnhill Manor), where he caught a train for York. This lady met him and drove him straight over to Norton (over 50 miles each way). After a two-hour session, she took him to stay the night with her and her husband. Next morning she brought him back to Norton for two hours and then drove him to York Station where he took a train home. We heard later that there were signs of real progress.

Sometimes our ministry to people a long way away took us to them. In 1976, the first time that Betty asked the Lord where he wanted us to go on holiday, she got Sudbury. We forgot there was one in Middlesex and thought of Suffolk. In the Farm Holiday Guide Book, there was a farm in Sudbury offering bed and breakfast. They wrote back that they were full for that fortnight, but suggesting we try their friends in Cockfield Green. We booked for ourselves and our youngest son. The first evening we got talking to the only other couple staying there. Out of the blue, the wife said, in a tone of voice that made it clear she did not believe it: 'A De la Salle brother told me that a woman's leg changed length last year in Manchester through prayer'. It would have been a shock to her if Betty had said, 'Well, I was there and it did happen'. But to hear Betty say, 'I was the woman that it happened to,' (out of all the millions in the country) sent her straight into tears. Then she said, 'We are having such a terrible time with our teenage son that we are losing faith in God. We are moving house 40 miles, which will give my husband a very long journey to work. We've come away this week because we are exhausted'. We prayed with them that night, took them to two prayer meetings during the week, and gave them the name of a priest who might (and subsequently did) help them all, and peace returned to the family. They had become Catholics and he was head of a department of RE at a teacher training college. They kept in touch. After a while he had retired and they told us in embarrassment that they had returned to the Anglican Church, and were again working in full-time ministry. We told them that we were just thankful that their faith in God had been restored. One of them died and the other got in touch. Then a daughter contacted us to tell us of the death of the other.

In 1978, when Betty asked the Lord where He wanted us to go on holiday, she received the name Ballybane. Even after searching maps, none of our Irish friends could locate it. I was due to present a research paper at an International Conference at Trinity College, Dublin, and we had the privilege of staying with Frances Hogan, whom we had known from when Betty and I had arranged her first teaching engagement in England in 1975. Then we began to wander around Ireland for two weeks. On our journey we learnt that the sister with whom the group had prayed just before my conversion experience was in Cork, so we headed there. We learnt that, although x-rays showed spinal damage, she had been without pain for 5 years. I am still in touch with her and she does an amazing amount of work with no pain.

When our car broke down, we were invited to stay at the convent in Cork for the three days until the garage could obtain the part. One of the sisters said, 'My sister and her husband live in Yorkshire, and I believe they need spiritual help. You may be the people'. A year or two later I was invited to be the speaker at a day of renewal in Birmingham. I was put up for one night at a community house of one sister and some lay people. The sister was the one we had met in Cork. She asked if I had to be at work the next day, Monday. I said, 'I had a strange feeling I had to keep clear of commitments but plan to get the first train from New Street to Leeds. Why are you asking?' She said, 'I have to drive to Durham tomorrow, lunching on the way with my sister. When I told them about you and Betty they didn't want to know. If I telephone now and ask if I can bring you, would you come?' I said, 'Yes'. After laughter on the phone they agreed. Following lunch, they asked if I would bring Betty and stay a few nights. They were a Catholic wife married to an Anglican Brigadier who was Clerk to York Minster. We stayed frequently with them after that over the years, and ministered to both of them, until both eventually died. We found Ballybane, within the city of Galway, booked into a guest house and began to talk about prayer with the owner, whilst still in the entrance.

My wife and I went frequently for a short break to a convent in Filey, where latterly the parish priest (now deceased) would ask us to be available after weekend Masses in order to pray with anyone who was troubled. A number of people came. Among them was a lady living well south of Filey, who then began to come a number of times to our home for prayer ministry. She would travel by three buses, and her total travelling time each day that she came was well over seven hours. We also prayed with a number of people who were staying at the convent, once at very short notice with a lady who was being met by car to be taken home an hour later. This led to her and two others booking into a weekend retreat which we were leading at a retreat house in Ilkley, and we received very grateful letters.

Some years ago we booked to stay a few days at Mount St Bernard Abbey in Leicestershire. The first evening that we were there, a priest from Ireland whom we had never met before asked if he could talk to us, and would we pray with him. Later that evening, members of an Alcoholics Anonymous group who were staying there began to talk to us. Much of our next few days was occupied with prayer ministry to them. One of them subsequently began to come to our home for further ministry.

There were many other intriguing encounters. Betty prayed with a lady in the toilets at a Roman site in South Wales; she gave a 'word of knowledge' to an unknown man at the end of a male voice choir in a church in Llandudno. On one occasion we were in an airport waiting for our plane to Medjugorje. Somehow I got talking to a mother and daughter who were waiting for a different flight. They asked for prayer ministry, so I went to fetch Betty. There was just time before our flight was called.

I was in East Berlin once, invited by the East German Academy of Sciences to give a paper at an international conference. As I was being driven back to the airport by an East German professor, he spoke of his distress at the division of Germany into two parts. When I spoke of my belief that God would not much longer allow the Communist control and would bring Germany back together, there were tears in his eyes, and for some years we corresponded about what the Lord would do.

In the late 1970s Betty and I were staying in Dun Laoghaire with a former colleague, now a professor at University College, Dublin, and his wife. They took us walking on the pier one evening. A nun and two ladies passed. Betty suddenly said, 'I think that was Sr Patricia'. They had been in nursing training at a Catholic hospital over thirty-five years before, and had not met since then. I said, 'Go after her and ask'. It was Sr Patricia. We stood and talked and told her where we were staying. Next day she rang up and asked if we could meet in the Pro-Cathedral.

She told us she had a great fear of travel and that it had got worse. She was due to go back to her mission in Sierra Leone, but she was not sure that she could overcome the fear sufficiently to be able to travel. We prayed with her. The root turned out to be an experience in childhood when she was on a train. As we prayed, she wept. Someone who was cleaning the church came to ask if she was alright. What were these two people doing to this sister to make her cry? She asked for more ministry the next day, and we met in the church where Matt Talbot's body is, and we continued the ministry. She was able to return to Sierra Leone and kept in touch, eventually dying back in Ireland.

Betty and I only ever had one holiday in Spain. At the hotel we got talking to a lady from the USA. Out of the blue she said, 'I'm going to ask if there is a room where we can go so that we can't be disturbed, because I need you to pray with me'. We had a long session. She wrote to us later that this had been the most outstanding spiritual experience she had ever had.

In the late 1970s, I received an invitation to visit, and to give a talk about my research, at a French government scientific research station in the Pyrenees. It was proving difficult to arrange my travel until a colleague in the French department, a fellow parishioner, suggested that I book to go on a pilgrimage to Lourdes. From there I could catch a train to Toulouse, from where a second train would take me close to my destination. They were willing to send a car to complete my journey. I reached Lourdes on Saturday, and on the airport coach was greeted by a priest from Lancashire, who remembered me from my helping to organise renewal conferences for priests. I left my hotel before breakfast Monday and was at my destination by mid-day. Returning the next day, I got in conversation, as best I could with my little French, with a man on the train and talked about God. I was in my hotel in time for the evening meal. That evening and others, I joined the priest in praying at length with several troubled people late into the night at the Grotto.

Telephone Ministry

A great many of those who come to our home telephone for additional prayer, encouragement and support in between appointments, or after they have stopped making ongoing regular appointments. We have also been in ministry to people we have never met face-to-face. Telephone calls for help have come from some of whom we had never heard; from Northern Ireland, London, West Midlands and elsewhere. I have even had a few sessions of listening and praying with a lady in North America via Skype.

In one case, telephone calls of well over one hour went on for a number of years. It was wonderful to listen to someone who, initially, was convinced that there was a conspiracy against her in her workplace, and who was struggling to hold onto God. Some years later, her confidence and trust had returned; she had even been able to accept promotion and more responsibility, and her peace of mind and faith in God was restored. Telephone ministry is very far from ideal, of course. For one thing, one loses almost all the non-verbal part of the communication, but it can be better than nothing until the Church provides more local ministry.

Before going on to discuss some of the things we learnt from many sources, and still continue to learn, we will look briefly in Chapter 4 at some of the experiences which we have had over the years which brought us slowly and unevenly, perhaps reluctantly, to the vital importance of this truth which St Paul wrote about in 2Co 12:9–10: 'When I am weak I am strong'.

Significant Points

- The Holy Spirit may have to disturb us out of a life to which we have become accustomed, and in which we feel comfortable.

- His call can be completely unexpected and in a direction which surprises us.

- He always has more to reveal and to teach us.

- He may well ask us to do something outside our experience, and beyond our present capabilities, so that we have to learn to depend upon His power.

Scripture for Meditation

For the message about Christ's death on the cross is nonsense to those who are being lost; but for us who are being saved it is God's power. The scripture says, 'I will destroy the wisdom of the wise and set aside the understanding of the scholars' ... God has shown that this world's wisdom is foolishness. For God in His wisdom made it impossible for people to know Him by means of their own wisdom. For what seems to be God's foolishness is wiser than human wisdom, and what seems to be God's weakness is stronger than human strength. God purposely chose what the world considers nonsense in order to shame the wise, and He chose what the world considers weak in order to shame the powerful. He chose what the world looks down on and despises, and thinks is nothing, in order to destroy what the world thinks is important. This means that no-one can boast in God's presence'. (1 Co 1:18–19, 20b, 21a, 25–29)

4

WHEN I AM WEAK I AM STRONG

When You Don't Know What to Say the Holy Spirit will Speak in You

One early example of the Lord acting when we are at our weakest came when I had gone reluctantly to the International Leaders' Conference in charismatic renewal in Rome in 1975. I had been held back at first from accepting the invitation by my feelings of inadequacy. A meeting of the European leaders was called and the other two representatives of England and Wales were not available. A dispute (in French) arose over two future plans. The priest who was translating for me became so caught up in the disagreements that he stopped translating. I just sat there letting it all flow over me because, although I knew what the two issues were, I did not know what arguments other people were raising. Suddenly, the senior priest who was chairing the meeting stopped them and said', 'Let us hear what Alan has to say'. I stood up (to gain an extra second) but I had no idea what to say. What I came out with completely settled both matters and there was no more discussion. As a direct result, I was invited that evening to have dinner with Cardinal Suenens, together with a Swiss priest and an American priest.

Jesus Himself said, 'Do not worry about what else you are going to say or how you will say it; when the time comes, you will be given what you will say. For the words you speak will not be yours; they will come from the Spirit of your Father speaking in you,' (Mt 10:19–20).

I had other providential encounters in Rome with a variety of wonderful people. A bishop from Central America (who later was forced to flee because of his support for poor people against rich landowners) told me that he had learnt more from meeting to pray with peasants in his diocese, than he had from all his years of studying.

One of the many people with whom I had the privilege to talk in Rome was David du Plessis, possibly the best-known member of the Pentecostal churches in the world. It was he who, when invited to a meeting of the World Council of Churches and asked the question 'What do you have in the Pentecostal churches which we do not have in the mainstream churches?', replied , 'Nothing, but whereas you have it on ice, we have it on fire'. It was some of that fire and a natural spring welling up within to speak of the power of God's love, to bring the Good News to them, which I was beginning to witness in Catholics as well. It was infectious; faith truly can be caught rather than just taught. The experience of being among 10,000 Catholics from 120 countries, wholeheartedly worshipping and praising God at the Catacombs of St Calixtus was profound and very moving. There was no sense of emotionalism or simply the witnessing of a musical performance, but clear feeling of everyone being lifted out of themselves to focus on God and being given a foretaste of Heaven.

Even my return journey from Rome, was an experience of being taken out of control. I was delayed in St Peter's Basilica by saying goodbye to people from different countries, particularly a lady from the USA with cancer, who wanted to talk. I walked quickly and soon became lost. The only person in sight was a priest. 'Will he speak English?' I wondered. He was a Jesuit from Farm Street, who took me to the bus stop. He became anxious that I was going to miss my charter flight, whereas I, completely uncharacteristically felt completely calm.

Eventually I reached the airport, presented my ticket and was told, 'Your flight goes from Fiumicino'. I rushed up to a taxi, gave the driver English notes plus all my lira, but suddenly retained 200 lira. I reached the airport well after departure time. There was a long queue. I was told that it was for the Leeds diocesan pilgrimage to a Marian conference, and that I was booked on it. The next moment Bishop William Gordon Wheeler walked by. My wife and I knew him well because we were members of the diocesan Ecumenical Commission and the Pastoral Council, and from other contacts with him. The flight had been delayed by a baggage handlers' strike, but just as I joined it, it began to move. There was a 200 lira airport charge!

'Perhaps I meant to speak to the bishop about my experiences?', I wondered, but decided that I would not approach him. The Lord could arrange it if He wished. I kept out of his way at Fiumicino, at Manchester airport and on the coach. People were being dropped at various places, and then the bishop and others got out at a presbytery. I was taken a few miles further, and dropped at cross-roads, where I was told I could get a bus to Leeds. I waited for ages, and then a car pulled up and offered me a lift. It was the bishop's car. All the way to my home the bishop was asking me questions about my experiences.

Desert Experience

For five-and-a-half years after the conversion experience in 1973, I had great awareness of God's presence through my senses, and it seemed easy to spend appreciable time in prayer each day.

Then, abruptly, it seemed as if God had left me alone, and all I could cry out was 'What did I do to drive you away?' I had absolutely no idea about how spiritual life might develop, and of how we need to be brought into some 'desert' experience in order that we learn to live and serve God by faith alone. I went to the Jesuit chaplain at the University for spiritual direction. In December 1979 I went very apprehensively—but in obedience to his suggestion—to an eight-day silent retreat at St Beunos. There, despite being unable to enter into the usual Ignatian meditation, I spent hours each day in prayer and I was given such a deep gift of peace that I hardly wanted to come home. It is because of God's infinite love that He takes us into the 'desert', so that we are completely dependent upon Him: 'So I am going to take her into the desert again; there I will win her back with words of love' (Ho 2:14).

The previous August, however, I was committed to organise, with my wife and another lady, the third six-day Charismatic Renewal Conference at Ampleforth, with four hundred people attending. Because I was so wretched at God's apparent departure from me, I could not relax and cope readily with all the problems which were brought each meal and tea or coffee time for me to solve. I felt totally unfit to deal with all the queries, or to be one of a ministry pair, as I had in the two previous conferences. In my distress, I felt that I wanted to go home and hide away from people.

Each afternoon, there was a long period of Exposition of the Blessed Sacrament in the church. In the crypt below, there were a good many pairs in little chapels ready to pray with those who, while praying in the church, realised they needed help. All I felt capable of doing was to stand at the foot of the stairs to direct people to a ministry pair who had become free.

Suddenly, I heard loud shouting, so I went to investigate. I only learnt the consequences later on. The man concerned, who went on to become a powerful witness to many others, published a full account fifteen years later in 'Voice', the magazine of the Full Gospel Business Men's Fellowship

International. Part of this is reproduced as Testimony 4A (p. 77). The fact that God chose to use me in this way at one of the lowest points of my life when I felt completely useless, is an example of 'not by might, nor by power, but by my Spirit, says the Lord of Hosts' (Zc 4:6).

Work Problems

Around that time I came very close to a breakdown. I had committed myself some months earlier to examine two PhD candidates. One, at a British university, was late in submitting a 300-page thesis, and had a date not far ahead to begin work in his own country. The other thesis, also late and of similar length, was submitted to the Australian National University in Canberra, by an Australian who had a flight booked to Heathrow, and an outgoing flight three days later to the USA, where he was due to begin work immediately.

In order to concentrate on such a thesis, without the interruptions in the University, I had always had to do the work at home. I knew how many weeks' work in my spare time would be needed. But there was simply nowhere near this time available. I couldn't sleep for worry so all my work suffered, and I was rapidly spiralling out of action. At 3am one morning, sitting in the kitchen unable to sleep, I picked up a little prayer book, and for the first time read the words of Jesus in John 15: 'Without me, you can do nothing'. I cried out for help.

A day or two later, I felt that I was being told, 'You have examined enough PhDs to be able to judge whether or not to award the degree, without doing so many hours of work.' All the work was completed without any further stress; I slept well and felt a deep peace. It was several years later that it dawned on me that I had been spending far too long on such theses in previous years, out of my own feelings of inadequacy and insecurity.

It was interesting to note that after 1973, when I became so involved in the Church, and when I stopped bringing work home for the evenings and weekends, my research output increased. After a few years I noticed that I was publishing more than twice as many papers a year as I had averaged over the previous twenty years. Yet I was spending far less time on research and I was much more relaxed. My ambition for promotion had gone, but it was then that the University made me a professor. Truly, if we seek the Kingdom of God, then all else (that we really need in God's eyes) will be added.

It is important to help people to realise that when they open up their lives afresh to the Spirit of God and seek deeper wholeness, then their progress will not be smoothly and continuously upwards. Human life generally involves going through ups and downs, physical, mental and spiritual variation, dealing with new external situations and problems and God revealing more ways in which we need Him to change and heal us. It is not surprising that as I found God blessing my professional life I was having to cope with personal problems.

Family Crises

Both my wife and I went through more suffering than ever before, after the decisive change in our spiritual lives began to occur in 1973. One night we felt that our marriage might end and we knelt down together and cried out to Jesus for help. Our marriage lasted fifty-eight years, and we grew in love and unity as the years went by. Unity in relationship with one another and with Christ Himself is needed in a pair of people used by Him to pray for the healing of others, because a lack of unity can result in there being little or no power of the Holy Spirit to be a blessing to others.

Another time, because I felt I would never change and that I was the cause of some disunity within our family, I said to Betty, 'You and the children would be all be better off if I were dead'. I had to go to London the next day and to remain for a few days, as part of a committee organising an international scientific conference. There I met an Italian lady who had exactly the same problems with a relative as I did. The Lord had recently revealed to her that she and a man with the same situation would be helped through the sacrament of Reconciliation. As soon as I returned to Leeds I asked a priest to give me longer than usual in the sacrament, so that I could talk in more detail. That family relationship was healed, and went on to be a very strong one.

Out of the blue, a very serious accusation was made against one of our sons, and two police officers came to our home to question him. They said it would be three months before a decision whether or not to charge him would be made. My earlier nature had been to worry and be anxious, yet during that three months we lost no sleep, and had no anxiety, despite our powerlessness to help. Some four years later, the accuser, whom we had never met or spoken with, telephoned in tears to ask for forgiveness for having told a lie.

Unlikely Candidate as a Listener

I would never have picked myself as a possible candidate for something which involves a great deal of listening. I was probably one of the worst listeners that anyone could have found. I was filled with feelings of inadequacy, poor self-worth and shyness, which kept me isolated from people. When someone spoke to me, I would interrupt them because I was afraid that, if I waited till they had finished, I would have forgotten what I had worked out to say next. I was so busy working out what comment I would make that I was not really listening to what they were saying. Worse still, when I met someone for the first time, I would often be thinking, 'What benefit to me can there be from my meeting and listening to this person?' Yet now I estimate that I have spent of the order of 10,000 hours listening to people. Truly, God picks the most unlikely people, in human eyes, because He puts His treasure in earthen vessels (2 Co 4:7) in order to show that it must be His power which is at work.

Awareness of Greater Weakness, not Strength

We have often been asked, 'Doesn't it drain you to spend hours listening to people with deep problems?' We have never felt drained. Tired? Yes—very sad for them—but we put all the burdens onto Christ. Only He can help them. We realise that we are being given a wonderful privilege, both by the person trusting us, sometimes telling us things which they have never told anyone else, and by God, who allows us to 'stand on holy ground', while He is helping one of His beloved wounded children. We often said, after someone left us, 'I wonder how many more of these amazing people God will bring here.

Grace always flows both ways, not in one direction only. One Monday morning we both awoke feeling below par. After Mass at 9.15 am, we had a 10am appointment. When this person had left at midday, we felt somewhat better. We had lunch and prepared for a second person at 2pm. By the time that person left, at teatime, we felt fine. They may well have been helped more by God than if we had felt really well, because then we might have been more in control and could have obscured God's working more.

One of the deep-rooted needs in most of us is to have to try to be in control. This comes from very early experiences of insecurity, where part of our natural defensive reactions, is to try to remain in control of the situation, out of fear that things may get worse, or even go into increasing chaos. This builds up great pressures in our unconscious mind and can use up much internal energy, and make it very difficult for us to relax and find inner peace and concentrate on someone else's needs. We have prayed with many people for the Lord to heal the deep origins of this so as to take away all the pressures, and set them free to allow Him to be in increasing control of everything in their lives. Teachers have been among those who find this particularly difficult to learn and to permit Jesus to make changes within them. If you are not in control of a class, then you can't do any teaching. Priests can find that their training in seminaries may have reinforced any past family, womb and early childhood influences, which combine to keep them prisoners of this need to be in control.

I have only described, in this and other chapters, a few of the many occasions when I was compelled to let go of control, such as with the mother and son in Leeds, and in the sheer tiredness of listening to someone for three and three-quarter hours, following four hours of listening earlier that day. On these occasions I have been forced to recognise my utter inability to know what to do or say, and to abandon temporarily my pretence of being able to rely on my own self-sufficiency and pride, so that the Holy Spirit was then able to work as He wanted, and someone was greatly helped.

We may be tempted to misunderstand some things we read or hear, as implying that God makes us stronger and stronger. Some examples are 'The Lord will give strength to His people', Ps 28 (Morning Office, Week 1, Monday): 'May you be made strong with all His strength', Col 1:9, (Evening Office, Week 1, Monday): '…that we may always draw strength from you', (Concluding Prayer, Evening Office, Week 1, Wednesday). If we supposed that we were really growing stronger, we would be in even greater dangers such as relying on ourselves in our old ways of pride and independence. We are meant to grow in faith, that at those times when we cry out to the Lord in humility and weakness, because of our need or someone else's, then He will always provide His power. It seems to me that as we go through life, we have experiences which cause us to learn more and more deeply that we are utterly weak and totally dependent upon God, as St Paul so clearly learned, and wrote about, particularly in 2 Corinthians 12.

I am struck by a quotation from Paul Tillich, given in the Glenstall Missal:

Both the Old and New Testaments describe our existence in relation to God as one of waiting. Waiting means **not** having and having at the same time. The condition of man's relation to God is first of all one of **not** having, **not** seeing, **not** knowing and **not** grasping. I think of the theologian who does not wait for God, because he possesses Him, enclosed within a doctrine. I think of the biblical scholar who does not wait for God, because he possesses Him, enclosed within a book. I think of the churchman who does not wait for God, because he possesses Him, enclosed within an institution. I think of the believer who does not wait for God, because he possesses Him, enclosed within his own experience. It is not easy to endure this not having God, this waiting for God, without convincing ourselves and others that we **have** God, and can dispose of Him. How can God be possessed? Is God a thing to be known and grasped among other things? Is God less than a human person? We always have to wait for a human being. Even in the most intimate communion among human beings, there is an element of **not** having and **not** knowing, and of waiting. Therefore since God is infinitely hidden, free and incalculable, we must wait for Him in the most absolute and radical way. He is God for us just in so far as we do **not** possess Him. We have God through **not** having Him.

It is vital in any area of the healing ministry to recognise the danger of our taking Him for granted, falling back into relying on the little that He has chosen to reveal to us; on the assumptions and presumptions we may have made as a result; or on our past experience.

An Example of the Experience of Others

Testimony 4B (p. 78) illustrates that many others are led to this experience of God working through them when they are at their weakest. It is a particularly poignant and courageous one, written by one of our parishioners, who even at the lowest point of his life showed concern for someone else. I regret that for most of my life I was centred on myself, not because of anything life-threatening like this man experienced, but because of feeling inferior and useless to others. Because of this and my pride, I was driven to put more effort and time into my work than a healthy balance would have indicated. I had needed God to change me in many ways over a long period, not least in becoming concerned about others and being set free of my old attitudes towards them.

As Frances Hogan says, each of us, at every moment, has only two directions in which to look:

- at ourselves and our problems, in which case our mind magnifies the problems, or,

- at Christ and like His mother we magnify the Lord.

If we choose (1) we may, in the words of Sister Michael, become a 'PLOM' (poor little old me). The man who wrote Testimony 4B (p. 78) is still continuing to choose (2).

Attitude Towards Others

By nature I was judgemental and critical towards the behaviours and attitudes of other people. As I have been made aware more and more deeply of my own weakness and brokenness, and of how totally I have to depend on the Lord; He has been gradually changing me, and still needs to do more.

I have often been struck by the realisation that when someone reveals to me their hurts and needs, I no longer have the judgemental attitudes I would once have had, or might still even have now, if I were to read about them in the press, rather than meeting them face-to-face. Instead, I am aware of being privileged by the person confiding in me and by God, allowing me to stand with them 'on holy ground'. I feel compassion and love for them. I'm not on some kind of superior level, but sharing in their brokenness and weakness, like the beggar who says to another, 'I've found a source of good food; if you'd like to walk with me, I'll show you where it is.'

Only Jesus can know intimately the deepest needs of this person, and only He has the power and the love with which to heal them, and is aware of just how difficult it is for them to open themselves up, and at what pace they are able to go. This takes all pressure off me and I can relax and help them to be as relaxed as it is possible for them to be at each stage of the process. Even if they are not in a place to be aware of this, at least I can try to avoid putting the slightest, even subtle, pressure upon them.

We had learnt a very clear lesson that the Holy Spirit never works through someone putting pressure on another person in November 1973. The follow-up meeting to that in the August in Littlehampton, where my life changed, was held in Birmingham. Again, about thirty people came. Those from the South had correctly diagnosed a need to relieve the pressure on one couple, by finding someone else to produce the national newsletter. They believed that they had the right solution, and were so sure that they tried to impose it without prayerful consideration and discernment involving everyone. Those of us from elsewhere instinctively knew that this was not the right solution. It fell to a well-known priest to voice this. There was great distress, and many tears.

Peace only returned well into the Sunday afternoon, with the decision to form a national committee. I was elected one of the original members of the National Service Committee for Catholic Charismatic Renewal in England and Wales. Humanly, that seemed to make no sense, when three months earlier I had been about to abandon any attempt to know God better; yet I served for eight-and-a-half years and the Lord did many remarkable things.

During one of the six-day conferences which we organised, we met together as a committee halfway through, and began to agonise over the deep suffering which was evident among many at the conference. It was one of the few occasions when the Lord seemed to use me to speak, when He said, in effect, 'I called them here; I know what I am doing; just relax and let me get on with it.' By the end of the conference the whole mood had changed to one of peace as the Lord worked through people meeting and praying together.

One of the great blessings is that the Lord called my wife and myself to minister mainly in our own home. There is no fixed agenda of a method or procedure or timetable. Within reason, I do not need to fix the duration of each session. I do not put pressure to make further appointments, but if they want to come I will continue to minister to them, not just over months, but we have in a few cases gone on for several years. Often they choose to return years later, as the Lord shows that the time is right to go into some deeper level of healing.

When the Lord calls people to minister during retreats, conferences, courses etc., as we ourselves have done many times, then clearly there is limited time, and if they live many miles apart, it may not be possible to meet up again. We have known the Lord do the most amazing healings on such occasions. However, it is vital that we do not seek to impose a goal, which is not out of the freedom of God's will being done and has more to do with our seeking the satisfaction of seeing some particular healing there and then, out of our own needs and pride. We should not be under any pressure, or impose it on those needing ministry, to accomplish any more than the Lord knows is right for that individual at any particular stage. Like St Paul, we need to accept that we just do the best with that part which the Lord calls us to do. 'Each one of us does the work which the Lord gave him to do; I sowed the seed, Apollos watered the plant, but it was God who made the plant grow. The one who sows and the one who waters do not matter. It is God who matters, because He makes the plant grow...We are partners working together for God, and you are God's field' (1 Co 3:5–6, 9).

Those who are called by God into the ministry of His love to others need to have come to love themselves and discover who they are, and then move on to accept themselves, and forget about themselves, in giving full attention to another person who is in need. As God allows us to experience His love, we begin to realise the tremendous worth of this damaged person, and to have reverence for them. It is this accepting, patient love God gives us which can begin to set them free. Perhaps we should also remember that God loves those who hurt them, perhaps very badly, and that they, too, are precious to Him and He wants to save them, and we are not sitting in judgement of them.

I believe that many who have experienced charismatic renewal are likely to be amongst those who are, or who will be, called into this ministry. Their experience of a real and deepening relationship with Christ, and of His love for them, should be setting them free of pre-occupations with self, so as to be available to be used by Him to help others. The various charisms can play an important role.

It is important that, if and when God calls, they step beyond concentrating only on the prayer group and renewal meetings. The test of a prayer meeting, it seems to me, is not so much what goes on in the worship in the meeting itself, as in the fruits which grow in the members' lives, as evidenced by deeper healing in their family relationships, and in their being set free to be used by God to bring deeper healing and faith to others outside the group.

In 1980, I was the official delegate of charismatic renewal to the National Pastoral Conference in Liverpool, and was invited to speak about this at the national leaders' conference held a few weeks later. Drawing on my meetings with many other delegates, also in renewal, who were becoming very active, perhaps in hidden ways, in their local churches, I took my theme from John 12:24–26, where Jesus says: 'I am telling you the truth; a grain of wheat remains no more than a single grain unless it is dropped into the ground and dies. If it does die, it produces many grains. Whoever loves his own life will lose it, whoever hates his own life in this world will keep it for life eternal. Whoever wants to serve me must follow me so that my servant will be with me where I am...'. Not everyone agreed with me.

This same passage of Scripture has played a significant role in one priest (some of whose teaching needs careful discernment) drawing attention to similarities, as though from a common inspiration of the Holy Spirit, between the twelve step programme for addiction and the Gospel message of Christ.[1] Each of these steps has been examined in the light of our need for healing, beginning with step 1: 'I accept that I am powerless. I have been trying to control my own life and I have not been succeeding'. It continues with exploration of much within each of us that controls our thinking and behaviour, but which has been hidden or partially obscured, and all of which needs transformation. In this present study of praying for inner healing, this involves discovering early roots which lie behind all our distress and difficulties.

Significant Points

- God can change our old reactions of anxiety and fear and inadequacy when we are suddenly out of control of the situation, and give us peace in which He can use us unexpectedly.

- However wonderful it is to experience God's infinite love for us personally, and His working in new ways through us, we have to go beyond depending upon feelings, so all that remains in the darkness of His apparent absence, is our faith.

- If we can accept and even welcome our total weakness and dependence upon God, we find a new depth of peace, and we can begin to serve in freedom and without the strain of our old burdens.

- God needs us to help others.

Scripture for Meditation

His answer was: 'My grace is all you need, for my power is greatest when you are weak.' I am happy, then, to be proud of my weaknesses, in order to feel the protection of Christ's power over me. For when I am weak then I am strong. (2 Co 12:9)

To Him who is able to do much more than we can ever ask for, or even think of, by means of the power working in us: to God be the glory in the Church and in Christ Jesus, for all time, for ever and ever. Amen. (Ep 3:20–21)

You are the people of God; He loved you and chose you for His own. Therefore you must put on compassion, kindness, humility, gentleness and patience. Be helpful to one another and forgive one another. And to all these add love which binds all things together in perfect unity. (Col 3:12–14)

Testimonies

Testimony 4A

'I fell further and further into debt. I became riddled with anxiety, nervousness and guilt. I was too tired to pray, couldn't think clearly and was constantly angry and short-tempered. Finally in the summer of 1979 my wife nagged and eventually succeeded in persuading me to attend a one-week charismatic conference. I took along my golf clubs and flatly refused to attend any prayer meetings.

By mid-week I had upset many people by my anger and arguments. They were excited about this personal Jesus. Finally I was so overcome with physical pain, mental anguish and despair that I reluctantly decided to give this Jesus a chance. With a cynical and impatient attitude I went to a ministry team, but when I thought that they were just trying to psycho-analyse me, I started to walk away, angrily calling them names. At that point a man alarmed by the disturbance I was creating approached me. I was about to reject him, too, when he told me to stand still, which I did, as I sensed some kind of authority within him.

Next he placed his hand on my head and spoke some words in a heavenly language. I fell flat on my back on a marble floor without injury. I lay there approximately 20–30 minutes. I could feel the collective rubbish; pain and confusion leave my mind and body. I sobbed for what seemed an eternity and then felt a tremendous peace. The Holy Spirit started to fill me with such joy and peace, it is beyond description. At that point, I too came to know Jesus in a personal way.

When I got up I was a completely changed person. I could hardly stand. Appearing to be drunk, all I could feel was a truly joyful and happy sensation within me.

Knowing Jesus has utterly changed my life. There is a constant joy in my inner being and a desire to share it with all those I meet, especially in my own church. The sheer happiness is beyond understanding.'

Testimony 4B

'This was going to be the best time of my life, going to Australia to run in the world athletic championships for the over forties, on Saturday, 29th November, 2003. Then, after work at the local hospital physiotherapy department, my world fell apart on Thursday, 27th. As I began my second job, as a back pain exercise therapist, I suddenly felt ill. Seconds later I had a major stroke and woke up in hospital.

Next day the doctors told me I had suffered such a severe stroke that they could not explain why I had not died that night. I told them that somehow I knew the Lord had other things for me to do than run marathons, though I wouldn't know what it is until the time is right. A few hours later this inner peace came over me. I thought that being in a wheelchair might just be the start of my life, not the end.

Next day the young man in a bed opposite was unable to eat or ask for help. For some unknown reason I managed to crawl into the wheelchair beside my bed and push myself with the one leg that worked. On reaching him I began to read the Holy Bible to him and looking into his eyes I could see the smile.

That's the reason why I survived this illness, so I could help others not to give up faith. The Lord is speaking to us, but we may not be listening. If we pray for help with an illness, don't give up, but listen for the meaning. As a well-known athlete, I had every reason to give up my faith, but what would have happened to Robert the little boy in Africa I have put through school? Let us remember that we still have the chance to help others like ourselves, no matter if it's cancer or some other debilitating illness. It may be our time to help others to get over such illness.'

Notes

[1] R. Rohr, *Breathing Under Water—Spirituality and the Twelve Steps* (Cincinnati: St Anthony Messenger Press, 2011).

5

DEEP EARLY ROOTS

The Real Problem

It is well known in counselling that the presenting problem is often not the real problem. Many people are unaware of the real root causes of their unease, while others may be in denial, or be unwilling to face up to them and to reveal them. In some cases, it will be genuinely hidden from their conscious mind.

We had an example of this on the course at Kinnoull. Apart from us there was only one other lay person. Besides several priests and brothers, most of the participants were sisters. In order to learn the counselling technique which we were being taught, we had to practice on one another. We were asked to work on real problems and not make anything up. One day, we were in threes, and it was the turn of Sister A to be counselled while Sister B observed the proceedings. I was to be the counsellor.

Sister A said, 'I have far too much work and I need to drop something. I am Superior of the convent; I am head of a department in a school, and I lead a big prayer group. All the people in need of help in this group come to me. For instance, last Friday, the day before I travelled here to Scotland, a girl in the prayer group had said 'Sister, I must see you before you go away'. So I taught all morning; got into the car and drove to the convent; I listened and prayed with this girl; then I drove back to school, arriving ten minutes after classes had begun again.'

I asked her if she had managed to eat any lunch. She replied, 'Oh, I didn't have time for any lunch. I think I must ask the Provincial if she will agree to my giving up my teaching post'. We began to use the counselling technique. All that happened was that she went into tears. Sister B tried to help her, but to no avail.

So I said, 'Let's stop using the counselling method, and ask Jesus to reveal what is really going on.' Within a few moments of our prayer, Sister A said, 'The problem is not overwork; it is another Sister'. Sister A and Sister C had been together in training college and convent for many years, and Sister C was always negative and hostile to any decisions Sister A had made. She continued, 'Years ago the Provincial came to me and asked me to become the Superior, but I refused because of the reactions of Sister C. Years later the Provincial returned and told me I had no alternative this time, and I reluctantly accepted the post.'

We were now in a position to pray for Sister A to be able to let go, to Jesus, all of her frustrations and other feelings and distress, and to be able to forgive Sister C.

Testimony 5A (p. 94), written by a man well into his seventies, is a further example of how one or more underlying roots may remain hidden for many years. It also shows that roots do not necessarily lie in incidents which would have seemed significant to any adults who were present. There is so much brokenness in mankind. It is sad that this man had to wait over 65 years before he received prayer ministry in which the root of his problem was revealed and healed.

Another example of a root which needed to be uncovered and then healed occurred well over thirty years ago. A very good friend, just married, expressed distress at something not being right in her marriage. A few weeks later, we were giving her a lift. Again she spoke, but with no explanation, of great unhappiness. We parked the car in the grounds of our church. 'Can you think of anything which may be responsible for this situation?' we asked. 'No,' she said. So we prayed for Jesus to reveal the root cause of the problem. Suddenly she said, 'It was a conversation with other children in the playground.' She did not need to say any more. We simply prayed for Jesus to heal the damage. She and her husband were very happy together for the many years until he died. The Lord can identify and release us from 'the little foxes' which have interfered with the free flow of His love in our lives. 'Catch the foxes, the little foxes, before they ruin our vineyard in bloom' (Sg 2:15). We had our own personal experience, through a sudden burst of depression in Betty, that underlying root causes of problems can be unknown or unrecognised for many years.

Betty's Suffering

My wife was ill a number of times over the years, requiring considerable periods in hospital. Then, at the age of 78, she suffered depression for the very first time in her life. She was ill for eight months and needed the help of a psychiatrist and a community psychiatric nurse. A number of anti-depressants were tried until, finally, one of the oldest - and now rarely used drugs - was prescribed for the rest of her life. She was well again until she was 80, when the illness returned and lasted for sixteen months, for two of which she was in a locked ward in the hospital. She went to the very depths.

However, when she gradually recovered, she would tell people that she had become like a new person, and in fact people became aware of an even greater boldness than before in proclaiming the goodness of God, and in inspiring others. Seven months before she died, she helped me to lead a weekend retreat. She began each of the four sessions by preceding my talk with a humorous and helpful reflection.

Betty received more frequent gifts of a word of knowledge, which would help to reveal an area or incident which the Lord was inviting us to pray about for Him to heal, after she became well again, than she had been getting before. Even while she was still in depression, people were continuing to come to our home for ministry. Frequently I would need to see them on my own, or Betty would only feel able to be present for part of the time. There were occasions when she would be in bed throughout the session, but she would be doing her best to pray for the person who was with me, in spite of how difficult, and sometimes impossible, it was for her to pray at all. Sometimes she would call from the bedroom, and when I went in she would give me some message or information which would help in the ministry. I continue to marvel at how many people still remember words which Betty spoke years ago, and which have had a great impact on them. Recently, one of these made it possible to find the root cause of a deep problem.

There was a great deal of prayer about the root cause of Betty's depressions. As far as we could discern, it was connected with the death of her father when she was eighteen months old. Her mother had to take her away from Norwich and leave her and her brother with her own parents in a very small remote village in North Wales, where the grandfather ran the village school. Because there was no work there, her mother had to leave them and live miles away with her own sisters. It was only when Betty was in her eighties that she got in touch with deeply buried hurts, including feeling abandoned and insecure.

As well as praying with her in the ways mentioned in the next sections, it was vital to pray for her to be healed of these damaged reactions, as described in Chapter 7.

It was after she had recovered from depression when Fr Jim McManus and I each gave a talk on healing at Ushaw College to over sixty clergy, including two bishops and the other main leaders of the Anglican, Catholic, Methodist, Baptist and URC churches in the North East, that, after giving a short testimony, she went back up to the microphone and urged them to tell themselves each day that he or she is a beloved child of God. She was also inspirational and challenging when, twice a week, she would introduce the evening programme at our inner healing prayer group.

She died after exactly forty days of very great suffering in body and mind in various hospital wards. I have no doubt that her suffering was united with that of Christ.

In order to look more deeply in this chapter and the two which follow into the factors and aspects involved in praying for inner healing, and in particular for the underlying root causes, it will be helpful to start with a definition of inner healing.

Inner Healing—a Definition

Fr Michael Scanlan had written in 1974 that, 'Inner healing is the healing of the inner person. By inner person we mean the intellectual, volitional and affective areas commonly referred to as mind, will and heart, but including such other areas as related to emotions, psyche, soul and spirit. Inner healing is distinguished from outer healing, commonly called physical healing.[1] He went on to discuss scriptural evidence for inner healing in the ministry of Jesus.

We had read his books and others, particularly by priests, during the 1970s, and we had gained valuable insights into inviting Jesus, who is God as well as man and thus outside time, to go back to heal hurts from the past and release us from burdens of pain locked up in memories in conscious and unconscious or subconscious parts of our minds. We don't forget the memories but we can be set free of the damage and be able to praise and thank God, as illustrated by Testimony 5B (p. 95), written by a lady from another parish after she came for a few sessions of prayer for inner healing. In her case, the Lord did not do the healing during her time of prayer ministry, but instead took her back to the place where the trauma had occurred. It is God who chooses when and how to heal.

Reading the books by John and Paula Sandford,[2] and attending a course which they gave in Durham, gave us further insights. Deeply based upon scripture, they focused attention on those early roots before about the age of seven. One particular aspect which they stressed was concerned with the consequences of how we perceived our father and mother early on, and how, perhaps unconsciously in some cases, we had judged them or perceived them in some negative way.

Honour Your Father and Your Mother

As we read in Ephesians 6:2–3, 'Respect (or honour) your father and mother' is the first commandment that has a promise added: 'so all may go well with you, and you may live a long time in the land.' We have had to minister to very many people where one or both parents treated them very badly, perhaps cruelly, with physical, emotional or sexual abuse, or who left them, or were never there at all, or showed no love or gave any quality time or care; even in some cases where their mother couldn't tell them which man (or of what nationality) may have been the father, or where they had no information at all about one or both parents. It is probable that no one, except Jesus Himself, had perfect parents and was left with absolutely no judgements or negative perceptions. Frequently people are left with some confusions and ambivalence, because they loved their parents, and wanted to believe that their parents were basically good and loving.

It is not the child's fault that they have carried into adult life negative perceptions of parents—they were innocent victims. However, they may have unwittingly gone against one of God's commandments which were not framed for our punishment or restriction, but to give us freedom to live in total peace with God and with one another. Thus the adult needs grace to repent on behalf of the child within, and to bring to Jesus on the Cross all their pain, anger, hatred, self-hatred, guilt etc., and then to ask for more grace to forgive the parent(s). It is not enough, however, just to ask God for the grace to forgive parents and for the gift of His love for them. We also need to open our hearts to receive the gift of honouring them. Our full healing of these childhood wounds depends on our living out that scriptural command to honour our parents. This is discussed further in Chapter 7, in the section on the power of the Word of God.

I don't believe, however, that I would ever fully have appreciated how an apparently mild negative perception of a very good parent, perhaps perceived quite unconsciously, could have such a powerful consequence on happenings in later adult life, if it had not been suddenly and clearly revealed to me in my own life.

One evening when I was in my late sixties, a friend called and she and my wife got me talking about my childhood. I realised for the first time that I had perceived my father as weak. The moment that was revealed, I could see how this had affected my 34 years on the staff of universities.

One after another, I had three heads of department who caused me difficulties because they were weak authority figures. When I was appointed Assistant Lecturer it was a temporary post, with pressure to get a Ph.D. My head of department offered to be my supervisor but gave no suggestions for a topic. While I was doing the research, part-time whilst lecturing, he only saw me about three times to discuss it, beginning with, 'Let's see; what is it that you are working on?' Suddenly, after only two and a half years (less than the time given to a full-time student) he required the thesis because a permanent post was to be advertised nationally, and success would help my chances. It was a nightmare to finish in time. I was extremely grateful that he had given this opportunity, but I really could have done with much more guidance and help. Then he retired. I found his successor causing problems to staff by lack of clear direction, and within a year of returning from Burma I moved to Leeds University. There, I found I had an even weaker head. In the early 1960s, I lay awake night after night, worrying because he would not stand up for me and authorise facilities which were needed to meet the demands of a government research contract which I had secured. I had to be treated for ongoing stomach problems as a consequence.

We pray for the Lord to reveal whatever negative feelings were perceived by the child. We invite Jesus into these memories to take the child in His arms so that they feel safe and loved, and able to express and let go to Him any feeling such as anger, hatred, bitterness, unforgiveness, disappointment etc. He touches their wounds with His wounds and, through His precious blood, draws their pain into His suffering on the Cross. We pray that He gives the child the grace to forgive parents, siblings, relatives, teachers etc. Sometimes the person can visualise Jesus in the painful situation, transforming the memories. Because He is all compassion, love and gentleness, and understands that they too are damaged victims, Jesus will not be condemning parents or others whom the child perceived as hurting or letting them down, but He will, in His own good time and way, invite them to repent and ask the child to forgive them. However, the Lord will give the child the grace to forgive them, whether or not they are ever aware of being asked for this by the offender(s). He wants to give the child more of His love for them, and to enable them to see them with His compassion and understanding, as being damaged through being victims in their turn, though this does not absolve them from being responsible for their actions. He then offers to give them the grace to forgive the offenders.

When we prayed with one man, whose childhood contained frequent family rows, he spoke of one particularly bad one, where he hid in a kitchen cupboard to escape. We prayed for Jesus, the light of the world, to dispel the darkness and take away his fear. He said the cupboard was now filled with light as Jesus held him. We asked him to open the door slightly and look out. He said that his father was standing there looking at him, and that he suddenly went down on the floor and took him out of the cupboard and into his arms. Then he said that his grandfather was standing in the doorway with a scowl on his face and had then turned and walked away. We realised that further prayer at an intergenerational Mass was needed for the deceased grandfather. Sometimes the person may need to let out feelings like anger, bitterness, betrayal etc., - whether against others, themselves or God - by privately shouting or punching a pillow or soft furniture. Betty would sometimes punch a pillow when she was in the depths of depression. We had to learn that what can be termed bitter-root judgements and bitter-root expectation can play a major but often long-hidden role in the pain which we carry, and in the damaged ways in which we react to other people and circumstances, as will now be explained.

Bitter Roots

Among the many ways in which conscious or unconscious judgements or negative perceptions, of one or both parents or of others, may affect the course of subsequent adult life is the bitter-root judgement. In Hebrews 12:15 we read: 'See to it that no-one fail to obtain the grace of God; that no root of bitterness spring up and cause trouble, and by it the many are defiled.' A different translation refers to 'poisoning a whole community' (family and beyond). If, for example, the perception deep in a little girl is 'my father is not there when I need him; I can't rely on him or trust him; he breaks promises and doesn't give me security or support', the consequence may well be that she believes any man or men who become important to her will let her down.

There is also bitter-root expectation which has some consequences, though less than those of the bitter-root judgement. That is where we have repeated experiences of negative behaviour towards us as a child, so as an adult we can have (perhaps unknown to us for a long time), the expectation that we will continue to be treated similarly as an adult. That can put a psychological pressure on others to fulfil this expectation, through our unconscious signals via non-verbal communication e.g. looks, glances, facial expressions, tone of voice, hesitations and pauses etc. The less the other person who is receiving these signals is strong and at peace in their inner being, the more likely they are to react negatively and continue the pattern. This, like the judgement, can be a significant factor in marriage, work and social situations.

These bitter roots will have formed during our early childhood, but there are three areas in which underlying root causes can affect us adversely. They are:

- effects of damage from past generations of our family;

- the time in the womb, including our conception and birth;

- the early years of babyhood and childhood up to about the age of seven.

Of those, the third area generally contains the most damaging and hurtful influences and is likely to require longer ministry than either of the other two. For this reason Chapters 6 and 7 are needed to deal with the many aspects of this period. In the rest of this chapter we now look first at our time in the womb and during delivery, and then at the healing of harmful patterns arising from the behaviour of people in the past generations of our family, in what is often called intergenerational healing.

The Time in the Womb

In addition to the hurts of the first seven years of life we had been learning early on from a variety of sources, including research by doctors, that a baby in the womb can suffer in a number of ways. If the mother has any painful experiences leading to a variety of negative emotions, such as anger, guilt fear, hatred, rejections and others, then the hormones are changed and the baby is affected.

86

We encountered many examples of this. One concerned us directly. When our oldest son was in his thirties, he told us that he was in difficulties with his work, arising from fear that he did not have sufficient information on a number of aspects of his responsibilities. Thus he had left unfinished many of these tasks beyond the dates when he had been due to complete them. My wife realised that his fear had originated in the womb. She had lost our first (and sixth) child in miscarriage. When she became pregnant again, she was fearful that she would lose this child, too. She was hospitalised for some time because the doctors were concerned. Our son accepted the truth of this. One day, walking in the woods, we sat on a seat and he asked me to pray for the Lord to free him of all the fear which had come to him. Over the years since then he has been able to take a more onerous post in an entirely different organisation, and to handle the challenges.

Another case involved a lady, strong in her faith. Some years after we met her, and were uplifted by her, she called for help. She was disconcerted because she now felt unwanted in her church. When we prayed, we discovered that the root was that her mother had not known that she was pregnant, until she had been in the womb for seven months.

One man, when we were praying for Jesus to heal his time in the womb, got in touch with anger that he, one of twins, was not acknowledged or welcomed through the pregnancy; because the doctors believed that there was only one child. Another man, during prayer, got in touch with the information that his parents had said, 'We can't afford another child'. That rejection, which we have known many to encounter in the womb, does very great damage. It seems likely that awareness of such a hostile reception may even precede the stage where medical knowledge would rule out any structures which can record memory in ways we can fully understand.

We have prayed with a number where abortion was advocated to the mother or sought by her, and almost happened. This threat to the baby's life has serious effects, and this played a major part in the story in Chapter 2 of the lady who sought prayer for healing, but deep down did not want to be healed.

Prayer is also needed for the delivery period. If, for example, a baby is struggling to draw the first breaths on emerging from the womb, then later in adult life there can be great reluctance to face and engage with changes and new challenges. It is as though, just as the baby is tempted to draw back into the womb where it had been safe because it is in danger of choking, then the adult tries to retreat back into older familiar and seemingly safer conditions.

For many years, we began our prayer at conception, with someone who was willing, because conception may have involved violence, lust, drunkenness. Then a priest invited a sister to give a mission in a nearby parish. She revealed that as a child she remembered her father beating her mother's head against a wall. The marriage broke. Later, he murdered someone and went to prison. Out of that background has come a wonderful sister who radiates Christ. Betty said to her that we prayed with people beginning at conception. Sister said, 'Yes, I used to do that till the Lord told me to start my prayer earlier'. We looked at her. She said, 'It says in Jeremiah 1, "Before I formed you in the womb, I knew you"'.

Later on, we realised that St Paul tells us: 'Even before the world was made, God had already chosen us to be his through our union with Christ, so that we would be holy and without fault before Him' (Ep 1:4). For years since then, we have begun our prayer with praising God that this person has been in the mind of God from all eternity, when they were completely whole and at one with Him, just as eventually they will be once again when they reach Heaven and live in the fullness of praise of God. Thus it seems to complete a circle of prayer from wholeness, through all the damage due to our own sins and those of others which we begin to encounter once we are conceived into a damaged family line, back to the eventual wholeness or holiness, for which Christ suffered and rose again.

Having prayed through the months in the womb for Jesus to heal any damage, and to give this new life total love and welcome and peace, we pray for easing of any pain or stress at birth, particularly where the birth was very painful and prolonged, or for example if the baby struggled to draw the first breaths because the cord was around its neck. We can pray for the Holy Spirit to breathe life into the lungs of a baby who is in distress. We then pray that the baby is delivered into the arms of Jesus. There he or she will receive love and security, with the assurance that the Lord will never leave them (though they may only sense rarely his presence through feelings). We then pray that the Lord will put His arms round baby, mother, father and siblings. Often that bonding could not in fact be complete, e.g. mother or baby needed separate medical care, or the baby was placed in an incubator because of being premature, or the father was absent. All of this can be healed and restored by Christ.

Intergenerational Healing

Beginning in 1982, books by Dr Kenneth McAll,[3] followed by books by at least two priests,[4] reminded the Church of the vital importance of praying for the dead, but now revealed that through such loving, forgiving prayers at a Mass celebrated specifically for this intention, God could bring healing of many kinds to those alive now.

It had, of course, long been known by doctors that many ills and damaging patterns tend to run in families, affecting some members and perhaps generations more than others. Dr McAll had, as a consultant psychiatrist, had many patients referred to him where conventional medicine had made little difference. He discovered that when his patients accepted his invitation to join in praying at a Eucharist for those in the family who had died, then very many experienced great improvements in their health. As one priest put it, out of love for our families, present and yet to be born, it is most important that we pray for God's mercy for those who have died. These patterns of damage do not need to be allowed to affect our children, grandchildren and others to come.

Dr McAll drew attention to the particular need for prayer for those who died in tragedies, wars, suicide, murder, accident, especially where there may have been little or no prayer for the repose of the soul of the deceased, due to circumstances, or due to the lack of faith in the family. The Jesuit brothers Dennis and Matthew Linn had given examples of physical and emotional healing in one or more living members of a family following prayer for miscarried, stillborn or aborted babies.[5] One example was a seven-year-old son whose hyperactivity and disabilities, diagnosed as permanent, disappeared weeks after prayer for three traumatic miscarriages.

When we lost our first child through miscarriage in 1952, we did not think to pray for that child. We read Dr Kenneth McAll's book 'Healing the Family Tree' when it was published in 1982, and immediately asked a priest to celebrate Mass in our house and we prayed for our first and sixth children, and my wife received names for them in prayer. My wife's prayer partner in the Lydia Fellowship, whose women members meet to pray for Britain, was an Anglican attending a Baptist church. There were difficult relationships in her family. When we told her about intergenerational healing, she drew up a family tree. All one side had broken marriage after broken marriage, including her first marriage. It seemed to go back to the suicide of a great-great- grandfather. Because a eucharistic service was rarely celebrated where she was attending, she gratefully came to the Mass in our house, to pray for the repose of the soul of this ancestor, and for all the family. It was wonderful to see improvements taking place in relationships in her family as time went on.

Since then, some 80–100 such Masses have been celebrated by a number of priests, at our request, for people coming to us for ministry. Latterly, they have been a regular part of our parish life, taking place three times a year on a Tuesday when we always have Mass in the evening.

Many people attending these Masses have witnessed to becoming aware of good fruits in the lives of family members. Three testimonies are given to illustrate this, 5C (p. 95), 5D (p. 97), and 5E (p. 97), written respectively by a parishioner who now ministers to others, a lady from another church and one from another diocese.

In 1991, our parish priest asked us to write the following account, which he checked and gave to every parishioner:

> We know that it has been the custom in the Catholic Church from the earliest days, to pray for the dead. There is evidence of this in catacomb and other inscriptions and epitaphs from at least as early as the 2nd century. The importance of praying for the dead was taught by may of the early Fathers of the Church, and is emphasised by our praying for them at every Mass today.
>
> Well-documented experience of priests and doctors has shown that following the loving prayer of the living during a Mass for those who have died in previous generations, there have sometimes been improvements, sometimes very marked ones, in the physical and emotional health of one or more members of the family.
>
> It may help us to think about this by reflecting upon experiences which we may have had of knowing someone who never seems to become free of the influence of one parent, say the mother. We can probably all think of at least one son or daughter who has shown signs of not being able to break away from the other's influence, and so is not free to develop fully and thus become what God gave them the potential to be. Thus there can be restrictive influences of varying levels between two living individuals. Such restrictive influences can continue to exist if one person, say the mother, dies. There is no doubt that we can cut these restricting influences by the authority and power of Christ through prayer,

leaving those concerned free to ask God's help to forgive and to be joined together by God's life-giving love.

In some instances, some things may not have been said or been done before death took place. This may have included forgiveness or reconciliation or telling the person that they were loved. Those still alive may be hurting from this and can pray to forgive and to be forgiven, so that the healing grace of the Lord can come into their life in a new and dynamic way, through their loving prayer for the dead.

Another area at which we need to look is that there has often been a lack of prayer for children who have died through stillbirth, miscarriage or abortion. These children are also part of our family trees and it is very right and loving to pray for them. In this way we invite the Lord Jesus into this area of family life where a particular healing may need to take place.

We may ask, 'Whom should we include in our prayers?' The answer is that we include not only those relatives whom we knew in life, but also those of earlier generations which cause patterns of unloving and unhelpful behaviour or attitudes which seem to occur in a number of generations. Many of us may have said something like 'Oh yes, that runs in our family'. Some families come from communities where throughout generations, even to the present day, there has been great bitterness, unforgiveness, injustice and even cruelty. We need look no further than in Northern Ireland to see this in reality. This reminds us that we need to pray for healing grace and forgiveness for all who have gone before us that they may find rest in the love of God. Some of our earlier ancestors, unknown to us, may have died in tragic circumstances or died alone without the prayer of others.

To prepare ourselves to celebrate the Mass on November 28th and pray in a special way for all who have died, you are invited to draw up a family tree on a piece of paper. Include those names you know, but don't worry about those you do not know because God knows all of them.

As we prepare the gifts at Mass, our family trees will be brought to the altar as a token of our prayer that Jesus will bring all the souls of deceased members of our families into the peace of God the Father as we pray for them in love and forgiveness.

If you wish to have your family tree returned to you, please place it in an envelope with your name on it, so that you can collect it after Mass. Anyone who has lost a child through miscarriage, still-birth or abortion, in addition to including them in the family tree, is also invited to write on a piece of paper a Christian name for the child, with or without a surname.

We began to see, years ago, that many of those coming to our home appeared to be, to the best of their knowledge, the only one in their present family who had any real faith in God, and sometimes they didn't know of anyone in the preceding generations, either. God, being outside time, is aware that, at a certain time in history, there will be one or more individuals in a family who will open up to His love and power. That is sufficient for God to pour out His love, mercy, forgiveness and peace into members of the family long dead, as this one person prays at a Mass for intergenerational healing. God always wants to heal more than just one individual. We are designed to be fully part of the Body of Christ. Thus He wants to heal the relationships with other living members of the family, and to free generations to come from the damage which has been running down the family line. But God wants to go beyond families, to heal church congregations, local communities, whole towns, countries and all of mankind. We all of us have an essential part in this great work of God. He hasn't made any spare parts.

The following prayer is one in which our present priest and his two predecessors have either led the congregation, or have asked me to lead them, at the bidding prayer time during all intergenerational Masses:

Prayer for Intergenerational Healing

In the name of Jesus Christ I renounce all the works of the devil together with any occult, freemasonry or witchcraft practices there may have been in my past family.

I consecrate myself to Jesus Christ, my Lord and Saviour, both now and forever.

In the name of Jesus Christ and with the authority of Jesus, I now break any curses and all psychic heredity and any demonic hold upon my family line as a result of the disobedience to God of any of my ancestors.

Father in heaven, I stand before you a sinner through my own faults. I bring before you my ancestors, and I ask forgiveness for their sins and mine. I forgive them for any disobedience to you which has brought harmful patterns into my family.

I ask you, Father, to give them a fresh opportunity to receive your pardon, and to be reconciled with you and with one another.

I pray that all present members of my family and any to be born in the future will be set free of disobedience to you, and of all harmful patterns of living, and through repentance of their sins and the gift of faith, they may come to know Jesus Christ as Saviour and Lord, and experience the power of the Holy Spirit working in their lives.

I praise and thank you, Lord, for everyone in my past family, including any babies who were lost, together with those alive now and those to come.

Significant Points

- We need to pray for discernment of the real problem and its root causes, which may well differ from the problem presented initially.

- The roots of deep and lasting damage are not always in obviously traumatic early experiences, but may lie in events perceived by the child in a entirely different way from how they were seen by any adult, if they were present and witnessed them.

- Some of the damage due to early experiences may not show up for a long time.

- God may do some healing without other Christians being present at the time.

- There needs to be greater awareness of the vital significance on our adult life of wittingly or unwittingly breaking the commandment to honour our father and mother.

- Much damage may be done at conception, in the womb and at birth.

- There need to be more Masses celebrated specifically for intergenerational healing, for the sake of past, present and future members of our families.

Scripture for Meditation

> No one patches up an old coat with a new piece of cloth, for the new patch will shrink and make an even bigger hole in the coat. Nor does anyone pour new wine into used wineskins, for the skins will burst, the wine will pour out, and the skins will be ruined. Instead, new wine is poured into fresh wineskins, and both will keep in good condition. (Mt 9:6–17)

> Since you have accepted Christ Jesus as Lord, live in union with Him. Keep your roots deep in Him, build your lives on Him, and become stronger in your faith, as you were taught. And be filled with thanksgiving. (Col 2:6–7)

> I ask God from the wealth of His glory to give you power to be strong in your inner selves, and I pray that Christ will make His home in your hearts through faith. I pray that you may have your roots and foundation in love, so that you, together with all God's people, may have the power to understand how broad and long, how high and deep, is Christ's love. Yes, may you come to know His love—although it can never be fully known—and so be completely filled with the very nature of God. To Him, who by means of His power working in us is able to do so much more than we can ever ask for, or even think of; to God be the glory in the Church and in Christ Jesus for all time, for ever and ever. Amen. Ep 3:16–21)

Testimonies

Testimony 5A

'All my life a small insult or rejection, real or imagined, has triggered in me a short-lived blaze of irrational anger. In November 1993, whilst attending a conference on the inner healing ministry, I asked to be prayed with for this problem. I am the eldest of three children. I had a brother 15 months younger and a sister 3 years younger than me.

I was 7 when my brother and sister were taken ill with scarlet fever. I was ok but I was isolated and sent to stay with my maternal grandparents some miles away. I could not go to school or play with other children. I well remember the loneliness as I stood at the shop door and watched the people and the trams passing, and listening to the church clock striking those long hours.

One day, as they improved, I was taken home to see my brother and sister and mother for a short while. My brother and sister were playing together but refused to play with me. They said 'you can't play with us—you didn't have it'. My mother was too harassed to 'fuss me' and I was quickly taken back to my grandparents.

When I was prayed with, I immediately re-lived that scene. I was the little lonely rejected boy. I burst into tears and cried out 'NO ONE WANTS ME'. I then experienced a wonderful sense of healing and peace. I was able to forgive those who had, quite unwittingly, hurt me. I also asked God's forgiveness for my bitterness and anger.

Since then these outbursts of anger have hardly ever arisen, and I am easily able to recognise them and control them, when they do occur.'

Testimony 5B

'I was sexually abused when I was 6 years old and I felt dirty and cheap. I was always inferior at school and felt different from my friends. I never felt accepted and wanted, and I felt I always had to do something to be accepted, but Jesus has healed me of something that I thought would stay with me forever.

One day I set off to take my little girl ice-skating, but the plans went wrong, and we ended up by walking home. On the way my little girl asked if she could go and play on the swings, and because she did not go ice-skating I said, 'Yes.' There was only my little girl and myself at the swings, and it dawned on me that this was the place where the abuse happened. As I was watching my little girl playing and giggling, I found myself opposite the exact spot where it happened, but instead of ignoring this place like I had before, I felt as though Jesus was telling me to look—**really look**, and then all of a sudden I felt a burst of happiness and joy from my head to my toes, and I wanted to laugh and swing. I felt like a little girl again; I could even see the man's face and I felt sorry for him. It only lasted a minute or so, but I know Jesus has healed me of that abuse and I can talk about it now without feeling ashamed, dirty and different because you see, it wasn't my fault. Thank you, Jesus.'

Testimony 5C

'Over the years I had always felt this recurring feeling of wishing I was dead; why was I here? I felt I would be better off dead, then I wouldn't have to face any problems or cope with life's difficulties.

I am a Christian and I hated these thoughts; they seemed to fly in the face of everything I had been taught by God in the Bible; nonetheless the feelings persisted and were very real.

I joined a little healing group in St. Joseph's and learned a lot about God's love and how He wishes to heal us even back through the generations. I had been to several intergenerational Masses and services, and although I found them hugely helpful, I still kept getting these horrible feelings.

Eventually, I asked for personal prayer from a couple in our healing group. They prayed that the root cause would be revealed by the Holy Spirit. After about half an hour of deep prayer, the lady said she had a word of knowledge from the Lord; she said she had received a picture of a man in a temper chopping up a table and threatening people. The lady asked if this made any kind of sense. I said it didn't, but later when I related to my mother the picture, she said that just such a thing had happened to my father by his own father, my paternal grandfather. To find out more I rang my father's sister, my aunt, and was horrified to find out that my grandfather, although very good to her, beat my own father severely all his young life, in fact, once hitting his head off the wall by swinging him by his ankles. I now realised why my father despised his own father and also hated all forms of corporal punishment. My father also seemed incapable, in his early days, of acting as a proper father. I often felt when a child, as though I were the parent not him; having said that, I loved him dearly.

I found out that my paternal grandfather was also abused by his own father. He himself was often put in the coal shed with his brothers to save them from a beating from their alcoholic father. So this seemed to confirm a kind of ancestral problem through the generations of the family. I then received more in-depth healing for myself and my ancestors on the paternal side, and can honestly say I have been completely healed of those negative feelings. Even though I have had many trials, as we all do, I feel able, with God's help, to cope and have never felt like ending it all, ever again. I am immensely grateful to the Holy Spirit who, through this gifted couple, healed me, and also I believe, my ancestors before me. God's ways are mystery, but are truly wonderful.'

Testimony 5D

'Some twenty years now I have been born again by God's spirit, but it is only recently that I have known the pure joy of walking with the Lord. This has been brought about by the special ministry God has given to St. Joseph's.

My family was all disjointed with all the traumas life had thrown at us and we had all retired into our own shells for protection. Gradually after I was regularly going to the healing meetings at St. Joseph's, God brought all of us to one of the Masses for Intergenerational Healing. My family and myself said the prayer for 'Intergenerational Healing' and even though part of my family didn't have a clue what it meant, God did a miracle! From that night on we have been much closer as a family and a warmth is beginning to emerge which had previously gone.

For myself, I am now experiencing being truly loved by God and know without a shadow of a doubt that He has a plan and a purpose for my life which is really exciting.'

Testimony 5E

'I suffer from a debilitating mental illness called obsessive neurosis (now known as OCD, Obsessive Compulsive Disorder). For eight years this illness has been particularly intense. My obsessions began early in life and my career at University was impaired and ten years of medication and a nervous breakdown ensued. The obsessions with cleanliness whilst bringing up my children left me distraught. The mental strain drains one of energy and leaves one feeling inadequate, helpless, depressed and totally hopeless.

Two years ago I came to St. Joseph's parish in Norton and through compassionate listening and prayers for inner healing, I believe God is slowly healing me. Last year I was able to accept a place at University and found the long car journeys were no longer a problem to me, whereas before I would have needed to re-check and re-travel out of fear of having knocked someone down. The peace, ease of events and positive feelings that I felt on re-entry to education, confirm that prayers are being answered and God has been at work. As the chains of this fearful illness loosen and the illness falls away, I feel that the means by which God is achieving this include the Mass for the healing of the family tree, prayers for inner healing through my childhood to the present, and prayers for the healing of relationships. I have been touched by the unconditional and non-judgmental gift of listening. I believe that the healing will be of my whole self and that the illness will have proved to be a tool, used by God, to achieve this.'

Some sixteen years after writing this, she is again coming for further ministry in one deeper area, but she has made a wonderful and total recovery from OCD.

Notes

1   M. Scanlan, *Inner Healing* (New York: Paulist Press, 1974), p. 9.

2   J. & P. Sandford, *The Transformation of the Inner Man* (Plainfield NJ: Bridge Publishing Corporation, 1982); Idem, *Healing the Wounded Spirit* (Plainfield NJ: Bridge Publishing Corporation, 1985).

3   K. McAll, *Healing the Family Tree* (London: The Sheldon Press, 1982); Idem, *A Guide to Healing the Family Tree* (Goleta CA: Queenship Publishing Company, 1996).

4   See R. de Grandis, *Intergenerational Healing* (self-published, 1989); J. Hampsch, *Healing Your Family Tree* (Everett WA: Performance Press, 1986).

5   M. Linn, D. Linn & S. Fabricant, *Healing the Greatest Hurt* (New York: Paulist Press, 1985), pp. 108, 129–130.

6

JESUS HEALS PAST WOUNDS AND SETS US FREE

Our True Selves

As explained before, prayer begins before conception with praising and thanking God, who knew us before He formed us in the womb. We can praise God that when we were only in God's mind we were our true selves because each of us is created in the image and likeness of God (Gn 1:26). We then begin to be contaminated with damage from our family line once we are conceived. There is further risk of hurt and ill-effects on us during pregnancy and at birth, through babyhood and into early child-hood. Clearly, we often go on being hurt and affected throughout our life, but our reactions and behaviour through adult life depend very greatly on the experiences up to the age of about seven, so that prayer ministry through all these early stages is needed, often more than once.

All of this damage, both the hurts we experience and our wounded reactions of emotions and behaviour to these disturbances, distort us further and further from our real selves. Praying for inner healing aims at the Holy Spirit - through the suffering, death and Resurrection of Jesus - progressively restoring us to our real selves, referred to frequently in the New Testament as the new creation. His final goal is our sanctification, which will ultimately be completed, after purgatory, when we are taken fully into the Father's presence.

There are many factors and ways by which we become distorted from our real selves through our own sins and those of others. For every one of these Jesus Christ has already done what is necessary to set us free, through His suffering, death and Resurrection: 'He endured the suffering that should have been ours, the pain we should have borne; because of our sins He was wounded. We are healed by the punishment He suffered' (Is 53:4–5). There is no other healer but Christ and no other place to come for healing than the Cross. However good secular counsellors may be at exposing wounded emotions and their causes, there is no healing without Christ and the power of the Holy Spirit working in us.

Nevertheless, it is important that we let God reveal all He wants us to know, using a variety of sources, so that for each person who is a unique, totally beloved child of God, He can guide us by His Spirit as to how and when to pray into all the areas of damage.

We are distorted, among other ways, by:

- an accumulation of emotions, many becoming buried through our defences,

- our damaged sinful reactions to the hurts,

- wrong patterns of thinking, attitudes ideas, desires, beliefs, habits, behaviours and

- striving to earn love and affirmation because we don't feel we are receiving it freely as a gift.

When, as a young child, we are driven to bury such emotions as angers and resentment, because our family is not comfortable with our demonstrating them, then we are no longer our real selves. Our real self is angry, resentful etc., but to avoid repercussions of disapproval or worse, we have to appear not to have these feelings. We are not being helped to learn how to control anger and other emotions. As Fr John Powell put it, 'We don't bury these feelings dead; we bury them alive'. Later in life these feelings can burst out, as we will discuss later. Children in the same family can of course vary greatly one from another. One child may give in under these pressures and develop a very poor sense of self-worth. Another sibling may, in effect, be developing an attitude of 'I'll get by within myself—I'll be self-sufficient'. There can be several different types of personality within this one family, but in many cases we end up 'putting on masks', trying to be what we think others want us to be, or to protect ourselves by stopping others getting so close that they can hurt us. Some of us may become excessively turned in upon ourselves, while others appear to be unduly confident and extrovert.

It has been remarkable, over the years, to meet the very large number of people coming who have said, 'I don't really know who I am'. Through the inner healing prayer ministry, we have seen so many coming to know, quite gradually, very unevenly perhaps, the wonder of their totally unique being. We all need God's power to a lesser or greater extent to come to a deep (not just intellectual) awareness of the wonder of our own being and just how precious we are to God our Father, so we can say, and really mean it, 'It was you who created my inmost self, and put me together in my mother's womb; for all these mysteries I thank you; for the wonder of myself, for the wonder of your works' (Ps 139:13–14).

Testimonies 6A (p. 120) and 6B (p. 120) are illustrations of this process at work. It is the most wonderful privilege to be allowed by the Lord, to walk with someone part of their journey of discovery. The first was written by a man who was obliged to work on Teesside for some months, far from his family. Through coming to St Joseph's, he said when he left to work near home, he had learned that a situation which at first seems to cause only problems to us can be used by God as an opportunity to bring us deeper healing and spiritual growth:

The second testimony is an example of how there is a right time for each individual to face up to the pain in them and become ready to take responsibility to allow the Lord to do more healing. We must never attempt to rush anyone, or put on the slightest pressure.

Both of these testimonies were written some years ago. Those who wrote them, and many others who have come for ministry, have been growing in inner peace as they are freed from damage in their early lives. They are becoming free to be their real selves, and can choose to reach out to others, rather than being constrained by the treatment or expectations of others, or by drives and compulsions within themselves. 'When Christ freed us He meant us to stay free. Stand firm therefore and do not submit again to the yoke of slavery' (Ga 5:1). Most of us need the help and prayer and support of others in the Body of Christ to become free and remain free. This is a work of the Holy Spirit, and in the next section we look at one important gift of the Holy Spirit, before moving on to other ways in which He works among us to bring healing.

The Gift of a Word of Knowledge

There were very many occasions when Betty received a word of knowledge. Generally the word or words would seem to have no significance at all to her, but if she had the courage to share them with the person needing prayer, then they would reveal some cause of pain and unease which the Lord wanted us to pray about. If the word(s) meant nothing, it didn't matter. The story has already been told of the man with depression, where the word 'ridicule' meant nothing at the time, but where the significance emerged later.

One of our earliest experiences occurred before we left Leeds. We had gone to a house of prayer run by sisters in Leeds one Saturday, to listen to teaching given by a man from abroad, who was used by God to pray for healing. He asked for volunteers to join him there on the Sunday, to pray with a lady who was being brought from Lancashire the next day for prayer, because she had been blind from birth or from very early on. Eight people turned up. He divided us into two teams: one praying in the chapel with her, and the other giving back-up prayer in another room. Every so often he switched the two teams. We prayed for several hours that day, with a break to eat in between.

During the afternoon my wife said that she had got a picture in her mind of a mound of earth. Someone else said they had thought of a grave. A third person said that they had in mind the trench warfare of the First World War. I then said that in the morning the word 'uncle' had come into my mind, but if you are praying for someone to see again, you don't pay attention to that. The man who was leading us then put the question to her, 'Did you have an uncle in the fighting in the First World War?' She said yes. Now that is not unusual. Both Betty and I had uncles killed in France or Belgium in that war. However, it was all we got in hours of praying, so we prayed for the repose of his soul, and she was taken back home.

Next day, our leader received a phone call from her. That evening, her sister, with whom she had had no communication for a long time, and who had previously shown no signs of faith, telephoned her to ask for prayer. It seemed as though the Lord saw this, and the prayer for the uncle, as a higher priority than restoring her sight. God is sovereign and He has many ways of surprising us and showing us that it is not we who are in control.

Another occasion, many years ago, a lady whose testimony appears as 5E (p. 97) in the previous chapter came because she had obsessive compulsive disorder, which was causing great difficulties and distress for her and her family. I telephoned two different people in the South to ask what had been written or learnt about the Lord healing OCD. They knew of nothing but both suggested I ask if there had been a curse in the family. When she came, Betty had a word of knowledge concerning a tramp at a garden gate. It transpired that he had been refused money by her parents and he had put a curse on the family. The breaking of that curse was part of how the Lord completely freed her from OCD. We were able to confirm, meeting her again some sixteen years later, that she was indeed healed of her obsessions.

A recent example was a man who was coming because excessive anger would well up in him, because children were playing football and riding about very frequently in his narrow road, and obstructing the way. He was driving his car towards them and only just stopping in time. It became clear that he had a great deal of anger because his father had treated him very badly indeed in childhood. A word came to me, which was 'bicycle'. I asked if it meant anything. He said, 'Yes'. His father had said he would give him a bicycle but it turned out to be a very old one in poor condition, which hurt and humiliated him. It seemed to reinforce his father's poor opinion and constant denigration of him. We prayed for Jesus to take the child's pain and anger and give him the grace to forgive.

Then, a few days later, he rang me. He remembered that when he had come for ministry seven years earlier, Betty had told him that she had a sense that there might have been another child in his family. He was an only child. That morning he had taken his mother shopping when something she said prompted him to ask if she had ever had another child. She said, 'When you were two years old, I had an abortion'. The news had sent him into tears and great sadness. I explained a little about post-abortion survival syndrome, whereby the siblings who survive, whether born before or after, can be affected by this loss, and the effects it can have on the mother. The next day he told me that he had looked up post-abortion survivor syndrome on the internet, and it had mentioned that a survivor can develop rage directed towards children. That was brought out after Betty's death, by a word of knowledge given to him by her some years before. A further example written by a man from another church and town who is very active in his church is given in Testimony 6C (p. 123).

Of course, as in this case, we are always praying for the whole person, body, soul and spirit, and this involves praying for Jesus to heal physical conditions and all the hurts ever experienced, not just the very early key roots. When someone speaks about physical symptoms which they have been suffering from for some time, we would always ask them when they first became aware of the onset of these symptoms. Then we would ask what had been happening in their lives, including of course family members, during the previous two years. Frequently they will remember some painful situation, perhaps involving such things as grief, or disappointment or anger, or rejection, which occurred during this period. We can then invite Jesus into this area of pain for them to let go of it into His suffering and ask for the grace of forgiveness.

Testimony 6C (p. 123), which is representative of many, is a clear example of how a man, then in his seventies, was still experiencing stress and tensions arising mainly from one particular experience in early childhood. Difficult or painful experiences in childhood can lead us in adult life to react out of the child within us. There may be many painful feelings which the child was forced to bury as automatic defences came into play to minimise further hurt and enable the child to survive what was happening. As a result, an adult can suddenly react out of the childhood state within who feels angry or resentful, or rejected, or unloved and unwanted, as we will now consider.

The Child Within

Sometimes we become aware that the Lord has not yet finished healing the past, by strong feelings coming up unexpectedly. Perhaps we had thought till then that the healing was more complete. I used to be a very angry person but gradually, over the years, I was being changed. Then, one day as we prepared to keep an appointment, a vital document could not be found. Betty's response was always to pray quietly for help. I, on the other hand, reverted to how I used to be—I became very angry. At the last moment we found the paper. Next day, Betty asked the Lord why I had become so angry again. The answer she received was that as a child I felt deprived. There were many things I couldn't have and couldn't do, because we couldn't afford them.

We can be triggered into reacting like an angry, rejected, disappointed, jealous etc. little boy or girl, by a variety of stimuli. Sometimes we know what it was that was said or done which acted as a trigger. Other times it is more subtle, like a gesture, tone of voice, a word which in our unconscious mind connects with some hurt from the past. It helps to look at the basic idea in transactional analysis. We can act out of one of three basic ego states (or 'ways of being me'): viz. the adult, parent or child. It is not necessary to pursue the deeper explorations of TA. One practitioner of TA running a professional counselling service, who wrote a handbook on the subject, came to us himself for some ministry.

In the few minutes it took my wife and I to walk to church, one of us, one day, suddenly reacted out of the child, and the other then spoke like a parent. The very next day, the other went into the child. If two people are talking quite normally in the adult state, and one suddenly is triggered into a reaction from the child, it is usual for the other, quite unconsciously, to react out of the parent state. In TA this is termed 'crossed communication', and we will all be aware of times when a conversation has ceased to be straightforward and constructive, and it becomes unhelpful, possibly even leading towards misunderstanding or argument.

This happens because, from our earliest beginnings, we automatically seek to avoid problems and the pain which may be involved in solving or dealing with them. This was clearly explained by Dr Scott Peck.[1] Our natural defences are necessary to enable us to bury, or partially bury our painful emotions sufficiently to enable us to survive whatever is going on in our childhood. Later in life we begin to realise that these 'buried' memories and emotions are intruding into our deepening relationship with God, and with one another. They are now seen to be affecting our behaviour and our peace. Sometimes they are so well buried that we genuinely do not know just what is in us.

An example of this was when a lady came from some distance, worn down by all the ways she was serving others. She felt she had to do these things—that if she didn't, no one else would be available. Betty felt that there was anger and disappointment in her. The lady seriously thought about that but said she did not think so. A little later, we began to pray with her. Suddenly her fists were clenched and she was shouting out her anger to God. She was one of a large family with little money. As a little girl, she longed to learn to dance. A brother felt that he might have a vocation to the priesthood. From the family they somehow found enough money to meet this obligation. No one listened to her. No one knew she longed to dance. Even if they had known they could not have afforded the lessons. It was truly wonderful to see the change in her after prayer ministry. She gave up the activities which had become a burden. Others came forward to provide this service. We have met her again over the years and there is a deep peace in her.

Much of the ministry is therefore to 'the child within'. We pray for Jesus to find the child at all times of hurt and need, to hold the child, listen to them (if old enough) as they pour out their distress, and to take all their pain to His suffering on the Cross. We pray for the grace to forgive (as we look at in the next section). We pray for the healing of the child's wounded reactions, and we pray for the adult to take responsibility to cooperate with God in becoming a new creation—their real self.

Discovering the main root or roots which need to be healed can sometimes be aided by first asking the person to identify the key emotion which keeps on surfacing, and secondly to identify, if possible, their very earliest recollection of experiencing that particular feeling, and of who caused it.

Inner healing is an ongoing journey towards freedom. For most of us it involves ongoing, supportive prayer with others. We need to look at this further. Of course the prayer for inner healing cannot begin until one has listened for a considerable time to the person who is in need. The quality of that listening needs to be examined now.

The Need for Empathetic and Reverential Listening

It is only God's love which sets people free, and as He gives that love to us and we experience it for someone, we begin to get in touch with the tremendous worth which that person has in God's eyes. Fr Pat Collins[2] has given deeply insightful teaching about listening. The love God gives us is a way of paying full attention to another; forgetting about ourselves; being patient and willing to go at their pace, without too many intrusive questions, so that they, and not we, set the agenda.

He points out the limitations of apathetic listening which is simply objective without any response on the level of feelings, and leads only to the giving of advice; and of sympathetic listening, where we may become part of the problem if we allow ourselves to take on the feelings of the other, say anger against some offender. Empathetic listening, however, where we can pick up on the other's feelings but don't enter into them, can enable us to respond with sorrow, understanding, compassion and love. We begin to receive reverence for the other, to understand that there is something sacred about their life and experiences as, in the words of Fr Pat, we begin to enter the sanctuary of another person's heart.

The following guidelines used by the Bloemfontein Samaritans in South Africa illustrate some of the essence of listening:

> You are not listening to me when...
> You do not care about me;
> You say you understand before you know me well enough;

You have an answer to my problem before I've finished telling you
what my problem is;
You cut me off before I've finished speaking;
You finish my sentences for me;
You find me boring and don't tell me;
You feel critical of my vocabulary, grammar or accent;
You are dying to tell me something;
You tell me about your experience, making mine seem unimportant;
You are communicating with someone else in the room;
You refuse my thanks by saying you haven't really done anything.
You are listening when ...
You come quietly into my private world and let me be me;
You really try to understand me, even if I'm not making much
sense;
You grasp my point of view, even when it's against your own
sincere convictions;
You realise that the time I took from you has left you a bit tired
and drained;
You allow me the dignity of making my own decisions, even
though you think they might be wrong;
You do not take my problem from me, but allow me to deal with
it in my own way;
You hold back your desire to give me good advice;
You do not offer me religious solace when you sense I am not ready
for it;
You give me enough room to discover for myself what is really
going on;
You accept my gift of gratitude by telling me how good it makes
you feel to know that you have been helpful.

One of the main aspects as we listen is to identify not only all the buried
hurts and feelings, but also all those people who were perceived by the
child within the adult to have hurt him or her, or to have failed to give
all the love and affirmation needed by the child. There can be no genuine
and lasting healing until the wounded person has become aware of the
depths of hurt, has brought them to Jesus to die with Him on the Cross,
has become ready to choose to forgive, and has travelled a long way along
the road to more and more complete healing and forgiveness. This then
is the next aspect which needs to be examined.

Receiving Grace to Forgive

Forgiveness is an essential part of the journey to wholeness and inner peace. In the past, clear teaching has not been readily available to all, but this has now been remedied.[3]

Some Christians may have interpreted the little teaching they received and some passages from Scripture as though God is demanding (almost putting pressure) that we forgive by saying, in effect, 'I won't forgive you unless you forgive others'. We have had to minister to people who have gone for help to some other Christian group, and have felt under pressure to forgive when they were not able, or not yet ready, to forgive, and have felt greater burdens like guilt, instead of peace and freedom.

The reality is that when the Holy Spirit convicts us of sins, including the harbouring of hatred, anger, bitterness etc. against someone, rather than seeking to forgive them, He does it in order to offer us the grace to be set free of the harmful consequences. So very far from the misconception that God, in seeing our sins, decides to exact some punishment, He sent His son to suffer and die to take our sins and all the damage and consequences. Thus He is always offering us grace to be freed of the consequences of infringing any laws He designed for our well-being, and offering us grace, coming from the Cross, to be healed and freed of unforgiveness, so that we can be reconciled with the Father and with one another. God is not threatening to withhold His forgiveness of us if we refuse or are not yet ready to forgive others.

As Fr Jim McManus wrote: 'In Christian forgiveness, the divine forgiveness comes first. Even before we return to God in prayer to ask for forgiveness, that forgiveness is already being offered. All we have to do is accept it. In truly accepting divine forgiveness, we should experience a conversion that opens our hearts to share forgiveness with others what we have received. Without this desire there has been no conversion, no acceptance of God's forgiveness, and so divine forgiveness cannot be retained.'[4]

One way to look at it is to think of sitting in God's presence in prayer with His love and grace to forgive pouring down upon us, as being a little like sitting in the sunshine. If we choose to go indoors, into ourselves with our bitterness, self-centredness, resentments, etc., then God's love and forgiveness are still pouring down, but we have cut ourselves off from receiving all He suffered and died to give us, His beloved children.

If our refusal comes from a deep wound within us, then the Lord is longing to heal that wound. If our refusal comes from a hardened heart, then, as Ezekiel 36 tells us, God is promising to give us a heart of flesh, instead of a heart of stone, so that He leads us to deeper conversion to Christ. By forgiving others we become more like God, and it is our destiny to become eventually fully part of God's life.

Testimony 6D (p. 125) speaks of someone learning how important this is. It is concerned with our call from God and our need to be enabled by God to forgive, once we make that choice and ask for His help. There are three directions in which we need grace. The first is to forgive others.

Testimony 6E (p. 125) is a wonderful example of a lady who allowed the Lord to do an amazing healing in her, and how, through her receiving the grace to forgive, new grace was offered to the offender. She only reached this degree of healing through deep extensive prayer ministry over many months, in which she was able to bring all the pain of her childhood to the Cross and receive the grace to forgive. There was evidence some years later that she had indeed been given new freedom and healing. She had noticed a change in attitude towards herself from a number of people in her church, including her own brothers and sisters. This hurt her and mystified her until someone explained that a woman in the same church had spread a serious slander about her. Her immediate reaction was to want to go straight to this woman in anger, but she turned to her pastor and accepted his advice to do nothing until she had prayed deeply about it. There came a day when she did go to the woman. What she said was, 'I love you,' and she meant it because the Lord had enabled her to forgive and to receive some of His love for this woman. The latter then broke down in tears and told her that she had spread the lies because relationships in her own family were bad and she was jealous of the good relationships which our friend had with her five younger brothers and sisters.

This is an example of how we cannot forgive someone until we have let go of our anger, pain etc., as Jesus takes it into His suffering on the Cross, and we have then asked Him to give us the grace to forgive, and for the gift of His love for those who hurt us. Then if He chooses and at the time He shows us to be right, we can go to the person with His love and respond to them as Jesus would, rather than with our old damaged reactions. In this way, the victory of Jesus on the Cross can set both victim and offender free.

The second direction in which we need grace is to do with our sense of our own guilt: it is often harder to forgive ourselves than to forgive others. Testimonies 6F (p. 126), 6G (p. 127) and 6H (p. 127) illustrate how important this is.

Sometimes the sense of guilt may come from actions like abortion. Some of the many women who have revealed that they had one or more abortions accepted our suggestion that they may get further help from Christians, in our area and church, who have specialised training in this area of need.

One lady had three abortions by the age of nineteen. She had prayer ministry from us and help from the qualified counsellors. She eventually moved out of the area, but has kept in occasional touch by letter, and is really making progress in a new life with God's help. In an earlier testimony she had written of sexual abuse by three men and physical abuse. 'I didn't trust people. My expectation was that the only time they wanted to have anything to do with me was to hurt me etc. I felt inferior and untouchable and hated myself. I hurt myself physically. I didn't deserve to be liked or loved. I couldn't receive the love and help people offered as I didn't know how to accept it and allow them into my life.' In a letter written some years later, she writes, 'I know I am a happier and more contented person and secure in myself'.

Testimony 6H (p. 127) is a glorious example of God rescuing someone from the very depths, healing them and then using them in powerful ways to help others. She is a wonderful child of God and an inspiration to others when they meet her. Among other things, she too needed God's grace to forgive herself for an abortion.

The third area in which we need grace is in our relationship with God Himself. Although God never does anything wrong and therefore does not need to be forgiven, many people feel (particularly in their 'inner child') that God had let them or their loved ones down. Unless they bring to Jesus on the Cross all their perceptions of anger and disappointment with God, for Him to take these burdens and heal the memories, then they are not able to trust God more and more completely.

One lady came years ago with her husband, who preached in the Pentecostal church which they attended. After one or two sessions, as she spoke of the horrendous pain and experiences from her childhood, we began to realise that she was angry with God. When we said this, she denied it, saying that her husband quoted scriptures to her to tell her she mustn't be angry with God. He agreed that he did so. After another session or so, the day came when she said, 'When I was a child, God the Father walked in and looked at the terrible things that were happening to me. Then he said, 'It's just too bad', and he walked out.' How could she, the adult, trust God until that was healed and the child in her 'forgave' God?

We, as adults, have each to take the responsibility of making the choice to allow Jesus to heal us. The alternative would be to go on incubating our pain, anger, disappointments, and grievances. It is of course not a quick fix, but a gradual process in which, as we will discuss in the next chapter, we need to pray with the authority of Jesus to become free of strongholds. The child in us needs ministry. For example, if a child hears that God is all-loving and all-powerful, and the child is suffering great agonies, then he or she is bewildered. Why doesn't God help? Perhaps He only helps other families, not mine? Perhaps there is something wrong with me and He doesn't really love me? People need gentle, compassionate help to work through all these things, but it is always our choice whether to ask for the grace to forgive and to open our lives to compassion, generosity, freedom and love, or to allow unforgiveness to poison us.

The Difficulty of Forgiveness

For many, forgiveness is neither quick nor easy. Some, when asked, 'Do you want to be able to forgive still say 'No'. We then ask: 'Do you wish that you could want to forgive?' So far only about three out of several hundred have said no to that question. Two had a loved one murdered. The other had a close relative commit suicide after she had convinced herself that if she prayed hard enough, he would regain good mental health. One day, please God, they too will accept His offer to release them from their prison.

People struggling with the difficulty of forgiveness can be helped towards the truth. If someone has injured me, I have the right not to let that injury poison the rest of my life. It is bad enough that I was injured in the first place without giving my offender the right to go on damaging me. Forgiveness is not condoning or excusing. It is not letting the offender 'off the hook', but permitting Jesus to release me, the victim, and take me 'off the hook'.

Jesus does not pressurise or invade someone's free will by forcing an offender to repent and to ask a victim for forgiveness. The story of the woman caught in adultery (Jn 8:3–11) illustrates the gentleness and compassion of Jesus, where he does not condemn either the accusers or the woman. Instead He brings about changes in them through their consciences. We must ask Jesus for his love and compassion, even for those who have hurt us most; they, like us, have been wounded and distorted from their true self. There is only one scripture in which Jesus links the offender asking to be forgiven with the victim choosing to forgive (Lk 17:4). In all the other passages, including the prayer to the Father which Jesus taught us, there is no mention of 'provided that they are sorry'.

Forgiveness is a process between me and God. Reconciliation would be a process between me and the offender, and such reconciliation may not be able to take place (at least in this life). Sometimes the two have been confused. It is of course true that Jesus says, 'Love your enemies', but he didn't then add, 'and welcome them into your home'.

Asking God to Give Us His Love for Those Who Hurt Us

Jesus asks us to go beyond asking him to give us the grace to forgive, when he tells us to love our enemies (Mt 5:44).

Fr John Hampsch suggests[5] that we close our eyes and, in prayer, imagine that we are alone in a room with one door, by which Jesus enters. I see His wounds and crown of thorns and ask his forgiveness that my sins contributed to His suffering. He immediately gives me his forgiveness and then goes out, returning with chairs which He sets up. He then brings into the room, one by one, everyone whom I perceive as having hurt me or let me down during my life.

Jesus then asks if I am willing to go with Him to each person in turn, not only to set me free of all unforgiveness, but to give me more and more of His love for this person, whom he is looking at with love and compassion. If I am willing, Jesus gives me His love for them, and puts one arm around me and one arm round the other. He invites me to tell this person in prayer how very much God loves him, or her, and that I am praying for them to accept this gift of love and salvation because I am longing to spend eternity with them in God's presence. Our ability to love others is greatly reduced or affected if we are unable or unwilling to love ourselves, as Jesus taught when he was asked about the commandments: 'Love your neighbour as you love yourself'(Mt 19:19). This is our next topic.

Receiving God's Grace to Love and Accept Ourselves

For years I supposed, quite wrongly, that if I were to love and accept myself, I would become self-centred. In Fr John Powell's programme 'The Fully Alive Experience',[6] he lists the most frequently encountered distortions in our vision. He identified 'I cannot love myself or admit my talents or else I will be egotistical' as one of the most common distortions. So I was far from alone in this misconception!

It is probably true to say that virtually every one of the many hundreds of people to whom we have listened, and with whom we have then prayed, have been to a greater or lesser degree unable to love and accept themselves. This of course has been due not only to wrong ideas, but, because so much damage has been done to most of us, we have been robbed of our sense of self-worth, or, more fundamentally, our sense of who we are in Christ, our true identity in God.

I was certainly over 60 before it dawned on me that loving and accepting oneself was at one end of a spectrum, whereas being self-centred was at the far end. I was probably over 70 when I began to accept fully the truth that God loves and accepts me totally as I am, and longs to give me the grace to love and accept myself. I had come to know that truth in my head earlier, and I could happily pass that truth on to others and pray with them to receive it, but I resisted it becoming real and true in the depths of my being. For some years before I retired, when Betty asked, 'Who are you?' I knew I was supposed to say, 'A beloved child of God' and really mean it, but I would say, 'I'm fed up'. I was angry at being 'got at' again; I had got it wrong again; I had failed her and God. I suffered depression; didn't like myself; didn't think I was any use to God or to anyone else. I was Betty's most difficult 'patient'—she certainly needed great patience—she often said 'You are so negative'. Since God was able to set me free, he can certainly do it for everyone else who is willing.

It is important to help people to look beyond and away from themselves to Christ, and to hold on to the truths revealed in the Scriptures, such as:

'You are precious in my eyes because you are honoured and I love you' (Is 43:4), and 'He will exult with joy over you. He will renew you by his love. He will dance with shouts of joy for you, as on a day of festival.' (Zp 3:17).

We recommend people to speak these truths to themselves, whether or not their feelings are in agreement, and we have given to very many people a sheet with verses 14–19 of Zephaniah 3.

Because, as Hebrews 4 tells us, the Scriptures are like a double-edged sword which can slip through the place where the soul is divided from the spirit, they can cut away the untruths of old experiences and set us free. If we keep speaking the truth with persistence, by a decision of our adult mind, to the wounded child within us, then gradually healing takes place.

We have often recommended that a person, from time to time, closes their eyes and in prayer imagines that the adult is taking the child they were into their own arms, and telling that needy child that he or she is totally loved and accepted by the adult. This is one of the many ways of 'living in the creative house' as Fr Jim McManus suggests[7] based on Jn 8:31–32: 'If you make my word your home, you will be my disciples and you will learn the truth and the truth will set you free.' (Jerusalem translation). This means that we are learning from the New Testament how God speaks and thinks, and that this is always positive and up building. 'Jesus Christ, the Son of God... is not one who is 'Yes' and 'No'. On the contrary, he is God's 'Yes'; for it is He who is the 'Yes' to all God's promises' (2 Co 1:19–20). We live in a world which generally promotes negativity, and we have become accustomed to speaking and thinking negatively, which means we are contradicting God—in rebellion. 'You love the destructive word' (Ps 52:4). Negative influences have caused us to 'live in the house of the destructive word'. We need to keep checking that we are repenting of that, and make sure that we are speaking and thinking positively. This point is developed further in the section on the power of the word of God in Chapter 7.

As we will discuss in more detail later, we have found that many who come for ministry would say that they have been 'baptised in the Holy Spirit' for years, and only now realise that they need inner healing. It is as though their adult has been living in the creative house, while their child is still in the house of the destructive word (Ps 52:4: Jerusalem translation). As inner healing proceeds, the adult and the child become more completely integrated, and the person is becoming more whole, with deeper inner peace not conflict.

Acceptance of our worth and dignity in Christ, with everything as free gift so that we cannot boast, is vital for us to be set free and receive the peace which only Christ can bring. But it is also necessary, because our ability to be used to show God's love and acceptance to others is impaired by our inability to love and accept ourselves. Jesus told us that when He said that the second great commandment is to love our neighbour as ourselves.

There is no need to give further testimonies about this aspect, because almost all those given in other sections have involved the person coming to a deeper acceptance and love for their own self. That is particularly clear in stories where there was sexual abuse and exploitation, because the damage to self-worth needs very deep ongoing healing. Many of the women who have come to our home were raped or sexually abused, and it is very moving and inspiring to see God gently restoring each of them to her very wonderful true self.

Fr Jim McManus describes[8] how 'our lack of self-acceptance or self-rejection is the root cause of our lack of ease, dis-ease, with self. If the person is in the destructive process of rejecting self, inner healing will be blocked'. He goes even deeper into this subject in a later book.[9] He shows[28], with the stories of a priest and of a sister, how they had wrongly supposed that the cause of their problem was another person's behaviour, as they had become convinced. The real root cause was their self-rejection, and, as God healed that, they found peace, whether or not any changes occurred in the other people whom they had blamed. He showed how he needed to help the priest to let go of his daily unrealistic expectation that two other priests would change and become his friends.

We have recommended to many people the three daily steps which he suggested:

1. Thank God for the wonder of myself. Then thank God for the wonder of anyone who is troubling me.

2. Thank God for all the good things He is doing in my life. Then thank God for all He is doing in the lives of these others.

3. Make allowance for all my own failures and ask God for pardon. Then make allowance for the failures of all these people.

(Of course, one needs to be praying also for the grace to forgive.)

An extreme form of struggling to love and accept oneself and to be free to reach out to other people is sometimes called 'performance orientation'. We have found that a high proportion of people coming for ministry (myself included) suffer from this problem to varying degrees of intensity, as will now be explained.

Performance Orientation

In the first of six residential weekends at Minsteracres, where we gave teachings on different aspects of inner healing each time, we spoke about performance orientation. Whilst delivering the talk, I was very aware from a variety of forms of non-verbal communication that this particular aspect of our struggling with self-acceptance was striking a definite chord with nearly everyone.

A small child will thrive on unconditional love and affirmation. If, on the other hand, my perception is that I am not receiving love and encouragement unconditionally, then to a greater or lesser degree I begin to get the message that I am only loved and accepted when I please people (generally parents), do certain things and avoid other behaviours or reach certain standards of achievement or what they regard as good behaviour and conformity. This begins to build up a lie, reinforced by many experiences, that I shall only be loved and fully wanted, when and if I perform to the satisfaction of others. The basis of this lie is fear. Fear of rejection, of not belonging, of failure, of not measuring up. If I only believe that I hear the message that I am loved and accepted when I am successful in meeting some standards and expectations, then I link together two statements which I should be receiving quite separately from one another. (1) You are loved. (2) Well done. The kind of message which can reinforce this distortion is 'Mummy and Daddy (or God) can't love you when you behave like that'.

This so painful to the child that my defences begin to bury, in my subconscious or unconscious mind, distressing thoughts like: 'If I fail to live up to what is expected of me, then I won't be loved or wanted, or, 'If people knew what I was really like inside they wouldn't like or accept me, so I mustn't ever reveal to others what is gong on in me'. We may learn to strive so that our behaviour reflects well on our family, though inside we may be angry or resentful, unloved and lonely. Even when our adult mind hears the truth that God loves us totally, unconditionally, just as we are, the child within needs considerable ongoing help for that truth to set them free of these early lies and distortions.

If we are doing things because we think we ought, or must, then we need to consult the Lord. He never puts pressure on us. He gently invites us to serve Him, and gives us the power of the Holy Spirit so that we do it in freedom, not in slavery to inner compulsions. There is a huge difference between what is sometimes described as 'working for God', where we are driven perhaps by inner needs and compulsions, using our own efforts and becoming exhausted, and on the other hand 'doing God's work', where through initial prayer and openness God guides us to the work which He has chosen for us to do, and we do it by the power of the Holy Spirit in great freedom and joy and gratitude to Him.

Fr Henri Nouwen[10] wrote movingly of losing his self-esteem, energy to live and work, his sense of being loved and even his hope in God. Then he was given the insight to let his father and father-figures go, and stop seeing himself through their eyes and trying to make them proud of him. He was told to let go of self-made props and trust that God was enough for him; to stop being a pleaser and reclaim his identity as a free self.

There are a number of indicators which help us to identify whether, and to what extent, performance orientation affects our life with God and others. When we have looked at these with people, we and they can see if, and to what extent, they are a victim of performance orientation. As we pray with people in all the aspects discussed in other sections, it is wonderful to see them being set free, but it is not generally a quick process. The Lord not only wants to give us more and more of His love for others and for ourselves, but for Him. As Jesus commanded, 'You must love the Lord your God with all your heart, and with all your soul, and with all your mind, and with all your strength' (Mk 12:30).

A Message of Encouragement

This is a message, believed to be from the Lord Himself and given on 1 September 2011 to 'Ann', a lay apostle to Direction For Our Times, and circulated to many groups around the world, and I have included it, whatever its authenticity is eventually decided by the Church to be, because it speaks of all the issues raised in this chapter:

> It is with joy that I speak with you today. When I contemplate your fidelity to my plan for mercy, I feel joy. When I contemplate your fidelity to holiness, I feel joy. Do not pause in your commitment to becoming holier. This calm movement into the spirit of gentleness and kindness should help you to view others with compassion, yes, but also yourself. Do you view yourself with compassion? Do you offer kindness and mercy toward yourself

when you contemplate your condition? My friends, My dearest friends, be careful to view yourself as I view you. Be careful not to view yourself in harsh light that seeks to condemn. If you are tempted against mercy for yourself, then truly, you are tempted against truth. Because it is only with mercy and love that I greet your present condition and your attempts to advance in holiness. I am love. I could hardly ask you to love others and then withhold love from you. That would be a flawed plan, destined to fail. My plan is perfect. I give you a receptive heart, you receive my love in abundance, and then stand for Heaven to be a well on earth which both stores and distributes love. Beloved apostle, search your heart today. If you do not find mercy and compassion for yourself in your heart, come to me at once and ask me to give these things to you. My plan for you and for the world will not advance as quickly as necessary if you do not accept your present condition and understand my perfect love for you. Your potential for holiness has not yet been fully achieved, of course, and I want you to advance. And I ask that you do so in confidence, joy and hope. Rejoice. I am with you.

Significant Points

- Many people who come for ministry do not know who they are. When they come to know deep down that they are totally loved and accepted by God, He can begin to make them into the new creation, which is revealed as their true self.

- The Church needs to pray more for the gifts of the Holy Spirit, such as a word of knowledge, and for wisdom.

- We also need to pray, as the bishop does at the sacrament of Confirmation, but making it a prayer for ourselves, 'Send your Holy Spirit upon us to be our helper and guide. Give us the spirit of wisdom and understanding, the spirit of right judgement and courage, the spirit of knowledge and reverence. Fill us with the spirit of wonder and awe in your presence. We ask this through Christ our Lord'.

- Many people need teaching that God offers us the grace with which we can go deeper into forgiving others, so that we are set free of their power to go on hurting us.

- We also need help to forgive ourselves and to let go of any perceptions that God may have been responsible for any of our hurts, so that He can give us much deeper trust in Him.

- God wants us to go beyond forgiving, and to ask for His love for others and for ourselves and for Him.

Scripture for Meditation

I want to get rid of my old self, which made me live as I used to, the old self which was being destroyed by deceitful desires. I want my heart and mind to be made completely new. I want to put on the new self, which is created in God's likeness, and reveals itself in the true life that is upright and holy. (Ep 4:22–24)

When we were baptised into union with Christ Jesus, we were baptised into union with his death. By our baptism, then, we were buried with him and shared his death, in order that just as Christ was raised from death by the glorious power of the Father, so also we might live a new life. (Rm 6:3–4)

There are different kinds of spiritual gifts, but the same Spirit gives them. There are different ways of serving but the same Lord is served. There are different abilities to perform service, but the same God gives ability to everyone for all services. Each one is given some proof of the Spirit's presence for the good of all. The Spirit gives one man a message of wisdom, while to another man the Spirit gives a message of knowledge. One and the same Spirit gives faith to one man, while to another man He gives the power to heal. The Spirit gives one man the power to work miracles; to another the gift of speaking God's message (prophecy); and to yet another, the ability to tell the difference between the gifts that come from the Spirit and those that do not (discernment). To one man He gives the ability to speak with strange sounds; to another, He gives the ability to explain what these sounds mean. But it is the same Spirit that does all this; He gives a different gift to each man, as He wishes. (1 Co 12:4–11)

Then Peter came to Jesus and asked, 'Lord, if my brother keeps on sinning against me, how many times do I have to forgive him? Seven times?' 'No, not seven times,' answered Jesus, 'but seventy times seven'. (Mt 18:21–22)

If you make my word your home, you will be my disciples and you will learn the truth and the truth will set you free. (Jn 8:31–32)

Testimonies

Testimony 6A

'I am learning to consider my life as a journey in which I come to know myself better and become progressively happier and more able to contribute to the world I find myself in.

I had a difficult start to life. I was not a wanted child, but was kept within a traditional family, however unhappy that was. At the age of 10, I decided that I wanted to change and have pursued that ever since. I have had varying degrees of success until I rediscovered a Christianity which said 'Jesus loves you'; instead of the one I had left which had said 'Thou shalt not.' I now know that Jesus' message is about healing and joy.

With this knowledge, I have progressively become a happier and more sociable person and achieve far more than I have ever done before. My relationships with my family and others get better all the time.

I have discovered some valuable lessons over the last decade, though this does not remove painful and anxious times, but I can now approach impending crises in a different way. Before, I would just try to attack my problems, and had limited success with the problems recurring. I now see them a little differently.

The choice we are faced with is to either just cope with life's hardships, or to see that we are sent them in order to receive healing through them, providing we are prepared to accept that help.

By using a mantra type (repeating phrase) meditation which focuses on Jesus, I have developed a relationship with Him which gives me peace in times of crisis. With that relationship, I can now be sure that when I have my darker times, my acceptance of His healing power resolves the issues at the time and more than that, is applying some permanent healing to the damage I incurred in my childhood. My life is sure of constant progression as long as I understand this.'

Testimony 6B

'I had been brought up in a Catholic family, but God was a distant figure; church was a familiar ritual with strong memories of the smell of candles and incense. By my late teens and early twenties, I no longer went to church. I was too interested in achieving my ambition in my chosen career. I met a married man and eventually married him and had children, but became increasingly unhappy because of his manic depressive state. Because our marriage was invalid as far as the church was concerned, we could not receive Holy Communion. This had a numbing effect on our lives and in time affected our children in a negative way. They never witnessed their parents receive Communion—they were different—no one to accompany them to the altar rails—an experience not fully shared. It all left its mark.

Eventually I went through a divorce and spent the next 7 years bringing up the children through their teenage years. It was a difficult time. By this time I had stopped going to church, as in one way I felt a failure; just another casualty on the way. Even in spite of this, I was strongly aware that God somehow still had His hand upon my life. Following the loss of my mother and the trauma of her sudden death, I started to attend Mass again and involve myself in church activities.

Then whilst abroad I met a man and the more I was with him the less involved I became in church. I always felt unsure what was the right thing to do. In my heart of hearts I knew he was bad for me, but I was quietly praying for his conversion, always hoping he would come to know Christ.

On one of my visits home I met a very good Christian friend who asked me to go to St. Joseph's parish in Norton for prayer ministry. I knew that I needed help, somehow along the line I had lost the plot. What was wrong with me? I knew that if I went for ministry, I must be willing to do what God asked of me. What if God asked me to give up this man? Could I handle that? I wrote a letter and arranged a meeting, but in the end I had to cancel this appointment. I just knew that I couldn't be dishonest with God. I had to go with an open heart and be ready to hear what God wanted of me. I was afraid I couldn't take what He would say; I wasn't strong enough.

I received a reply to my letter cancelling the appointment saying that my difficulties were understood and that I would be prayed for. That was that for quite some years.

One thing I have learnt with Jesus, is that He is very patient with us. He will bring us to the point of acceptance where we are willing to receive something new from Him. Though I had put the offer of prayer ministry on hold, so to speak, God hadn't put me on hold. Somehow He was looking into my heart and my life and seeing the yearnings that I had. I still wanted a Godly life. I still wanted to worship Him and be around His people, and began to attend an Anglican church in the town where I lived abroad.

My relationship with the man I was living with started to deteriorate quite badly. He was becoming more and more hostile towards me and spending more time away, and it then became increasingly obvious he was having an affair. Soon afterwards he was diagnosed with cancer. He had two operations, but was then treated with chemotherapy and radiology. When I prayed with him his reaction was hostile and he accused me of being crazy. Eventually I was unable to stay there and returned to England, tired and broken.

I was now ready to go to St. Joseph's. Surprisingly I was led prayerfully back into the first 10 years of my life, dealing with the root causes of my problems. In this process, the Lord Jesus was invited into those buried memories of my childhood, when I was sexually abused by a close family member and by a family friend. Over the course of similar meetings, through love and prayers, I was able to bring the people who hurt me to the person of Jesus Christ and to the foot of His cross.

In the middle of the night I was able to pray a prayer where I brought my life under the Lordship of Jesus. I asked Jesus to be Lord of all and brought all my family and friends, time, work, sexuality, possessions and abilities ... all these areas into His hands, into His Lordship, so as to choose **life** in all the areas of my life. The following day I had many blessings given to me and I attended a Mass for the healing of my family.

Since then, rather like the prodigal son, I have found that I have come back to my Father's house. A house which is creative and full of blessings. Now I have resumed daily communication with Jesus, praying and reading Scripture. Through this and keeping a prayer journal I can see how Jesus has touched and continues to bless my life, bringing healing into my relationships with my children, and back to my parents and beyond. I have prayed in particular for healing in my relationships with men, both past and present, so in the future I am no longer a victim, but victorious in whom I have been created to be. Since leaving the man I had lived with, I have been able to visit him, to wish him well and to be his friend. Of course I continue to pray for him daily.

This could not have happened, I am sure, without the love of Christ shown through prayerful ministry. Of course, like anyone else, I have my problems—but the difference for me is that I bring all my cares to Jesus and learn more to trust Him—sometimes I fail, but I know He uses even my failures. He is faithful indeed.

The one thing I have learnt is the importance of daily prayer and renewing my relationship with Jesus, bringing all my relationships, past and present, into is light. And, so now, I look forward to see how He will provide for me and my family in the future. Any real heartaches and cares I bring to Him. I continue to value the gift of friendship with Christians, the sacraments of the Church and the gift of perseverance, keeping my eye on the goal, which is the Lord Jesus Himself.'

Testimony 6C

'Up to three years ago (January 2007) I had been suffering (for several years) from atrial fibrillation—irregular heartbeats, involving fast, slow and erratic or missing heart beats. At its worst I wondered if I would soon die, but everything changed on the 2nd January, 2007 when my heart was prayed for by two devoted Christians in Norton—but first some background.

The prayer for healing started several months earlier when we met to consider root causes of the stress and tension within me; for instance, one prayer minister received a word of knowledge; 'staircase'! This reminded me of the occasion (I was about two years old and my mother told me about it later) when my mother was overcome by fumes from a defective gas water heater in the bathroom. She crawled away, collapsed on the floor and then slowly recovered at the top of the stairs. I stood horrified below. She asked me to fetch a neighbour, but I said 'please get dressed first' and in any case could not open the door. Fortunately (and to her surprise) she recovered sufficiently, as she lay on the floor, to crawl to the bathroom and switch off the boiler.

In our prayer time after this revelation (mid 2006), I felt Jesus was with us and that He was healing the little boy so that the distress in the memory was swept away. After about six sessions (during 2006) tackling root causes of heart problems, the miracle day arrived. All I knew beforehand was that something important was going to happen. It did.

They prayed for all the main parts and functions of my heart, and all the distress in my memory. As usual, the whole session took about an hour. I felt so close to God that I needed a quiet recovery time afterwards.

Over the following month, the 'heart episodes' gradually became less frequent—from well over 100 times a day down to just a few. I'm very glad that the improvement was so gradual. Here was a daily humbling reality: the presence of the love, power and gentleness of the Lord. After a few more weeks, I visited my G.P. who checked my heart and cut my medication down to a third. He said he didn't want to 'risk reducing the medication further as it seemed to be working well.'

But why was there occasional residual fibrillation? What kept coming to mind was that I'd been 'broken-hearted' and now needed to address accumulated problems of 'forgiveness and reconciliation' and 'lifestyle'. I kept thinking and praying about each of these factors and did the best I could practically—with the help of further prayer ministry. This involved steady persistence on my part, fuelled by the conviction that God surely couldn't want an incomplete miraculous healing!

In October 2009, I saw a newspaper article which described new research. 'Stress during pregnancy can harm a baby's development, leading to long term problems.' As I read the article, the revelation dawned '…that's my mother … that's me, that's me!'

The way ahead was clear. I needed to ask for further prayer for healing.

Ten days later (20th October, 2009), the generational healing day arrived. I explained, the best I could, the deep feelings experienced by my mother during her pregnancy: loneliness, missing her work, living in a strange place, cut off from family, rejection and deep sadness.

In the prayer time, Jesus was invited to come into my home to be with my mother and me—to take away all the hurts from us both and to cleanse me entirely from all effects of stress and trauma in the womb.

When I returned from ministry, the world looked and felt different. At first, I felt a bit frightened. I had to get used to a new me, to work out, with the Lord's help, how to respond to people and intimidating situations that previously I had avoided. I was no longer afraid of certain sorts of people and situations—and I had to fight off the temptation to be rude back when people were rude to me.

The changes were difficult to describe, but I no longer feel partially cut-off. The world looks and feels closer to me and I want to experience it more closely. I'm in the process of building up new attitudes and a new lifestyle (including '… six days shalt thou labour …'!). I felt at first that this was all as much healing as I could cope with, but isn't it wonderful? In a world with so much sin and sickness, it's just wonderful to experience the pure, personal love, power and gentleness of Jesus.'

Testimony 6D

'Forgiveness is at the very core of our salvation (Mt 6:14–15). Through Jesus we were forgiven, healed and reconciled to God. With the help of people at St Joseph's and the grace of God, I have begun to learn to put forgiveness into practice in many areas of my past and present life situations. This is resulting in the beginning of healing and restoration for me and my family.

Recently I heard on the radio an interview with one of the men who had been held hostage in Iraq. This is what he said: 'Forgiveness is letting go of the issue we have with a person or persons. This creates space for something else to happen like healing and restoration that otherwise wouldn't happen. By not forgiving, we become full of resentment, anger etc., which make us unable to move forward'.

I've learnt that forgiving is not a one-off thing, but a process we engage in with God, which brings healing to our lives and others.'

Testimony 6E

'When I was born my mother almost lost her life giving birth to me. She totally rejected me from birth until my grandmother encouraged her to 'just look' at the child she was leaving behind at 10 days old.

This was the beginning of a life that was to prove to be a very painful and traumatic existence. My father was at the time of my birth in the Air Force. He came home for good when I was 3 years old. In the first three hours of meeting him, on the train journey home, I was painfully aware of my unwanted presence as he wanted to be alone with my mother.

Shortly after his homecoming I was blest with a little sister and every year after for six years the family grew steadily. After each pregnancy my mother was advised by the medical profession not to have any more children as her health deteriorated with each birth.

With her seventh child God called her home taking the child with her, leaving six children motherless and leaving myself to the mercy of a very broken and confused father who changed his attentions from his wife to eldest daughter, me!

I received his attentions both physically and emotionally from the age of 8 years old, just before my mother's death, until my sixteenth year when meeting my future husband gave me the courage to end the relationship. I was married three years later at 19 years and gave birth to two wonderful children when I was 23 and 25 which has proved to be one of the greatest blessings God has bestowed on me.

I started the long painful climb towards finding the beautiful child within 15 years ago when Jesus called me to live my life fully in Him. The climb at times seemed almost too much to bear and I would not have recovered as fully if God had not provided wonderful people along the way who were prepared to be the hands and heart of Jesus, using their gifts of sensitivity and love in healing ministry to bring me gently back to God, teaching me to trust and live in Him.

I sometimes still have 'ups and downs' and struggle at times with very traumatic memories of childhood sexual abuse, nursing my sick mother from 4 years old and eventually finding her dead in bed, also bringing up five brothers and sisters into their adulthood and coming to terms with myself as God created me to be. I thank God every day for the healing I received through His body, the people who prayed with me and touched my life with the power of His healing presence.

God has enabled me to feel His presence and in turn, through my experiences of life, to touch others with His power through my hands and heart to help them in love. I firmly believe that if I had not received this freedom and healing, I would be a very unhappy and confused individual. Thank you, Lord Jesus for the healing ministry and your Body on earth.'

Testimony 6F

'Two years ago a Christian friend told me that God had a plan for me. I was at that time a sceptic. Although I had been baptised and confirmed as a Catholic I was so aggrieved with the Church that I had left. I came in time, to find Buddhism. I felt at last something without a guilt trip attached, but my friend still insisted that the Lord had a plan for me. As I was talking to my friend one day, I suddenly asked, 'What about forgiveness?'

My past had been a chequered one and I could not see how I could possibly be forgiven for certain aspects of it. He talked about redemption and of the sacrifice that was made at the Cross for me and how we can place all our burdens there. We also spoke of the prayer that I could use that would mean I asked for forgiveness. Yet I still could not let my past sins go. I could not let my burden go to the Cross. Then it came to me—it was not enough that I prayed for forgiveness—I needed to experience a

symbolic, yet physical, act of forgiveness to accentuate the process. Words alone held no comfort of my being a 'new creation' in Christ.

I arranged a visit with a priest who was a great help with my problem. The process of confession, the repenting of my sins and ultimately the forgiving blessing by Him, gave me the much-needed reconciliation I needed. I am still on that journey and much, much, nearer to the Lord's plan.'

Testimony 6G

'When my son was born 32 years ago, I became ill with severe post-natal depression, which lasted over 2 years. I did not bond with my baby and consequently was not a good mother. Then my marriage ended in divorce and for the next 21 years I was admitted to hospital many times. In 1997 I was prescribed more modern medication and my health improved, but I still felt guilt and self-hate. Eighteen months ago I started to attend the ministry of prayer for inner healing and through wise and loving counsel I found a new way to pray for my son and also for forgiveness for myself from God.'

Testimony 6H

'I came from a family of drinkers, particularly on my mother's side, but my father too was a drinker. In drink, he was violent and abusive to my mother who did not drink. He found me difficult to deal with whereas my sister was his favourite. My mother and I lived in fear of him and I felt unloved by him. Even as a child I longed to be able to protect my mother, but had to watch her becoming crippled emotionally and physically, and I felt helpless. My father came from a Catholic family, but neither he nor my mother had any faith. On just one occasion, I went with other children from the street to a Sunday School on Palm Sunday. I came back excited with a palm cross, but was told by my parents that there was not going to be anything to do with God in this house, and was forbidden to go again. For a while from the age of four, I was sexually abused by two uncles.

By my teenage years I longed to get away from home and escape from all that was dysfunctional in my family. I felt some peace in being creative as I learned hairdressing, after being accepted for an apprenticeship as a frightened and insecure 15 year old. Because of all the pain in my family life I was unable to chat freely with ladies on whose hair I was working, and I longed for something positive in my life about which I could speak. I felt that if I could find a boyfriend it would give me something positive to chat about. That began a further downward spiral in my life as I searched for some love and happiness in the wrong directions. I began to go to pubs and clubs, and at 17, whilst drunk, I met an older man who was going through a divorce, and I felt an overwhelming need to possess him. At 19 I had my first child by him, but he began to be violent towards me while I was still pregnant.

Three years later I became pregnant again, but without telling my husband, I decided to have an abortion. Life with my husband and the effect on our child seemed so bad that I didn't want to inflict this on a second child. Despite this I stayed with him and we married when I was 24. Because of my parents' marriage I accepted violence as being part of being loved, as though it was better than being alone and unwanted. For a while we lived apart and I began to be hopeful that I could face life alone with my daughter. Then his mother died and I felt that it was my duty to give up my dream of a new life, and that I must go back to care for him. Two more children followed.

I turned more and more to drink to try to avoid feeling worthless and useless. At 29, in order to escape my husband's violence, and as though I was looking for a second prince charming to rescue me after the failure of the first one, I ran off to London with another man, feeling bad at leaving my children with my husband. For some time we lived rough in various squats and then slept in doorways in The Strand. The man I was with was violent and I also found myself becoming violent, particularly when I felt I needed to protect myself. I reached the point where I felt like killing myself, because of guilt over the children and because life was not worth living. One day, about 5.00 am, a lady put on the pavement beside me, a cup of tea and a sandwich. That helped me to have a little reason to believe that perhaps life could become worth living.

After a few years with him on the streets and in squats, I realised what a damaged and even perhaps evil person he was. He forced me to become a prostitute and he was my pimp. I was still living in fear, now of my very life. That went on for two years, until the death of my husband. I returned to the North East and took two of my children to Brighton, leaving the eldest with my husband's family. I had no idea how irresponsible I was. I just kept hoping that somehow things would get better. For a while, with the two younger children and the pimp, we lived partly by begging, being re-housed when we became homeless. Somehow, my one visit to a Sunday School, and the joy I had experienced at receiving the palm cross, had sowed a seed of hope and faith.

My husband had come from a Catholic family and I felt in some way that I and the children might be helped by his prayers now that he had died. Before long, however, I was unable to cope and the two children were taken into care. The youngest was only three when her father died, and she was alone with his body, when he died, until the other two returned from school. All of this made me fearful for the damage being done to them, and I felt guilty that I was now letting them down again when they had to be taken into care. At least, however, the authorities promised me that the children would be taken to church. The nursery to which my youngest was taken was called after Mary Magdalene, and somehow I must have heard of her, because it connected in my mind with my guilt, shame and remorse.

Because of my children being taken into care, I began to be helped by various agencies, and it was a doctor who put me in touch with A.A. In my desperation over the children, I went to one meeting and stopped drinking for 6 months, while I battled with my partner's drinking. Even though there was so much pain and struggle, this period of 6 months stands out as bright, as I began to seek help for issues from childhood. Not being drunk, I could think more clearly and I began to learn about such things as co-dependency. I began to dare to believe that there was a God and I began to cry out to Him. It took a further six very painful years of drinking during which I returned to the North East, agonising over the children going into and out of care, and dealing with my obsession with my partner, and suffering his violence, until finally I left him. I was now alone with my children coming and going. I was still searching for love and approval and got involved with several other men, who turned out to be sick or even evil.

I continued to cry out to God and was letting go of much of the denial which began in my childhood, as I went for counselling. God was now beginning to help me through other people, one of whom was a Catholic teacher who taught my children. I realised that I had met her when I was 19 and had helped her in a family crisis. Now she was helping me, taking me to prayer groups and to church and introducing me to other Christians. I was still drinking at this stage, but over 12 years ago the grace of God's love enabled me to stop drinking, as people prayed for a miracle for me.

Over these years, God has been doing more and more healing in me and giving me the power to forgive others and myself. I was able to open up to other Christians and admit the abortion, and began a process of prayer in which I was gradually able to let go of my guilt and shame, and to know that God had forgiven me and I was able to receive the grace to forgive myself. A Scripture passage which means a lot to me is, 'So if the Son sets you free, you will be free indeed.' (Jn 8:36).

The culmination of the healing process was when I was guided to come regularly for prayer to the group for inner healing at St. Joseph's, Norton. One of the ways in which God is now using me, is that I am involved in helping others in the AA group and an Al-Anon group. I now know in the depths of my being that I am a beloved child of God and that He wants to make use of me to help others. I am now happily married. Five years ago I was baptised and received into the Catholic Church, and I now realise how vital it is to me to receive Holy Communion and the sacrament of Reconciliation. My children are a wonderful blessing to me and I thank God for the healing that He is still doing there. I am being delivered of my obsession with seeking perfection by my own efforts, and now have a tremendous trust in God, who will protect and take care of us in every way.'

Notes

1   M. Scott Peck, *The Road Less Travelled* (London: Arrow Books, 1990), pp. 13–16.

2   P. Collins, various tape cassettes and CDs.

3   J. McManus & S. Thornton, *Finding Forgiveness* (Chawton: Redemptorist Publications, 2006).

4   *Ibid.*, p. 46.

5   J. Hampsch, various tape cassettes.

6   J. Powell & L. Brady, *The Fully Alive Experience – Participants' Personal Notebook* (Argus Publications, 1980).

7   J. McManus, *Hallowed Be Thy Name* (Chawton: Redemptorist Publications, 2009), p. 29.

8   J. McManus, *Healing in the Spirit* (London: Darton, Longman & Todd, 1994), pp. 92–94.

9   J. McManus, *The Inside Job—A Spirituality Of True Self-Esteem*, (Chawton: Redemptorist Publications, 2004).

10   H. Nouwen, *The Inner Voice of Love*, (London: Darton, Longman & Todd, 1997), pp. ix, 5.

7

CONTINUING OUR JOURNEY

Ongoing Process

With so many potential roots of early hurts, which tend to give rise to a repeated pattern in various ways in later years, prayers in many of the areas outlined already are likely to be needed more than once. Often people think they have received enough healing and then return some time later, shocked to have found that feelings such as deeper anger, resentment, disappointment are now emerging, and they think that they have stopped making progress and gone backwards. It is in fact progress, as the Lord uncovers deeper layers, and so more prayer is needed. Of course, the person should not be continually seeking to hark back to the past because the Lord wants to free us of all burdens from the past and also remove any burdens like fear and anxiety about the future, so that we can live in peace with Him in each present moment.

However, this is a process that takes time—in fact it really takes a lifetime, because being freed from all the effects of our own and other people's sins, and becoming sanctified by the Holy Spirit is never totally completed in this life. Passages in the Old Testament, where the people of God faced numerous enemies obstructing their way to the Promised Land, can speak to us of God healing us of many things in preparation for our eventual arrival in our heavenly home. An example is: 'The Lord your God is with you; little by little He will drive out the nations as you advance. You will not be able to destroy them all at once for, if you did, the number of wild animals would increase and be a threat to you'. (Dt 7:22). Perhaps if our healing were quicker we might be threatened by such things as pride or independent self-sufficiency.

One day in ministry with a young man, I realised what the Lord was saying was wrong in him. When I explained, he burst out in anger, 'Why doesn't God push a button and set me free?' He didn't keep the next appointment, and hasn't come back. It says in Galatians 2:19–20, 'I have been put to death with Christ on His cross, so that it is no longer I who live, but it is Christ who lives in me'. Some people seem to think they need make no effort but expect Jesus, through His victory on the Cross working to produce in them the fruits of love, joy, peace, patience, kindness, goodness, faithfulness, humility and self-control. But these fruits do not just grow instantly and automatically. Galatians goes on to show that it is dependent upon our cooperation: 'Those who belong to Christ Jesus have put to death their human nature with all its passions and desires' (Ga 5:24). This is exactly what is discussed in this next section.

In a number of passages, St Paul reminds us that this is something we have to be determined to work at with the power of the Holy Spirit right through the rest of our lives: 'Keep on working with fear and trembling to complete your salvation, for God is always at work in you to make you willing and able to obey His own purpose' (Ph 2:12–13); and 'I have done my best in the race. I have run the full distance, and I have kept the faith' (2 Tm 4:7). In the letter to the Hebrews, we read 'Let us rid ourselves of everything that gets in the way, and of the sin which holds on to us so tightly, [binding!] and let us run with determination the race that lies before us. Let us keep our eyes fixed on Jesus, on whom our faith depends from beginning to end.' (Heb 12:1–2). We hear it again in 1 Timothy 6:12: 'Fight the good fight of the faith; take hold of the eternal life to which you were called'.

Yet in spite of these Scriptures, in a number of Churches people have been taught that when they invite Jesus to come more fully into their lives so that they experience personally the love and gift of salvation which God has for them, and they are baptised in the Holy Spirit, then they become a new creation and they are set free of their old life. One very well-known Christian teacher and writer published a book in 1993 about this. It seems to be concluded in some evangelical circles from such Scriptures as 'When anyone is joined to Christ he is a new being; the old is gone, the new has come' (2 Co 5:17), that we now have total freedom and new life, once for all, instantaneously or in a very short time, and that our old creation has gone, so our past with its hurts is dead and thus does not need healing. The author appeared to be willing to pray with a person about the healing of past hurts on one occasion only after baptism in the Holy Spirit, and then did not expect them to speak again about any of it, and said that he would stop them if they tried to do so. There has not always been sufficient recognition that upon baptism in the Holy Spirit great changes can occur quickly in our conscious mind, but it takes much longer for changes to occur in our unconscious or subconscious mind.

In recent years, an increasing number of people have been coming to our home from evangelical or Pentecostal or other churches where they say they have experienced being baptised in the Holy Spirit. They have not found there any ministry of inner healing, but they now realise that they need this. In some cases they have been confused or even hurt by the attitudes or teaching. Testimonies 7A (p. 161) and 7B (p. 163), written by a young couple coming separately and together to my home, are examples which typify the needs which are being revealed in a number of people. Both of them are now being called by God in powerful new ways and in a very different church to the one to which they had belonged, which has greatly surprised them.

We come now to a very important aspect of our co-operation by which we can, in the words just quoted from Galatians 5, 'put to death our human nature' or, in the words of Hebrews 12, 'Let us rid ourselves of everything that gets in the way'.

Destroying Strongholds of Damaged Reactions

Many people have used phrases like 'I'm bound to get it wrong again', or 'I'm bound to have problems when I meet him'. Sometimes phrases spoken casually do reveal a deeper meaning. We tend to go on reacting in the same old ways, driven by processes in our unconscious or subconscious mind, coming from influences which have fixed our attitudes, habits, ideas and behaviours.

Many years ago it had seemed to us that prayer ministry could gradually release people from their old damaged reactions, as though new 'grooves' were being formed within their unconscious or subconscious brain. We had not then heard of neuroplasticity and ingrained or grooved neural pathways forming within our brain very early on. With the advent of functional MRI, sometimes with automatic image registration, there is much research within cognitive neuroscience, looking at cognitive, behavioural or neuropsychological outcomes. This goes beyond studies following brain injuries, and already includes such studies as cognitive behavioural therapy (CBT) on some children as it affects certain reactions. One recent study[1] published by the Association of Psychological Science in 2011 used EEGs to show much reduced levels of anxiety in some adults with social anxiety disorder following sessions of group CBT. As some patients were taking medication, it cannot yet be claimed that psycho-therapy is changing the brain. However, as the lead researcher wrote, 'If the brain does not change, there won't be a change in behaviour or emotion'. It will be interesting to know if research will in due course include studies of the brain by functional MRI or EEG before and after prayer for inner healing.

Just to take one aspect of binding now, and then consider others later. If we think and speak negatively, whether about ourselves or about others, we cause binding and we can find ourselves in effect contradicting God or being in rebellion against Him. There is nothing negative in God, so we have spoken out of 'the house of the destructive word', rather than out of the 'house of the creative word' (Jn 8:31–32), and we have not used our awareness from Scripture as to how God speaks and thinks. (See the previous chapter, and the section on the power of the Word of God in this chapter). The letter of St James speaks of the power of the tongue, so our spoken words have real power. Even our unspoken negative thoughts exercise some binding, as discussed by Derek Prince in his book 'Blessing or Curse'.[2] Word curses can range greatly in severity from relatively minor ones which we may inflict upon ourselves, e.g. 'I don't like my appearance' through to major curses coming from a source with evil power. We should pray with the authority of Jesus to break the power of any curse as soon as we become aware of it.

Our youngest son's first appointment was to teach RE in a Catholic secondary school. Distressed by the lack of interest and faith of the pupils, he resigned without finding another job. He was looking for supply or short-term contract work, but was hoping to transfer to primary teaching. He came home and said, 'I will never teach RE in a secondary school again.' We said, 'You have bound yourself, can we set you free?' He said, 'Yes'. We asked him to say to God that he was sorry for speaking negatively, and we prayed, 'In the name of Jesus Christ, and with the sword of the Holy Spirit, we set you free from the power of your negative words'. Within a few months, he rang to tell us he had a permanent post. 'Secondary or primary?' we asked. 'Secondary,' he said. 'What is your main subject?' we asked. 'RE' was the reply. For two years he taught RE in a secondary school, but he was then given the chance to move to primary teaching, where he still works.

Even St Paul was puzzled that he wasn't free: 'I do not understand what I do; for I don't do what I would like to do, but instead I do what I hate. Though the desire to do good is in me, I am not able to do it. I don't do the good I want to do; instead I do the evil that I don't want to do' (Rm 7:15–19).

But St Paul keeps encouraging us, e.g. 'Since you have accepted Christ, live in union with Him. Keep your roots deep in Him and become stronger in your faith' (Col 2:6). So we are to move deeper into union with Christ, which means inviting Him into deeper and deeper layers of our soul—our mind, will and emotions—so that He is increasingly becoming Lord in all these areas.

Many years ago, Betty, while we were praying with a man, had a picture in her mind of a mummy. If a live person has layer upon layer of binding upon them, then they become rigid and helpless like a mummy. We keep on through our life, repeating our old damaged reactions to people and events. So we are stuck and helpless. Like Lazarus we have to be called into new life by Jesus, and then Jesus asks the others to unbind him. That is what Jesus is asking us to do as He gives us His love for one another, so that we can pray for inner healing.

Defensive reactions automatically build up in layers in us from our earliest beginnings, and were necessary then for us to survive pain and distress, but later in life we begin to realise that they have become barriers which keep us from being free to grow into deeper loving relationship with God and with one another.

Self-protection, self-preservation and self-justification are actually sins. An extreme form of self-preservation is a mummy! When I am hurt from my earliest days the defences build as I try to avoid being hurt again, e.g. an unconscious decision not to let people get close to me in case I again become vulnerable to them. That means that our style of relating to others has more to do with self-preservation than self-giving, which is sin, because we are trying to protect ourselves rather than trusting the God who made us and died for us to be our only protection. It is as if we are saying to God, 'I trust you with some things, but not with the deepest parts of my being where I need to protect myself, because I am so afraid of being hurt that I might fall apart'. Naturally the child cannot realise this, but every time we do it automatically and instinctively, another layer of defensive reaction is added, which further binds us.

This process has been described by Liberty Savard in the first of her three connected books, *Shattering Your Strongholds*.[3] She writes:

- something traumatic happens in my life, which is a fact

- this leads me to develop a wrong pattern of thinking
- which helps me to justify a wrong behaviour
- which causes me to erect a stronghold to protect my right to this damaged reaction
- which perpetuates my pain by keeping the trauma locked in and God locked out.

Until we take our self-protective layers off the vulnerable areas of our own wounded souls, God can't heal our wounds, resolve our doubts, and neutralise our fear and pain. When we prevent Him from doing that, we limit our usefulness to Him.[4]

Yes, things have been done to you, said to you and taken from you—no one can deny that. But the condition of your soul today is not the product of these things. Your soul's condition today is due to how far it refuses to let go of its reactions to the things of your past. Your soul actually keeps alive all the effects of need, pain and confusion, by keeping your worst memories on artificial life support.[5]

This is very good news because we do not have to remain a victim. We can use our free will to take the authority of Jesus to destroy these damaged reactions, so that gradually these layers are peeled off like Jesus asked them to do with Lazarus and we become more and more free. We are not entitled to say, 'How can you expect me to be any different when you look at how badly treated I was as a child?' We have to take full responsibility for our actions and how we live our life.

Father Pat Deegan, who has an extensive ministry of teaching and praying with people for inner healing, emphasises[6] that we have to own our emotions which will never be healed until we stop blaming others, and we accept how things are and let go of all regrets and 'if only'. We must accept responsibility for our own spiritual growth because we cannot abdicate that responsibility to anyone else. We are each responsible for our own reactions to the sins of other people against us and for our own happiness. As he says, our happiness is an inside job, and he suggests putting a note on our mirror, 'You are looking at the face of the one who is responsible for your happiness'.

Liberty Savard was led to a deeper meaning in Matthew 16:19 and 18:18, which helps us to take that responsibility and to let go of our damaged reactions as we regularly and persistently bring them in prayer to die on the Cross with Christ using His authority. This gradually fulfils the Scripture 'And those who belong to Christ Jesus have put to death their human nature with all its passions and desires' (Ga 5:24). We have recommended the prayers which she has suggested, to hundreds of people and strongly advise that they should pray them daily, both for themselves and for their loved ones. Very many have told us how important and powerful they found them.

These prayers, the putting on the full armour of God (Ep 6), together with other prayers listed in Appendix 5, are ones which we strongly recommend people to pray every single day. Over twenty years ago, a doctor living some distance from us would offer our address to some patients, and say that they might be helped by prayer ministry, and a number did come. The doctor would say, 'If they give you a prayer or a Scripture passage, treat it as you would a prescription from me; you don't just take it sometimes, but every single day'.

Here is a shortened version of the prayers which Liberty Savard recommends:[7]

You can pray this prayer for yourself or those who are dear to you. Simply present the person you are praying for to the Lord in the space marked *.

> In the name of Jesus Christ, I bind myself and * to the will of God, to the truth of God, to the mercy of Christ and the work of His cross with all of its mercy, truth, love, power, forgiveness and dying to self, and to the mind of Christ.
>
> In the name of Jesus Christ I bind Satan and loose his hold on anything he has ever stolen from me or *.
>
> I repent of any wrong attitudes or thoughts. I renounce them now and ask your forgiveness Lord.
>
> In the name of Jesus Christ, I loose and destroy any wrong pattern of thinking, attitude, idea, desire, belief, habit and behaviour that may be still working in me or *. I tear down every stronghold erected to protect or justify wrong feelings against anyone.
>
> In the name of Jesus Christ, I loose the power and effects of any harsh or hard words spoken to, about or by me or *.
>
> I loose all generational bondages and associated strongholds from myself and from *. Amen.

The term 'stronghold' comes from 2 Co 10:4–5: 'The weapons we use in our fight are not this world's weapons, but God's powerful weapons which we use to destroy strongholds. We destroy false arguments; we pull down every proud obstacle that is raised against the knowledge of God; we take every thought captive and make it obey Christ'. A stronghold in this context can be defined as something we rely on to defend our right to believe something. We may rely on a stronghold of denial to protect our right to avoid facing the pain and doing something about it. We might rely on a stronghold of distrust, to protect our right to build defensive walls, because we fear that no one can be trusted.

There are great numbers of possible strongholds in us, apart from self-protection, self-preservation and self-justification, such as anger, bitterness, hatred, unforgiveness, pride, jealousy, fear, confusion, self-indulgence, denial and many other things.

For years, since Savard's book became available to us, I have prayed these prayers every day for those strongholds which the Lord has so far revealed in me, and for my family, though I do not presume to know their strongholds. Whilst Betty was alive I prayed them for her, naming those strongholds we had become aware of in our prayer.

It seemed as though the two long depressive illnesses which she suffered in her later years owed much to the death of her father when she was eighteen months old. Her mother had to move her and her brother from Norwich to a tiny isolated village in North Wales, where her grandfather ran the local school. In order to find work, her mother had to leave her and go to a town to live with sisters. So she, in effect, was deprived totally of her father and almost totally of her mother for some years, until her mother re-married. Betty became aware in prayer that she had felt abandoned and insecure—two strongholds. Another big stronghold in her was disappointment. I had wondered for years why an apparently small disappointment would affect her so much. Again, in prayer, Betty was led to a memory of when the children of this village school were given the rare treat of a day's outing. She was the only child not permitted to go. She never knew why, but it seemed cruel and surprising and unjust when she was the granddaughter of the head teacher.

Testimony 7C (p. 164) talks of strongholds being diminished and removed over a period which, sadly, preceded a great loss, but where these prayers played a part in this wonderful lady facing the suffering. She is greatly used by God to pray with others for healing.

The first part of the strongholds prayer, where, with the authority of Jesus, we bind ourselves and our loved ones closer to God, may remind us of the prayer in the version of the Stations of the Cross by St Alphonsus: 'Never permit me to separate myself from thee again; grant that I may love thee always, and then do with me what thou wilt'. In this context, the use of the word 'bind' is a healthy one, rather like the way in which a mother in some countries may bind her baby to her breast, thus leaving her hands free to do her work. The same word 'bind' also has negative connotations when it refers to our being bound so that we are not free, and some aspects of this negative binding will now be discussed.

Other Forms of Binding

We always recommend strongly that, immediately following the daily prayer for destroying strongholds, people pray, in the name of Jesus Christ, to cut all the emotional bonds and soul ties between themselves and all the significant people in their life. This is particularly important for those in our close family, and they can occur not only between those who are alive today, but can also involve binding coming from family members who are dead. This can arise not only from emotional and relational damage in our family, but could also come from involvement of past family members in such activities as freemasonry or occult practices. Prayer at a Mass for intergenerational healing may also be needed in the latter cases.

Many times, an adult in our home for ministry has referred to some recent conversation with a parent or another close relative. Something, it may be a tone of voice, a look, a particular word, has triggered a difficult negative reaction in them. They may have felt suddenly like the small, resentful, angry child, or made to feel inadequate, unwanted etc. In some way, what went on, perhaps with no conscious intent on the part of the other one, parent or some other, triggered subconscious or unconscious memories of incidents or words or feelings from childhood, when they were made to feel similar emotions. It may reveal that they need further prayer for healing of memories and emotions, and to ask for the grace to forgive more deeply, and for the Lord to help them to love and accept themselves.

For years, immediately following the stronghold prayers, I have prayed to cut all these bonds between myself and Betty while she was alive, between myself and other close family members, and then between these various pairs of the family. For years, we did people a disservice by supposing, wrongly, that, having prayed once, these bonds remain severed. Then it dawned on us, through listening to people and to God, that they very easily re-grow, especially if we have further contacts e.g. by telephone or by meeting.

As we daily cut away these unhelpful emotional bonds, we are praying that God gives us more and more of His pure love in place of our always imperfect love for everyone in our family; a process which will only be complete when eventually we are in the fullness of God's Life. Soul ties are more difficult to define, but probably include such things as 'I (or we) couldn't talk to Mum (or to him) about that!' It is as though there are 'no-go' areas between us. We are cutting away impediments which hinder the growth of God's love between us.

In order to emphasise the vital need for anyone involved in prayerful ministry to others to pray for protection, unbinding and cleansing for themselves and their family, Testimony 7D (p. 167) has been included. A lady gave a very powerful talk to the inner healing prayer group at St Joseph's, Norton, which was based on very hard and painful lessons which she had learnt after she was clearly called by the Lord to help someone in trouble. The testimony is a very brief summary, depersonalised so as to avoid risk of any possible hurt to anyone, which summarises stages and lessons learnt over an extremely painful period of fifteen years. It is further evidence that when someone faithfully seeks God's way through suffering, He finally brings wonderful healing and reconciliation to all concerned. Her sharing with the group also illustrated the vital importance of wanting complete forgiveness and, if possible, reconciliation, and of anyone undergoing prayer ministry being helped to depend totally on the Lord, and not become dependent upon, or unduly reliant upon, those persons providing the ministry. It is important to pray to cut emotional bonds and soul ties between those praying and those in need, as well as breaking the power of any inner vows.

Another way of looking at our being released from some of these bonds besides cutting them is to think if them being untied. Any individual can be affected in ways known fully only by God, by many disobediences to God, broken relationships, sinful behaviours, unforgiveness, prejudices, hates, anguish, rejections and loneliness, involving not only themselves and those in their lifetime but many in their past family. It had occurred to my wife and I many years ago that it was as though there were many entanglements or knots in the bonds which needed to be loosened and untied in the families of so many who were coming for ministry. It also seemed to us that Our Blessed Lady as a 'mother to us in the order of grace'[8] would be likely to be given a role by God in the untying of these knots as part of His work of healing and freeing His children.

It was only very recently that I realised that St Irenaeus had written about this role of Mary. 'The knot of Eve's disobedience was untied with Mary's obedience; what the virgin Eve bound through her disbelief, Mary loosened by her faith'.[9] Some devotion to Mary in this area of our need of her help has remained in parts of the Church. In Perlach in Bavaria the Church of St Peter has an image of Our Lady as the undoer or untier of knots which goes back to 1700. Many of these bonds and knots may have their origins in relationships and events in earlier generations of our family of which we are completely ignorant. Also, the various hurts and emotions arising from many sources, particularly in our early life, have become entrenched and tangled together within each one of us. There is no area of human hurt, however hidden or sensitive, in which we need hesitate to ask for Our Lady's help, so that healing can occur without our doing any harm with our ignorance, tactlessness or clumsiness.

A delicate question, which we have to be sensitive in asking, is whether or not this person ever had sexual intercourse outside marriage. If that has happened, then bonds have been established which need to be broken by the authority of Christ, and we pray that anything which was lost in joining with the other partner, is fully restored by Jesus as part of their becoming whole and free.

An example of discomfort being triggered by something seemingly as minor as a tone of voice occurred following a twelve-week course of teaching which we had given some years ago. It was attended by 97 people and was strongly supported by our bishop, and a number of priests recommended parishioners from a wide area to attend. Following the course, a lady in a senior position in her profession asked to come to our home for ministry. In one session she spoke of being upset by something said by a man in one of the plenary sessions of the course. She did not know what he had said. She did not know what he looked like, not being able to see him in the large group, and she did not know why she was so disturbed. We identified him as a Superintendent Methodist minister from another town. Why was she so troubled? She herself had been married to an Anglican priest. They had fallen out with the authorities and left the Church. They then joined a Pentecostal Church where they again had trouble with the leaders and left that. Then her marriage broke. She had been affected by the tone of this man, because it awoke subconscious memories of how various church leaders had hurt her.

Other influences outside the person which need to be broken are the intergenerational bonds, and the need for prayers at a Mass has already been discussed. Sometimes these unhelpful bonds have formed during our lifetime in our dealings with someone in our family who is now dead, but there can be other influences known only to God coming from earlier ancestors. These sometimes require prayers for deliverance. Mention has also been made of curses. Of course we can use our own tongue to bless or curse, and we may have placed a binding on ourselves by saying such things as 'I'll never be able to do that' or 'I'm too stupid'. But curses of more sinister kind can come upon us or our families, and need to be broken. Whenever we celebrate a Mass for intergenerational healing, at the time of bidding prayers, the priest or I lead the congregation in prayers which include freeing ourselves and family from any possible curses. People may also of course need individual personal prayer ministry as well.

Our first experience of a curse came in 1975, when, in an almost circular church, Francis MacNutt made what we later realised was an unwise move. He went round and prayed briefly, mainly in tongues, with everyone in the front row. He then asked each of them to turn, lay hands on, and pray with the person behind, until, row by row, everyone had had some ministry. Immediately after that, a lady in the core group of our prayer group, a most peaceable woman, became belligerent. So much so that she upset another member to the extent that I was told this other lady had packed her case and gone to the car park to drive straight home. I intercepted her in the car park and persuaded her to stay. We prayed with the one who had become difficult, in order to free her.

We then investigated. The person who laid hands on the one who changed character was a lady not long in the North from living in London. She was a wonderful Christian with deep faith. Whilst in London she had gone to a Moon group, with the idea of praying for them to see the error of their ways, repent and turn to Christ. They had discovered what she was doing, and they put a curse on her. Later she herself was completely set free and was a great inspiration to others.

At one time, we were prepared, if someone requested it, to pray with someone with laying on of hands, on behalf of someone not able to be present. Then we learned that this could give rise to a risk. If the absent person being prayed for needed deliverance, some evil spirit might then affect the one being prayed for on their behalf. Of course, it is perfectly normal to pray for absent people without making it prayer by proxy.

In order to be able to deal with our own difficulties, and where appropriate to help others, we all need to be praying for God to give us more clarity and truth in our thoughts and attitudes, and in how we perceive people and situations: to be able to see them as it were more through the eyes of Christ and with His love and compassion and understanding, less clouded by our own weaknesses and damage. One aspect of this is to ask God to heal us of what are sometimes called distortions in our vision.

Distortions in Our Vision

Whilst still in Leeds, we attended a weekend at a house of prayer. The subject was The Fully Alive Experience programme of Fr John Powell SJ. We were introduced to the way in which we, probably every one of us, absorbed statements which became unconscious attitudes or imperatives, which go on affecting our behaviour through our adult lives. They tend to govern many of our ways of living, but, if we can identify them and look carefully at them, we realise in fact that they are all lies. They can be responsible for many of our unconscious automatic ways of dealing with situations. They can cause internal pressures and drives. We say to people: 'If you are doing things because you think you *should* or *must* do them, then check with God in prayer—this doesn't sound like serving in freedom and peace.'

From his work as a psychologist and priest, Fr Powell identified[10] distortions in vision about (1) self, (2) others, (3) life, (4) the world around us and (5) God. We were given workbooks, and in prayer began to get in touch with ways in which these (mostly) hidden influences had been stopping each of us from being free to do what God wanted.

Typical examples about self include:

- I must keep peace in all my relationships or else I will be failing in my duty'. Of course, the phrase following or else may not be identical for different individuals. For some it might be 'or else I will not be able to think of myself as a good Christian'. However, it is not possible to go through life without, on

occasion, needing to stand up to someone, perhaps even confront them with the truth, in the right way and time. Thus if we
are driven by this particular lie, we are liable to fail to stand up
for the truth when God wants us to do so.

- I should always think of others' needs before my own or else I
  will be self-centred.' That can put great strain on us as we are
  driven to do things for others which perhaps God is not wanting
  us to do, maybe at a time when we need to conserve our own
  strength and spend time with Him. It may lead to tiredness,
  frustration, anger, perhaps asking ourselves, 'Why aren't they
  more grateful when I'm doing all this for them at great cost to
  my own health?' That would put pressure on them. We would
  not be serving them in freedom and peace. Another closely
  related example is, 'I have to please others and satisfy their
  expectations or else I am not a caring person.'

An example about life is, 'Life must be fair to me *or else* I will be angry
and bitter'. We do great disservice to children if we give them too much
emphasis on expecting that everything must always be fair, or otherwise
someone is to blame.

We frequently give these lists to people who come here, and they can
examine carefully in prayer if they have been driven by some of these
unconscious lies. Then they, and we, can pray with God's authority to be
freed. These lies can be picked up by children through repeated attitudes
and words, particularly in the home and school. Sadly, many brought up
in Catholic homes and schools have been given a distorted 'image' of what
God is like. We have had to pray to free many from God being a stern
policeman figure who is constantly watching for every misdemeanour,
recording it in his book, waiting to confront us with the list when we die.
Common distortions about God include: 'God is only conditionally loving
so I'd better meet His conditions or else He won't love me'; 'I have to be
perfect or else God will write me off'; and 'God never seems to hear me
or answer me when I pray and therefore He must be disinterested, cold
and distant'.

Have some of us, becoming aware of the power of God to heal, slipped
unwittingly into a false image of God? Could we, by our actions and
words, be unconsciously treating Him as a kind of genie who can be
summoned up to do our will if we pray? Have we lost our reverential

awareness of the awesomeness of God? I have certainly been asked to pray with a number of people who went to other churches for help, and became more damaged by what followed. When they did not seem to be healed in the way and in the time expected, they began to experience rejection in various ways. In some cases they were blamed for not having enough faith, so now they became burdened by guilt as well. Others found that those offering the prayer ministry not only stopped, but then deliberately avoided them. Some were made to feel that they must leave the church because they were harming its image by not being healed, and in some cases they lost their faith in God and in any church. Have we in some ways forgotten, and acted against, the primacy of love and the sovereignty of God?

It is very important that people are set free of any false images of God, and of any fear of Him, which are likely to have their roots in what they were told as small children and in their childhood perception and experiences of their own father. Until they receive this healing from Christ it is very difficult, perhaps impossible, for them to trust God enough for them to surrender their whole being and life more deeply, and to obey the call of Jesus. 'If anyone wants to be a follower of mine, let him renounce himself and take up his cross and follow me' (Mt 16:24). It is this ongoing surrender and self-offering to God which is the next topic to be looked at.

Daily Self-Offering—Dying to Self

Jesus commanded us to die to ourselves that we might live more fully for Him. In the words of Eucharistic Prayer IV, 'And that we might no longer live for ourselves, but for Him, He sent the Holy Spirit from you, Father, as His first gift to those who believe, to complete His work on earth, and bring us to the fullness of grace'.

For a number of years we had been saying to some of the people coming for prayer ministry, 'Your will is like the horizontal beam of the Cross, while God's will is like the vertical. You will remain at cross-purposes with God and stuck in your old reactions and ways, until you decide to surrender and align your will fully with God's will'. After years of saying this, it came as a surprise to us to read the following quotation from the writings[11] of Luisa Piccarreta, an Italian mystic who died in 1947, and whose cause for beatification has been opened. This came to her in prayer on November 18th, 1913:

I was thinking of my poor state and how even the cross is banished from me. And Jesus in my interior said to me, 'My daughter, when two wills are opposed to each another, so it is with Me and the creatures when their will is opposed to Mine, I form their cross and they form Mine— Thus I am the long shaft that runs vertically along the cross; and they are the short shaft, both of which, when crossing each other form the cross. Now when the soul's will unites itself with mine, the shafts no longer remain crossed, but united to each other. Hence the cross is no longer a cross. Do you understand? What is more I sanctified the Cross, the Cross did not sanctify me. Therefore it is not the Cross that sanctifies, rather it is the union to My will that sanctifies the Cross. Accordingly even the Cross can bring about good only insofar as it keeps itself connected with My will'.

Many of those who come ask such questions as 'Why has this happened?' 'Why did God allow that?' Again for many years we had said, 'All the time you keep asking 'Why?' you will get no answer but will just torture yourself. If you change your question to, 'What are You saying to me, Lord, in this difficult or painful situation?' or 'What are You asking me to do now that this has happened?, then you will get an answer'. Again, it was a surprise to read the following passage given to Luisa in prayer on 30 January 1909:

Daughter, in almost all the events that happen, creatures repeat and always say Why? And Why? Why this sickness? Why this state of soul? Why this punishment? and so many other whys. The explanation of the why is not written on earth but in Heaven, and all there shall read it. Do you know what the why is? It is egoism which gives continual food to self-love. Do you know where the why was created? In Hell. Who was the first to pronounce it? The Devil. The effects that the first why produced, were the loss of innocence in Eden itself, the war of the implacable passions, the ruin of so many souls, the evils of life. The history of the why is long. It is sufficient to tell you that there is no evil in the world which does not bear the mark of the why. The why is the destruction of Divine Wisdom in souls. And do you know where the why will be buried? In hell, to make them restless forever, without giving them peace. The art of the why is to wage war against souls without giving them rest.

It is said that to get to know God better we need to get to know ourselves. We can hardly make a truly meaningful offering of ourselves to God if we do not know what is in us. It would be rather like giving a gift to someone and saying, ' I hope you will like this present but I don't know what it is'. God reveals more and more about our weaknesses, strongholds, sinful obstacles, as time goes on.

There is a deep need in all of us to try to remain in control, stemming from our instinctive building of defensive walls out of fear. The degree of this need will be greater in some through being reinforced by life experience, such as those who are teachers, because no teaching is possible without control of a class of children. It takes time and ongoing persistent prayer as we grow in trusting God, to let go gradually of our need to be in control and to surrender ourselves more completely to Him. A prayer such as 'I offer myself as a living sacrifice to God, dedicated to His service and pleasing to Him' (Rm 12:1), prayed for example as we approach receiving the Lord in Holy Communion, can play a part in this. A sacrifice is not in a position to argue or bargain any more than clay can do so. 'Who can resist God's will? But who are you, my friend, to answer God back? A clay pot does not ask the man who made it, "Why did you make me like this?" After all, the man who makes the pots has the right to use the clay as he wishes, and to make two pots from the same lump of clay, one for special occasions and the other for ordinary use' (Rm 9:19–21).

We need to be committed to making continuing daily steps of self-offering and receiving more grace, rather like the steps of a dance we are enjoying with God. In Zephaniah we are told that if we are deeply committed to doing God's will then 'He will exult with joy over you; He will renew you by His love; He will dance with shouts of joy for you'. Our steps in this dance of love with God are greatly strengthened by:

- time spent in prayer each day;
- the Sacraments of the Eucharist (daily if possible) and Reconciliation;
- meditation on the Scriptures;
- daily praying the stronghold prayers, cutting away all bonds and putting on the whole armour of God (Ep 6); and
- checking, a number of times each day, that we are 'living in the house of the creative word'.

The prayerful support and sharing of a trustworthy group can be a big help as well.

A few years ago, our former parish priest, as well as starting the inner healing prayer group, had prayerful indications which were confirmed by three people within two days, and started another group which meets every two weeks. It is one of a number of groups meeting internationally to pray the rosary and share as they listen to a monthly message given to 'Ann', a lay apostle, in Direction for Our Times. An example of one of these was given at the end of Chapter 6. No matter what decision the Church may eventually make about these messages, the people in the group feel greatly blessed by praying and sharing together. The members of this group and those in the inner healing prayer group do find that the loving prayerful support of the others and the sharing of experiences are helping them greatly on their journey. 'Following in Christ's steps, those who believe in Him have always tried to help one another along the path which leads to the heavenly Father, through prayer, the exchange of spiritual goods and penitential expiation'[12].

Whatever the nature of the path on which God leads us, involving us with other Christians in various ways, which may include regular group meetings, one vital factor will always be present, and that is our deepening and prayerful engagement with the Scriptures. It is to this that we turn next.

The Power of the Word of God

As Hebrews 4:12–13 tells us, 'The word of God is alive and active, sharper than any double-edged sword. It cuts all the way through to where soul and spirit meet, to where joints and marrow come together. It judges the desires and thoughts of man's heart. There is nothing that can be hidden from God.'

For years, we have recommended people to pray passages of Scripture every day, because they have the power to bring about deep changes within us. Fr Cantalamesa writes[13] of two examples of healings taking place, through repeatedly reading some Scripture. The following passages have been adapted to a personal prayer by the substitution of personal pronouns, and we have the passages printed out ready to give those who come to our home for ministry:

I offer myself as a living sacrifice to God, dedicated to His service and pleasing to Him. This is the true worship that I should offer. Help me not to conform to the standards of this world, but let God transform me inwardly by a complete change of my mind. Then I will be able to know the will of God, what is good and pleasing to Him and is perfect. (An adaptation of Rm 12:1–2)

I ask the God of our Lord Jesus Christ, the glorious Father, to give me the Spirit, who will make me wise and reveal God to me, so that I will know Him. I ask that my mind may be opened to see His light, so that I will know what is the hope to which He has called me, how rich are the wonderful blessings He promises His people, and how very great is His power in us who believe. This power working in us is the same as the mighty strength which He used when he raised Christ from death and seated Him at His right side in the heavenly world. (An adaptation of Ep 1:17–20)

I ask God to fill me with knowledge of His will, with all the wisdom and understanding that His Spirit gives. Then I will be able to live as the Lord wants and will always do what pleases Him. My life will produce all kinds of good deeds, and I will grow in my knowledge of God. (An adaptation of Col 1:9–10)

I want to get rid of my old self, which made me live as I used to, the old self which was being destroyed by deceitful desires. I want my heart and mind to be made completely new. I want to put on the new self, which is created in God's likeness, and reveals itself in the true life that is upright and holy. (An adaptation of Ep 4:22–24)

I ask God from the wealth of His glory to give me power through His Spirit to be strong in my inner self, and I pray that Christ will make His home in my heart through faith. I pray that I may have my roots and foundation in love, so that, together with all God's people, I may have the power to understand how broad and long, how high and deep, is Christ's love. Yes, may I come to know His love, although it can never be fully known, and so be completely filled with the very nature of God. To Him who, by means of His power working in me, is able to do so much more than I can ever ask for, or even think of; to God be glory in the church and in Jesus Christ for all time, for ever and ever. Amen. (An adaptation of Ep 3:16–21)

With everyone who comes, we stress the importance of 'living in the house of the creative word', which was explained in the section Receiving God's Grace to Love and Accept Ourselves in Chapter 6. We have frequently suggested putting a piece of paper somewhere it will catch their eye a number of times each day e.g. on the fridge door. On it, they could draw two little houses: one blocked in to represent the 'destructive house',

149

the other left white for the 'creative house'. Thus they can check, many times, whether or not they have been speaking and thinking in the same positive and up-building way that God speaks through the Scriptures. We suggest that if they keep finding that they have slipped back into negativity, they have a 'light' attitude, perhaps having a laugh that they need so much help from the Lord. This way we focus on Christ and His power to change us, rather than the negative way in which I used to react when looking at myself. My reactions for years, when realising that I had again got it wrong, were to be even more negative with thoughts or even words such as 'I never get it right'; 'I'm hopeless, I've just done it again'. Thus I spiralled down into deeper negativity and feeling guilty. It took many years of Betty's love, encouragement and prayers for me to speak words of truth from the Scriptures to my inner being, so that the child within was gradually set free of poor self-worth and negativity. I long to see others set free far more quickly. Another way of representing this is:

Creative House	**Destructive House**
Open to grace	Blocked from grace
Speaking and thinking the truth as revealed in the Word of God	Speaking and thinking negatively contradicting God in rebellion
leading to	*leading to*
Trust	Doubts
Peace	Fears
Hope	Hopelessness
Praising God	Thinking God has let us down or rejected us
I'm a beloved child of God	I'm no good

There are many references in both Old and New Testament to the great power and dangers of the tongue: e.g. 'I said, 'I will be careful what I do and will not let my tongue make me sin" (Ps 39:1); 'Finally Job broke the silence and cursed the day on which he had been born' (Jb 3:1). There is a very eloquent description of the power of the tongue in James Chapter 3. Even our negative thoughts have power, as evidenced by: 'You speak words of blessing, but in your heart you curse him', (Ps 62:4). This has been examined in some detail by Derek Prince.[14] We have the choice either to curse or to bless.

We have prayed, with the authority of Jesus, to free large numbers of people from curses which they have uttered in words or harboured in thoughts, as well as from curses spoken against them or against members of their family, perhaps in some previous generation. If the person has himself or herself been responsible, then we invite them to ask God for forgiveness for speaking or thinking negatively, and then pray: 'In the name of Jesus Christ and with the sword of the Holy Spirit, we cut you completely free from any binding from your own words or thoughts'. An example of our doing this with one of our sons was cited earlier in this chapter.

When praying with people for healing of deep early roots, they may well get in touch with having said or thought as a child, 'I hate such and such a person' or 'I wish he/she/I had never been born'. Both of these become understandable, when, through prayer and listening, one gets in touch with the perceptions of a very small child. It is not uncommon to uncover the latter reaction stemming from a baby or very small child experiencing reduced attention from parents following the birth of a sibling. It is a vital part of their healing that these are uncovered and acknowledged and brought to Jesus to let go of into His suffering. That involves the adult asking for forgiveness from God on behalf of the child within. We can then pray for Jesus to give the child the grace to forgive these people, often close members of the family, and then ask Him to help the child to desire to receive His perfect love for each one. All of this getting in touch with painful feelings can be done in silent prayer. If the person does speak out that they hated someone or wished someone had never been born, then they should be saying it quietly and privately to the minister(s), perhaps in sadness that it happened, but in gladness that they were being set free. They would certainly not be encouraged to shout it out to others, which would amount to expressing a curse. Ephesians 4:29 reminds us of this:

'Do not use harmful words, but only helpful words, the kind that build up and provide what is needed, so that what you say will do good to those who hear you.'

All of this is particularly vital when it is one or both of our parents who caused hurt to us as a child. This issue was discussed in Chapter 5. When someone, during ministry, does express negative emotions and perceptions, or gets in touch with them in the perception of the child within, then we can quickly cut everyone free of any binding of the spoken words or negative thoughts with the authority of Jesus Christ.

Appendix 2 lists a number of feelings and habits of behaviour which can poison a person's life in many ways, in how they feel and act, and how they respond and relate to others. With each of them is given at least one scripture passage which can be used prayerfully, preferably daily, to combat the troublesome conditions, and act as an antidote as part of the person cooperating with God to become free.

One of the many lessons which we learn from the Scriptures is to desire to keep our focus on God, not on how we feel or what we are enduring. If we keep praising God even in the most difficult of circumstances, then we are in the right place and attitude to receive grace from Him to work through our situation. One of the many wise and helpful things which Frances Hogan has taught is that every person, at every moment of their life, has two directions in which to look. Either we look at ourselves and our problems, in which case we magnify the problems, particularly if we do not talk to anyone else and our thoughts just go round and round so that we become more confused and anxious. The other direction is to look at Christ and, following the example of His Blessed Mother in the Magnificat, we magnify Him. We look further at this now.

Power in Praise of God

It is vitally important to help and encourage people to praise God, whether they are feeling like it or not. Betty often praised God with tears running down her face with suffering. God is entitled to our praise for who He is, quite apart from praise because of all His infinite love, goodness, mercy and gifts to us. When we are praising God, we are focusing on Him instead of being turned in upon ourselves and our struggles, and we are opened up afresh to His love and power.

In the 1970s, Merlin Carothers wrote a series of books beginning with 'From Prison to Praise' and 'Power in Praise'. Large numbers of people read them and some wrote letters, some of them published in 'Answers to Praise', full of thankfulness and telling how God had been working since they praised and thanked God constantly. However, for some the situation had not improved, or had become even worse. Those were people who had not been ready or able to receive God's grace to forgive themselves or others, or to know that they had been forgiven by God.

It is very important that we should thank God constantly for all His gifts and blessings to us, but it is not enough to express gratitude after we discover how He has brought us through difficulties and crises. The Scriptures constantly emphasise the vital role of faith, and we are not expressing faith if we merely look back at what God has done. 'To have faith is to be sure of the things we hope for, to be certain of the things we cannot see' (Heb 11:1). The more we have a positive attitude in the midst of suffering and difficulties, expressing joy and faith as well as thankfulness, the more we can be used by God to attract others to faith in Him and to be a help to them, as the Lord intends us to be to one another.

Freeing Ourselves Through Christ may Help Free Others

Just as the Lord 'comforts us in all our troubles' (2 Cor 1:4), we in turn may become a source of comfort to others, as in the case of Testimony 7E (p. 169). This is true of many of those who have come for prayer ministry to our home, some of whom are now being used powerfully by the Lord to reach out to others. We should expect this to be happening because of the Scriptures and the teaching of the Church.

> This witness of life, however, is not the sole element in the apostolate; the true apostle is on the lookout for occasions of announcing Christ by word, either to unbelievers to draw them towards the faith, or to the faithful to instruct them, strengthen them, and incite them to a more fervent life.[15]

Pope Paul VI was explicit: 'The Church exists in order to evangelise: all Christians are called to this witness and in this way they can be real evangelisers: finally the person who has been evangelised goes on to evangelise others' leading to 'a total interior renewal which the Gospel calls metanoia; it is a radical conversion, a profound change of mind and heart'.[16]

Of course this whole process depends entirely on the power of the Holy Spirit and the extent to which an individual is open and willing to surrender to the will of God. There are some who seek prayer ministry where to a varying degree there is an underlying atitude of asking God to solve or at least alleviate some problem or discomfort, so that they can return to their old way of life, only pleasing themselves and perhaps forgetting God until the next crisis occurs. In my experience, people at this stage of their journey may give up after one or two sessions. Many of us, too, may have waited a long time before we were ready to be thoroughly disturbed and challenged by God, and so we should not be judgemental of others. Instead we should ask God for the discernment to find a balanced blend of gentle encouragement and firmness, and go on praying for them after they stop coming for ministry. We can only do the best we can, and leave any further outcome to God and others. As St Paul said, 'Each one of us does the work the Lord gave him to do: I planted the seed, Apollos watered the plant, but it was God who made the plant grow (1 Co 3:5b–6). God is patient and will offer each one further opportunities to stop asking for 'a patch on an old coat', as Jesus put it in Mark 2:21, and allow Him to bring their old being to death on the Cross with Christ so that they can begin to become the new creation of their real self through ongoing surrender and metanoia.

Often during the process of praying for deeper inner healing, which is a vital part of this metanoia, as we invite Jesus to transform the painful memories from the past, people become aware of, and are troubled by regrets about choices which they made, and the damaged ways in which they have been reacting. We always try to help them to desire that Jesus frees them from all regrets, blame, guilt, or wishing that things had been different, or that they had received healing earlier in life. We encourage them to let go into His suffering on the Cross of every burden of that kind as God forgives them and completely forgets any guilt and sins, as the Scriptures tell us in so many places. They can then begin to live in the creative house in each new present moment, set free from the burdens of the past and also any for the future, such as fear and anxiety. They can come to realise that Christ is somehow redeeming all the painful past, and through their suffering being brought to die with Him, He is preparing them to help others in ways and with a compassion and love which would not have been possible if they had not endured and accepted all that had happened. Nothing is lost or wasted if we invite Jesus into everything within us and in our life and accept the truth. *'Bless the Lord, O my soul, and all that is within me bless His holy name'.*

One very significant way in which we have found that God can use people to help others is through their being in the same place of employment. A very appreciable number of those who have come to us have spoken of their concerns about others in the same place of work. In these cases, after we had, perhaps during an appreciable number of sessions, prayed for the Lord to heal all root causes of unease, we would reflect with this person about how they might respond to situations at work. Two examples of this are given in testimonies 7F (p. 170) and 7G (p. 171), both written by fellow parishioners.

As well as the reference to holy water in Testimony 7G (p. 171), there had been previous occasions when its use was a blessing. In 1980 a priest came from another town to have a meal with us. He wanted to ask questions about charismatic renewal because he had concerns and reservations. He must have been convinced because he rapidly became involved locally and nationally. He spoke of serious anxieties about the behaviour of children in the primary school in his parish and the ways in which this was being handled. We suggested he might sprinkle holy water through the school and pray for God to bless everyone involved and to send angels. Within a short time he told us how wonderfully the situation had improved.

There have been a number of people who spoke about work colleagues because their behaviour had been having a disturbing or damaging influence on them and on others. Two ladies from the same parish came separately to us many years ago. Apart from their own individual backgrounds and experiences for which they needed prayer, they both spoke of their concern that three other members of staff in the care home in which they worked were attending spiritualist meetings and talking about this while at work. At our suggestion, they talked to their parish priest who then spoke to the proprietors of the home, who also attended his church. As a result, our two friends were reprimanded and for a while thought that they might lose their jobs, and the other three continued their involvement in spiritualism. The two women went on praying for the protection of all those in the home, and with the authority of Christ bound into His hands any powers of evil involved, and discreetly sprinkled holy water. After a while, one of the three ladies became frightened at what happened in one spiritualist meeting and stopped going. A second re-married and she no longer went to the meetings. The third ceased to work in the home after her marriage broke, lost her home and drifted from job to job. We reminded our friends to go on praying for them out of God's love.

Whatever is happening in the life of every Christian it is vital that we look beyond the physical world in which we live and recognise that there is a cosmic battle but that Jesus has won the victory in His death and

Resurrection. 'In all things we have complete victory through Him who loved us. For I am certain that nothing can separate us from His love; neither death nor life; neither angels nor other heavenly rulers of powers; neither the present nor the future; neither the world above nor the world below - there is nothing in all creation that will ever be able to separate us from the love of God which is ours through Christ Jesus our Lord' (Rm 8:37–39). The knowledge of the reality of spiritual warfare need not cause us any fear, but we should use all the protection which God provides for us.

Spiritual Warfare

No matter what course our life is taking, we are in spiritual warfare. We may become more aware of the reality of this in our personal and family lives, as we do our best to grow towards deeper union with Christ. For years we have strongly advocated that those coming for ministry should, first thing every day, put on the six pieces of armour described by St Paul in Ephesians 6. When we put on the belt of truth we are praying for Jesus, who is The Truth, to completely enclose us, so that we really live in Him, who is already in us through the indwelling of the Holy Spirit. It reminds one of St Patrick's breastplate prayer. Each piece of armour is needed.

It is vital that we realise that putting on the armour is quite unlike putting on a protective garment against rain or wind. It is not a passing act which, once done, we can assume it goes on protecting us without any further action on our part. It involves actively living out our relationship with, and total dependence upon, God from moment to moment.

In having the truth as a belt around us we are entering more and more deeply into our union with Christ, upon which everything true and right in our lives depends, as is brought out in a number of verses in Ephesians 1 and 2. Only God is righteous and, if we are truly putting on the breastplate of righteousness, we must constantly desire the help of the Holy Spirit to bring us closer to doing the will of God at all times. Verse 16 in Ephesians 6 shows us that we have to be active in using the shield of faith to protect ourselves and loved ones from the burning arrows shot by the Evil One. We are not just meant to read the word of God, the Scriptures, but to use them actively as the sword of the Spirit to free and defend ourselves and others. Putting on the helmet of salvation helps us to live out the free gift of God's total love and mercy for us, and to pray that our minds be renewed more and more completely. The shoes of the readiness to announce the Good news of peace reminds us that we need to be more and more completely evangelised so that the Lord can use us any way He chooses to evangelise others, with love not pressure. Verse 18 of Chapter 6 does emphasise our need to be active all the time in this process:

> Do all this in prayer asking for God's help. Pray in every occasion as the Spirit leads. For this reason keep alert and never give up; pray always for all God's people.

All this activity involves deep peace and trust, without any anxiety or fear or stress.

When people return for further ministry, I ask if they are remembering to put on the armour each day (for themselves and for the protection of their family, especially if they are a parent or grandparent). If they say they only remember it on some days, I ask how many times in the last year they have left the house barefoot. When they say it was none at all, I ask whether they are really concerned to protect the sole of their foot, rather than their immortal soul.

Some years ago we had gone to Sheffield to attend the Golden Jubilee Ordination Mass of a priest who has been a close friend for many years. There we met a lady who is a primary school teacher. She told us how she teaches the children to put on the armour every day. One day she asked a little boy if he had put the armour on that morning. He replied, 'I slept in it all night, Miss'.

Sadly, this awareness of the reality of spiritual warfare does not seem to be widespread in the Church. For over two years before we left Leeds, we met weekly in our home at the suggestion of our curate, with him, a nun and another lady, to intercede for our parish. One aspect which came strongly to us was to pray for people to be cut free from the roots of apathy and passivity.

It is as though many of those Catholics who still attend Mass unconsciously have on their chest a notice bearing the words 'Do Not Disturb'. If they meet difficult problems they may pray for God to solve them so that they can return to the busy routines, pressures and pleasures to which they are accustomed. If they are uncomfortably confronted with questions, the answers to which they cannot remember from their childhood, then they may ask a priest to give them the answer. They believe that if they attend Mass once a week then they are doing all that is required of them, and they have no idea of the abundance of God's love, power and blessings which He is longing to pour out on them and their family.

Pope Benedict XVI, reflecting upon Gethsemane, wrote:

> The Lord says to his disciples: 'My soul is very sorrowful, even to death; remain here and keep watch' (Mk 14:33–4). The summons to vigilance has already been a major theme of Jesus' Jerusalem teaching, and now it emerges directly with great urgency. And yet, while it refers specifically to Gethsemane, it also points ahead to the later history of Christianity. Across the centuries, it is the drowsiness of the disciples that opens up possibilities for the power of the Evil One. Such drowsiness deadens the soul, so that it remains undisturbed by the power of the Evil One at work in the world and by all the injustice and suffering ravaging the earth. In its state of numbness, the soul prefers not to see all this; it is easily persuaded that things cannot be so bad, so as to continue in the self-satisfaction of its own comfortable existence. Yet this deadening of souls, this lack of vigilance regarding both God's closeness and the looming forces of darkness, is what gives the Evil One his power in the world. On beholding the drowsy disciples, so disinclined to rouse themselves, the Lord says: 'My soul is sorrowful, even to death'.[17]

Questions need to be raised and answered, however, about any ways and extent to which the Church has been and still is contributing towards this drowsiness, through what might be termed 'sedation' of the laity. This can arise in many ways: for example, by (i) a lack of emphasis on and guidance in praying towards a deepening loving relationship with and growing focus and dependence upon Christ, coupled with negative messages received in childhood from Church and home; (ii) a lack of proclaiming and witnessing to the power of the love of God working today in myriad ways in the lives of people in our local church as well as elsewhere, so that most people have insufficient expectant faith; (iii) a lack of ministry of the healing power of Christ, so that many are burdened by covering up or burying unhealed and unshared hurts and stresses; (iv) a lack of teaching in many areas including the reality of spiritual warfare, and a lack of warnings about specific dangers such as many forms of occult and new-age practices which Catholics sometimes pursue alongside their church attendance - 'My people are destroyed for lack of knowledge' (Ho 4:6); (v) a lack of proclaiming the power coming from Christ's death and resurrection, by which those baptised and called by God can be guided to pray correctly and responsibly for minor exorcism (deliverance), and can learn to pray for other aspects of a growing and healthy spirituality.

This 'sedation' is also likely to owe much to the attitude of most of the Church and its leadership towards the role and any effective involvement of the laity, despite all that is written in Vatican II documents. Through such things as fear and the need to retain control within the priesthood, the laity are not helped 'to become mature people reaching to the very height of Christ's full stature' (Ep 4:13).

It is sadly true that many people attend Mass weekly, but have little or no contact throughout the week with other Christians. Perhaps a few superficial remarks are exchanged on Sunday, but there is no community group in which they can learn to know and trust others, so that they can begin to reflect and share and pray with others at real depth. Any teaching which they receive is generally limited to the variable length and quality of a weekly homily. There are few if any opportunities in most parishes for teaching on any aspect to be developed and reflected upon over weeks or months.

In all of these areas the training and attitude and morale of priests play a vital role, and in the next chapter the duty of lay people to pray out of love for their priests is emphasised. It should not be seen as a grudging, critical, half-hearted duty, but as a joyful and grateful response to the gift of God of priesthood and the men who respond to it, and a desire to ease the burdens placed on them and to grow together as one people of God.

Significant Points

- Praying for inner healing is not a 'quick fix', but a lifetime process in which we need to cooperate with the Holy Spirit, as He works within us towards our being more and more sanctified.

- Every one of us is likely to have many strongholds within us, but we can pray with the authority of Jesus to destroy them in ourselves and in our loved ones.

- Whenever we come to the end of any stage of prayer ministry we should pray for the Lord to cleanse us to free us from all binding and powers of evil, to come afresh to us with the Holy Spirit in every area of our being and to protect us and our family.

- We need to pray the stronghold prayers, and pray to cut emotional bonds and soul ties for ourselves and others every day.

- We have unconsciously taken on a number of wrong ideas and attitudes which operate in our subconscious or unconscious mind, to place us under inner drives and compulsions, which prevent us from being free to serve others in the love of God.

- The state of our soul today is determined by the extent to which we refuse to let go of our damaged reactions to past hurts, not by the hurts themselves, so we can't hide behind being a helpless victim.

- We need to keep checking a number of times each day whether we are 'living in the house of the creative word' or 'the house of the destructive word'.

- It is absolutely vital to put on the armour of God every day for ourselves and our family.

- For a list of some important daily prayers, please refer to Appendix 5.

Scripture for Meditation

The Spirit produces love, joy, patience, kindness, goodness, faithfulness, humility and self-control. There is no law against such things as these. And those who belong to Christ Jesus have put to death their human nature, with all its passions and desires. The Spirit has given us life; He must also control our lives. We must not be proud, or irritate one another, or be jealous of one another. (Ga 5:22–26)

The weapons we use in our fight are not the world's weapons, but God's powerful weapons which we use to destroy strongholds. (2 Co 10:4)

Truly, I say to you, whatever you bind on earth shall be bound in heaven, and whatever you loose on earth shall be loosed in heaven. (Mt 18:18)

When He had said this, He cried with a loud voice, 'Lazarus, come out'. The dead man came out, his hands and feet bound with bandages, and his face wrapped with a cloth. Jesus said to them, 'Unbind him, and let him go'. (Jn 11:43–44)

The Word of God is alive and active, sharper than any double-edged sword. It cuts all the way through to where soul and spirit meet, to where joints and marrow come together. It judges the desires and thoughts of man's heart. There is nothing that can be hidden from God. (Heb 4:12–13)

Testimonies

Testimony 7A

I became a Christian twelve years ago in an independent church through an Alpha course, at the age of twenty. My baptism in October 2000 was also the day I met my husband, as he was getting baptised at the same time. We have been married for ten years and are blessed with two beautiful children aged five and two.

I did have some experience of faith when I was younger and attended a Roman Catholic Church quite often, but I struggled with really knowing and believing the story of Jesus. I knew about God but I didn't really know Him.

I struggled as a young person and became very depressed. I remember being prescribed anti-depressants and beta blockers as young as fifteen to try and help my depression, whilst also having to visit a psychologist at hospital over one-two years for counselling. This was my first severe episode of depression. A few years later I faced a second dark episode after my mother was attacked and raped in the street.

When I first started the Alpha course, at which I felt I really became a Christian, I was still taking anti-depressants, but after a year or so of knowing God's love, acceptance and encouragement I gradually weaned myself off them.

Coming to faith in Christ totally changed my life. I was a student at the time, living it up at university, and I didn't expect to encounter Jesus at all, but after I saw my mum become a Christian on an Alpha and some of the peace it brought to her broken life I became intrigued by the Jesus she talked about. After making my initial commitment to follow Jesus whom I now believed in, and knew believed in me, some supportive Christian friends at university helped me to strengthen my faith.

God began a healing work in those earlier years which He has now intensified. He has shown me the great depths of His Father heart and how I have a valuable place in His love. Throughout my childhood I struggled with a sense of loss and rejection that I buried so deep even my closest friends didn't realise. I was raised in a single parent home after my parents separated when I was born, due to an affair my dad had. My mother later married when I was seven years old, but that relationship ended in divorce a few years later. I have few childhood memories of my dad, but one particularly painful one was of me as a young girl aged about six sitting by a window in my home, staring out, wondering if this was going to be the weekend my dad would come for me. Occasionally he would come after my parents first ended their relationship, but he suddenly stopped all contact when I was about three years old. I hadn't seen him at all in three years but still kept a small hope that he would come back for me. That hope drained and became a wound that would harden my heart. The rejection in that memory haunted me so badly that I buried it so deep that the first time I spoke of it has only been in the last couple of years. Through prayer ministry and the support of my husband, God began healing these pains with many others I had, but it wasn't till I started the counselling prayers of inner healing with Alan that I now really understand what it is to be free. Free from the power of those memories, and the numbness and hardened independent heart it had helped produce in my life. I have experienced intense healing: it has been a real Godsend! I began the inner healing at a really difficult time; it has eased so much pain and burden for me. I literally feel like Jesus has been there in my living past and healed me at the point of trauma, leaving me free from the effects today.

After understanding the power and importance of inner healing I pray it for my children and family and have seen the fruit with my own eyes. Allowing Jesus to reach inside and touch areas that may never have been talked about has been a journey of discovering peace and wholeness for me. I was taught that once you were a Christian, you were a new person and then shouldn't have any hang-ups with the past, but whilst some pains were healed at my conversion many still remained, so I found myself denying or burying them. It's only now that I know the freedom and the means of having them really healed.

One of my favourite verses in the Bible is Romans 12:2, which talks about 'being transformed by the renewing of your mind'. I really feel my mind is being renewed. As past hurts are healed, the defence mechanisms those pains caused are falling away, and I am seeing and understanding others and the world around me in a freer and renewed way.

Testimony 7B

Her husband's story:

I first became a Christian in 1996, after I had broken up from a relationship, which left me depressed and with no direction in life. I found a leaflet on the floor that offered a free booklet explaining the meaning of life, and I filled it in and posted it off. Some weeks later a man showed up at my door, and I invited him in. It became a regular meeting once a week where he explained the gospel to me, about how Jesus had died on a cross for my sins, and how God had raised Him from the dead to offer me forgiveness and eternal life through a relationship with Jesus Christ. I asked Jesus to forgive me for living my life my own way. Before then I was drinking a lot on a regular basis and taking recreational drugs to numb the pain and rejection I had experienced from childhood. I was bullied in secondary school as well as witnessing violence in the home between my mother and father while I was growing up, which left me with deep emotional scars. This new start in life with Jesus filled me for the first ten years with much joy and set me free from bad habits and destructive behaviours which I was powerless to break before I became a Christian. In the next few years I met my wife at church, and we married and moved to Manchester in September 2001, where I took a degree in theology to train for Christian ministry. After four years we moved back home to Teesside and started a family, in which God blessed us with two beautiful children, a boy and a girl.

From 2001 until 2011 my wife and I were both very active in church leadership within a Pentecostal/charismatic tradition, which involved preaching in the UK and abroad, leading discipleship groups, Alpha courses and Gospel meetings, as well as my working full-time as a mentor in a large secondary school. The pressure of all this activity led to strain on my relationship with my wife, increased stress at work, and conflicting issues within church leadership. I had a nervous breakdown, which resulted in many negative buried emotions coming to the surface that I had never really dealt with. These had unconsciously led me to make choices that I was not really happy with, and which backfired on me and increased my feelings of self-rejection. I was desperate for help. All the knowledge I had of spiritual warfare and living free in the spiritual life that I had taught others was of no help to me.

A friend then recommended a ministry of inner healing led by a man called Alan, who had more than thirty years' experience of helping people to experience a deeper freedom of God's love and healing to mind, body and spirit. My experience of inner healing was the real stepping stone in helping me become more fully healed from the emotional burdens of the past. It revealed that I had buried strongholds of rejection, aggression, jealousy, judgementalism, fears of being controlled, bitterness and self-hatred, to name but a few. The inner healing also contributed to the restoration of my marriage, which subsequently resulted in my wife seeking inner healing, and, later, her mother. One of the best things that has happened through the process of inner healing is a new self-awareness of myself and, more importantly, of God. It has totally transformed my thinking and my relationship with God, leading me to experience His love and healing more deeply and understand His will for my life more clearly.

Testimony 7C

I started seeing Alan and Betty for ministry several years ago and was a part of the St Joseph's group for a year. I was continually surprised that areas of my past life that I was confident had been dealt with or did not need healing, would crop up in my sharing. I realised that childhood experiences and early family relationships were in need of Christ's healing. Over months I received healing of memories and self-image and was freed from the spirit of fear as I learned more about its roots and about the strongholds I had built to protect myself from unresolved pain and loneliness. I had unknowingly built these strongholds to keep the pain out, but began to learn that strongholds keep the pain and trauma in and God locked out. As Alan and Betty prayed, I learned more about binding and loosing. I began to put this into practice in my daily prayer, binding myself to His love, His will for my life and loosing, stripping away anything not of God, my own sinful nature, my wrong thinking and attitudes, behaviours and habits.

I began to see that the Lord helps us to do this and promises: 'You will seek Me and you will find Me because you seek Me with your whole heart. Yes, I say, you will find Me and I will restore you to your land' (Jr 29:13).

I know that I am very much work in progress and I continually fall short. But I also know now that I am a beloved child of God and His love is always with me, forgiving a repentant heart over and over again. I can hear and see Betty smiling at me and asking, 'What are you?' and waiting for my reply, 'I am a beloved child of God!'

In 2008 my husband, John, suddenly became seriously ill and we were confronted with our worst fear, that of losing one another. Over the next eighteen months, as he underwent debilitating treatment and had to face his own mortality, I had to face the possibility of life without him. We spent time with Alan and Betty and other Christian friends as we faced the unthinkable.

It was a time of suffering, loss and heightened emotion as we battled with sudden loss of health and opportunity, work and relaxation, and all the real and simple pleasures of life we can all take for granted. Worse still, separation from each other, family and friends. I know that many people have experienced similar scenarios and it was a terrible time in many ways. Just as Jesus wept and grieved, we continually felt bewilderment, disbelief and shock. But it was also a time of great joy and blessing as we worked through things together with the support and prayers of so many people. In the midst of fear, anxiety and loss, the Lord blessed us and we learnt daily to use His strength rather than our own weakness. We began to put this knowledge into practice as we experienced how to live in the moment where God is, the God of our now.

We began to experience as never before, how the present moment is all we have (and indeed all we need). I Am Who I Am, says the Lord. This was incredibly challenging with the pressures that each day brought, but it gave great freedom to know that the past is over and the future yet to come—that we can totally rely on His love in the eternal present. During this time, John gradually came to know the Lord and, as he deteriorated physically, his inner transformation was wonderful to witness as he opened himself to the Lord and, despite the doubts and the low times, was gifted with an inner peace and joy expressed in a great love and compassion for others, and a need to be reconciled, to forgive and be forgiven.

I now continue this daily challenge of living in the moment now that he is safely home. One would not choose to experience illness and death in our lives, but it does present us with an opportunity to grow, to completely trust in the Lord for everything, to know that we are all, whether we know it or not, on the journey home. We are travelling moment to moment, grace to grace. We don't need to worry about the future as we walk into it with Him and we receive the grace we need as we need it and not before. Through the ministry of prayer for Christ's healing, I know that God sees the bigger picture, He truly knows what is ultimately best for us. Death is not a disaster but an experience of the fullness of life in Him. There will always be this tension between our will and desires and God's complete love and knowledge of us, knowing what is truly best for us. We hope that our desires are His, too, but as I know His will is healing and He is complete love I can relax and praise, floating in the sea of His love. It does not take away the pain and loss but it consoles and heals in deep and wonderful ways as we discover He is with us at our deepest point of need and we are eternally held.

Never before has The Communion of Saints meant so much—not only an article of faith recited in the Creed but a joyful reality in my life. I know that my husband (and Betty) are now living in God's absolute presence, in the very fullness of life. This is the great Communion of God, through the Spirit, at one with Christ, surrounded by angels and saints. As Christians, we are still in communion with those who have died and, as we are in God and He is in us, and our departed loved ones are in Him, we are all part of His love, destined to be forever united. It is wonderful to think that our loved ones intercede for us much more effectively now than when they were in this life. We can relate to them, speak to them through Christ and pray for them, as they surely pray for us. In fact, their prayers are so much more powerful as they now live with God in the fullness of truth. The bonds of love still exist and indeed are strengthened as they continue their care of us in the heavenly realm.

In the same way, God has given us each other to channel His love and healing, and I am so grateful for Christ's body here on earth, supporting me in so many different ways practically and spiritually. John continually marvelled at the body of Christ in action, so touched by people he had never met, and would never meet this side of Heaven, generously praying for him, sending uplifting messages and doing acts of kindness. In fact, it was one of the first things which made him realise his lack of faith as he was so overwhelmed with the goodness of people he did not know, and he wanted to know about what made them behave in this loving way.

Betty and Alan have taught me that we need to be real before God—He is big enough to take our anger, lack of faith, admitting our pain and uncertainty, our jealousy and resentment. None of us can move from human frailty and sin to trust and acceptance on our own—it is purely grace, God-given. As God gives me the grace to accept and embrace my loss, over and over, I find not emptiness but His fullness. Every loss, united to Him, brings gain. Somehow, as we experience pain and suffering, our thankfulness can increase. The grief is still at times difficult to bear and I feel his loss continuously. It can be raw and many will know the depth of ache and longing that such loss inevitably brings. But Betty and Alan have taught me not to live destructively but creatively, praising rather than continually petitioning and pleading. The Lord has lavished His love on His children and when we state the truth, that God is love, that truth has the power to transform me and all people, despite our weakness and uncertainty. If we choose God we choose life, there is no negative in Him. If we use faith to assert this truth in our lives, the gifts will follow. God acts first and we can then respond and accept His love.

I am grateful to Alan and Betty for showing me that I do not need to let go of all that I had with John, I do not need to 'move on', as the saying goes. Rather, my past is changed and healed and my life transformed through the wounds of Jesus and, as in some small way we share His suffering, we will experience resurrection.

'We know that in all things God works for good with those who love Him, those whom He has called according to His purpose' (Rm 8:28). Alleluia!

Testimony 7D

Throughout a stormy relationship, spiritual forces have been evident. But when unhampered by incomplete forgiveness, Jesus calmed the storm.

The start:

The Lord spoke, urging me into action. Initially I argued but eventually obeyed and He brought about a new friendship. I learned that at times the Lord can be irresistible.

Lord's intervention - and the Enemy:

The Lord spoke again and, as before, I briefly resisted and then obeyed. He used me to provide help in an emergency. But I was taken into a situation where my dormant fears became active. I sensed the Enemy unsettling me - *did He really heal you?*—but my faith told me that as the Lord had brought me into that situation, He would protect me.

Prayer ministry:

The Lord has given me gifts to bring comfort through prayer—I accepted and exercised these gifts. But I was careless and did not always pray a cleansing prayer after ministry, exposing the person I had prayed with, myself and ultimately my family, to attacks of the Enemy.

The Lord's provision—and the Enemy:

The Lord provided a solution to a pressing family dilemma—through someone I had been ministering to, but the Enemy stepped into the area of vulnerability I had unwittingly opened by not praying a cleansing prayer.

Inner vow—and the Enemy:

Feeling defensive, I made an inner vow, thus inviting an attack from the Enemy - and weakening my ability to recognise this.

Forgiveness - and the Enemy:

The Lord prompted me to forgive a serious, unprovoked attack against myself and my family. I obeyed in part but did not resist the Enemy's temptation to hold onto evidence of the wrong-doing.

Cutting soul ties:

Despite forgiving, I still felt severe anxiety, and no peace. I still felt bound to the other person and needed to be freed.

'Truly I tell you, whatever you bind on earth will be bound in heaven, and whatever you loose on earth will be loosed in heaven'. (Mt 18:18)

Although I knew I had the authority to cut these soul ties, I felt too entangled and sought help from another to pray this. Although the person I had felt bound to was not aware of the prayer, it led to an immediate reconciliation, seemingly sealed by taking communion together. But there was still a sense of 'incompleteness'.

Illness - Lord or Enemy?

I suddenly became ill in the night. Was it an attack of the Enemy or brought about by the Lord? Either way, as I considered I might be dying, my sole concern was that the 'evidence' of wrong-doing that I had kept hidden in my drawer, should not be found by my family. This sudden illness reaped wonderful fruit because I decided to destroy the evidence.

'Don't you see, you planned evil against me but God used those same plans for my good'. (Gn 50:20)

'And we know that in all things God works for the good of those who love him'. (Rm 8:28)

Total forgiveness and reconciliation:

As I forgave more fully and shredded the 'evidence', it somehow created a 'sacred space' where the Lord moved powerfully to bring about true reconciliation. He showed the person who had wronged me exactly how I had experienced the offence. This, in turn, brought about deeper, authentic repentance in her and she sought confirmation of my forgiveness. I learned that despite the prayer to break the soul ties, and even the shared communion, the retained 'evidence' had caused some bonds to persist but when I humbled myself to destroy this evidence, the final negative bonds were broken—I had finally denied the Enemy access to disrupt the healing process.

Reparation:

The Lord continued to work in this 'sacred space' and uncovered lies and theft. Money had been demanded of me under false pretences. He insisted on reparation and the money was returned to me. In order for this to happen, I was placed in a location where I was physically vulnerable and the Enemy again caused dormant fears to become active. *Have you really been healed?* But I believed in the Lord's protection. Meanwhile...

The Lord hears every prayer, even the most casual murmur:

I casually prayed about our inability to help when another friend requested financial assistance, murmuring that as we had had unprecedented demands on our savings, we would need an unexpected windfall in order to help. Our wonderful Father hears every prayer! The money which had been 'stolen' from us was unexpectedly returned and then immediately passed on to the other person in need. I learned that the blessings of true forgiveness can be boundless, and believe they can reach beyond generational and geographical confines.

This relationship was brought about through my obedience to the Lord, and put in jeopardy by my carelessness. The restoration process began with a degree of forgiveness, and was hastened when soul ties were cut. But it remained incomplete whilst I held onto 'evidence' of wrongdoing, thereby giving the Enemy access to the wound. Total forgiveness led to true repentance, reparation and reconciliation - and a widespread blessing! Alleluia!

Testimony 7E

I was introduced to a prayer minister by a friend, eighteen months ago. At that time I was feeling very low and was dwelling too much on the bad times in my past life. Even at our first meeting I felt very much at ease. In prayer, I was taken back with Jesus to when I was in my mother's womb, and from being a baby on through the very volatile childhood which I had experienced with my parents, with all the rows which had left me very tearful. I have had a number of sessions during which the layers of my very bad past have been coming off. I have found great comfort through the prayers, and I have not been looking back to the past so much. If I do get depressed and low for a day or two, I don't let it last like I used to do. I am much improved and I am very grateful to God my father for all the help He has given me through Jesus Christ. I am putting on the armour and praying the stronghold prayers every day. In the last few months, over a dozen people have begun to open up to me about their troubles, and are grateful that I listen to them. I have begun to pray for many people, particularly those who live in the same block of flats. One lady, towards whom I had previously been judgemental because of her drinking, has now disclosed to me the reason for the pain in her.

Testimony 7F

On 8 December 1983, the feast of the Immaculate Conception, I received an audio tape from a friend in Liverpool. Somebody had recorded a talk by a priest and for me it was amazing. He said Our Lady was appearing in a small village called Medjugorje as the Queen of Peace. She first appeared on 24 June 1981 on the Feast day of St John the Baptist and I remembered the words 'Prepare ye the way of the Lord'.

From the moment I heard the tape I believed and consequently could not stop spreading the GOOD NEWS. At the time I was working in a hospital and as I travelled to work I started praying for Our Lady's intentions. She said, 'I know that you are not able to love your enemies, but I beg you to pray at least fifteen minutes each day to the Most Sacred Heart of my Son and to my heart, and He will give you the Divine Love which will enable you to love your enemies.'

So as I travelled to work each day I started to pray the peace rosary for every single person in the department. This is an ancient Croatian custom. It starts off with the Creed, followed by Our Father, the Hail Mary, and the Glory Be seven times, finishing with 'Our Lady, Queen of Peace, pray for us'.

It was not a happy department, some women were actually fighting with each other, the language was appalling, sometimes they were drinking, and there was no peace. By this time I was acting supervisor. The situation got gradually worse, and when I was asked what I was going to do, I replied that I was going to Medjugorje to pray for peace in the office. When I was in Medjugorje I prayed as I had never prayed before, but when I came back to work I could feel the peace in the department.

I continued every day to pray for every member of the office. I mentioned each person by name but I simply prayed, 'Blessed Lady, I place them into your Immaculate Heart. Please give them your motherly blessing and take them to your son Jesus'. So it was every person in the office was prayed for every day for years. There were many miracles as staff requested to be moved into other offices, or they would apply for a position elsewhere and against all odds would get jobs out of the area.

You have heard that it was said: Love your neighbour and hate your enemy. This I tell you: Love your enemies, and pray for those who persecute you, so that you may be children of your Father in heaven. (Mt 5:43–45)

Testimony 7G

The power of spiritual prayer can take time to manifest itself. One experience I had was helping a colleague at work. My colleague was upset and stressed because he had not gained the promotion he thought due him. At the same time, he could not accept the changes in his status because his boss had left who had promised him the promotion.

The situation grew worse for him as the stress of the change proved too much. He left with a stress-related illness for a long period of time. We then moved to a new building where I joined the team.

I came to my new job in a new building as part of a new team. I was under pressure as well because more of his work was coming to me. At the same time, my role often put me in conflict with the organisation and colleagues. The role I had required me to do the right thing in law and for the organisation. However, colleagues and senior managers often wanted to work outside the law and wanted me to bend the rules or overlook them.

Faced with this situation and the growing stress it was creating, I discussed it with my spiritual adviser. We prayed on it together and he suggested that I was facing a spiritual battle beyond the organisational battle. What was needed was to join that battle and seek God's help. What the prayer revealed was the need to defend myself with holy water. I went to work that week and sprinkled holy water around my work station and then around the room to protect me from the challenges that the devil was presenting.

What he recommended as well was to put some holy water around my colleague's work station and to pray to God to help him. I said that I would. Although my colleague at first continued to struggle with the strains and stresses of work, he finally found peace when he made the decision to retire. His early retirement led to an immediate change in his mental and physical health. He went from someone being troubled, stressed and feeling undervalued to a person full of life with a renewed zest for life.

Looking back on it, I can see that my situation and my colleague's situation improved in the days and weeks after the holy water and the prayers. The counselling and work recovery stress reduction programmes were not working because what was needed was a spiritual intervention because there was spiritual turmoil. The change was not instantaneous but there is no doubt in my mind that through prayer and God's intervention my colleague is now happier and healthier.

Notes

[1]   V. Miskovic, D. Moscovitch, D. Santesso, R. McCabe, M. Antony & L. Schmidt, 'Changes In EEG Cross-Frequency Coupling During Cognitive Behavioral Therapy For Social Anxiety Disorder' in *Psychological Science* 84/2 (2011), pp. 194–200.

[2]   D. Prince, *Blessing or Curse* (Milton Keynes: Word Publishing, 1990).

[3]   L. Savard, *Shattering Your Strongholds* (North Brunswick NJ: Bridge-Logos Publishers, 1992), p. 90.

[4]   L. Savard, *Breaking The Power* (North Brunswick NJ: Bridge-Logos Publishers, 1997), p233.

[5]   L. Savard, *Producing The Promise* (North Brunswick NJ: Bridge-Logos Publishers, 1999), pp xvi-xvii.

[6]   P. Deegan, various tape cassettes and CDs.

[7]   Savard, *Shattering Your Strongholds*, pp. 131–132.

[8]   Vatican II, *Lumen Gentium*, 61.

[9]   *Ibid.*, 56.

[10] J. Powell & L.Brady, *The Fully Alive Experience—Participants' Personal Notebook* (Argus Publications, 1980), p. 14.

[11] L. Piccarreta, *When The Divine Will Reigns In Souls* (Jacksonville: The Center For The Divine Will, 1995).

[12] Vatican II, *Sacrosanctum Concilium*, 6. See also Pope Paul VI, Apostolic Constitution *Indulgentiarum Doctrina*, 5.

[13] R. Cantalamessa, 'Spiritual Healing' in *Prayer for Healing* (International Colloquium, Rome: International Catholic Charismatic Renewal Services, 2003), p. 223.

[14] D. Prince, *Blessing or Curse* (Milton Keynes: Word Publishing, 1990), p. 147.

15　Vatican II, *Apostolicam Actuositatem*, 6.

16　Pope Paul VI, *Evangelii Nuntiandi*, 14, 21, 24, 10.

17　Pope Benedict XVI, *Jesus of Nazareth—Part 2* (London: Catholic Truth Society, 2011), pp. 152–153.

8

MINISTRY TO PRIESTS AND RELIGIOUS

Priests Needing Personal Ministry

In various ways, priests from at least seven different dioceses have come to us for a great variety of reasons, and were very grateful that they could talk in confidence and pray about situations in their lives. Whilst in Leeds, we had both been members of the Diocesan Pastoral Council and vividly remembered the priest chosen by the Bishop to lead a retreat for all clergy of the diocese, giving his subsequent report. He said, 'My overwhelming impression from that retreat is the utter loneliness of the priests'. This had helped us in being given even greater compassion and love for priests. In the Vatican II Decree on the Apostolate of the Laity, we read: 'Lay persons of a genuinely apostolic spirit supply the needs of their brothers, and are a source of consolation no less to the pastors than to the rest of the faithful' (cf. 1 Co 16:17–18).[1] Priests need all the loving support that their people can give.

Our parish priest, one of the most senior in the diocese, was not an easy man for people to relate to and work with. We had begun to realise how wrong and damaging it is to criticise and judge priests and to grumble about them. We asked God's forgiveness and began, with some sisters of St Gemma's Hospice, to pray for him. Then I attended the first charismatic renewal conference for priests, which I had helped to organise. With 460 priests there, the one next to me in the lunch queue, seeing Leeds on my name tag, asked me the name of my parish. I told him, and then I said, 'I know God can do anything, but I don't think he could get our parish priest to a conference like this'. 'I know he couldn't,' he replied, 'I'm his nephew'. I then looked at his name tag—he had the same Christian name and surname. I hadn't known he had a nephew. Over lunch, he said to me, 'My uncle could never give love or receive love in the family'. At the follow-up conference the next year, this same priest from Scotland was there. I asked whether he knew that his uncle was ill in hospital. He had not known but drove there at once, arriving at the same time as our curate. Together they prayed with our parish priest.

Our hearts went out to him even more and God gave us more and more love for him. He had never been in our house in nearly twenty years. We asked him for a meal. On the doorstep, he said, 'What have you got me here for?' In other words, people only want me if they want to demand something—they don't want me for myself. We said, 'We just want you to enjoy yourself and we'll enjoy having you here'. At the end of a relaxed evening, he gave us a long Latin blessing and gave Betty a hug— something I never thought he could do. We said to him, 'We are praying for you every day'. He replied, 'I can feel it'. He said to Betty one day, 'If Alan wants help with his work in renewal I'd be glad to help'. I regretted never taking up the offer.

A while later, Betty and I spent an hour praying in St Columba's Chapel on Iona. People looked in but did not stay, so Betty asked the Lord why they went straight out. Then she felt she heard, quite distinctly in Monsignor's Scottish accent, 'They haven't heard the call of the Master'. She sent a card to our curate, saying that she had something to tell Monsignor. Later that week, still on holiday, we heard that he had become ill on the day we were on Iona, and died a few days later. We were sad not to see him again in life, but joyful to think we'll meet again. For the last year or so of life people had been remarking on changes in him. For example, for years his fear of death had come through in many homilies. That disappeared.

The second year, 1997, that Betty asked the Lord in prayer where He wanted us to go on holiday, she got 'Peebles'. There was a farm in Peeblesshire offering bed and breakfast. One day, at a remote beauty spot, we met a priest who spoke about the scenery in Austria. I told him how the Lord had sent people to Graz to pray with Carmelites (see next section). He said, 'I want nothing to do with charismatic renewal: it is all emotional people'. Half an hour later, he amazed us by asking if we would go to Mass in his church, and, instead of his giving a homily, would we answer his questions about renewal. The Saturday night, he appeared at the farm and asked if we would go to Mass next morning in both of his churches, and do the same thing. This we did. He was a very lonely man, now long dead, and he asked us to go back and to stay with him for some days the next year. One day he asked us if we would drive him to the presbytery of a friend of his. We had only been talking a few minutes with his friend, the superior of the community, when he suddenly poured out great distress and hurt and he asked us to pray with him.

In another Scottish diocese, the Bishop asked us to give a weekend of teaching to help build up the healing ministry in his diocese. He was so pleased with this that we were invited back the next year to give a weekend in a different town. For these weekends we stayed in a convent, where a year earlier we had been invited to do joint ministry with a Church of Scotland minister. Each of us teamed up with a local person, and in the week we ministered to thirteen Catholics and thirteen Church of Scotland members. We hoped that this would lead to ongoing joint ministry between the Churches, but the minister had a hard time because of his contacts with Catholics, and had to move.

In February 1977, I was among twenty-eight people, eighteen of whom were priests, including Bishop Langton Fox and Abbot Ambrose Griffiths OSB (later our Bishop), who were invited to a five-day study of deliverance and exorcism, at Hawkstone Hall. At that time, we did not have in England, Wales and Northern Ireland, any priest with sufficient knowledge and experience to lead the conference. Instead we had invited Rev Christopher Neil-Smith, exorcist for the Anglican diocese of London. Several of the priests subsequently became diocesan exorcists.

At the end of our time there, Christopher told me that he had prayed with more than half the participants, mostly priests, for deliverance. I had travelled to Shropshire with two priests very active in the Church, one of whom was clearly not his usual self on the journey there. When we returned, he was back to his usual full peacefulness and purpose.

People should pray much more for their priests out of love, and out of thankfulness to God and to them for their sacrifice and service. Those prayers should include praying for their protection. Our own now-retired parish priest told us years ago that the three main aims of the satanists in this country (and perhaps elsewhere) are (1) breakdown of priesthood and seminaries, (2) breakdown of Christian marriages and (3) violence in the streets. Independent confirmation of this came twice. A couple from our parish visited the husband's brother in South Wales. The latter had recently been discharged from hospital, where a man in his ward said that he was fasting for these three aims. Then we met someone who had been in a hairdressers', when another woman refused coffee because she said she was fasting for the same three intentions. One way that a priest may become oppressed can be when someone, themselves oppressed, is dying.

Evil spirits will seek to go to some living person, and priests are present at more death-beds than other people.

Priests can be subjected to much negativity, sometimes overt, but sometimes grumbling and gossiping in a more hidden way. We need to repent of ways in which we can make the problems worse and become part of them. Where people genuinely feel that changes in the attitude or behaviour or teaching of a priest would benefit everyone, then instead of grumbling or speaking to others, far more could be accomplished by bringing the problems to the Lord in prayer, asking for the power to forgive and for the gift of His love for the priest. They might sometimes be guided to speak directly to him, but in love rather than in anger or criticism, and in ways which can also give affirmation and encouragement. I need to be reminded of advice given to us by a priest years ago, to pray at each homily for the priest to be anointed by the Holy Spirit to speak, and for the congregation to be anointed to listen deeply. He pointed out that sometimes people claim to have heard something quite different from what he said.

For some years I and many others have been praying daily the following prayer for our priests:

> Lord Jesus, You have chosen Your priests from among us and sent them out to proclaim Your word and to act in Your name. For so great a gift to your Church, we give You praise and thanksgiving. We ask You to fill them with the fire of Your love, that their ministry may reveal Your presence in the Church. Since they are earthen vessels, we pray that Your power shine out through their weakness. In their afflictions let them never be crushed; in their doubts never despair; in temptation never be destroyed; in perse-cution never abandoned. Inspire them through prayer to live each day the mystery of Your dying and rising. In times of weakness send them Your Spirit, and help them to praise Your heavenly Father and pray for poor sinners. By the same Holy Spirit put Your words on their lips and Your love in their hearts, to bring good news to the poor and healing to the broken-hearted. And may the gift of Mary Your mother, to the disciple whom You loved, be Your gift to every priest. Grant that she who formed You in her human image, may form them in Your divine image, by the power of Your Spirit, to the glory of God the Father. Amen.

Experiences with Religious

We have prayed with very many sisters over the years. In the 1970s, on holiday in North Wales, we found Talacre Abbey, an enclosed Benedictine community. Whilst in their 'shop' buying sweets made by the sisters, the nun who was serving us suddenly said, 'This morning one of the community was banging the table and saying, 'We need the Holy Spirit in this place'. We spoke briefly of some of our experiences and were asked for our address and telephone number. A few months later we received an invitation to speak for an hour about praise of God, at a day of renewal to be held in the Abbey in the following January. We accepted.

Only later did we hear how the day came about. The only two sisters who attended an ecumenical prayer meeting, encouraged a lay person, Shirley, to ask if they could have a day of renewal. Shirley asked for permission to see the Abbess. A sister disappeared through a door and eventually came back with the message, 'The Lady Abbess will see you a week on Tuesday at 3 o'clock'. These two sisters, sensing that the Abbess was going to refuse, pointed out that the Abbess had received a form from the Council of Major Superiors. Among other questions were some about their contacts with local people. The sisters pointed out that it would fill up one of the embarrassing spaces on the form, if the Abbess agreed to the request. Reluctantly she did so, but she said to Shirley, 'Of course the only two members of the community who will attend will be the two in the prayer group'.

The Friday night before the Saturday day of renewal, such heavy snow fell in Leeds that I couldn't get the car out of the garage. Our phone having been put out of action, I phoned from next door. I told the Abbess that we couldn't come. 'Oh dear,' she said, ' we're really looking forward to your coming. Can't you come by train?'

Next morning we left very early, walking through unbroken deep snow. Thankfully a bus took us to the station. When we reached Manchester, the train we wanted was crossed off the timetable, and this was at first confirmed verbally. Eventually, however, we did get there. The snow was very thick in North Wales. Seeing this, we later learned, the Abbess phoned our neighbours to tell them to stop us coming—the day was cancelled. The neighbours put down the phone, came to our door and found we had gone. Then they thought, 'Who was it that phoned us?' All they knew was that we were Roman Catholics and that they had heard Prestatyn mentioned. They asked the operator to get them in touch with

Catholics in Prestatyn. They got the parish priest. It took him some time to work out that it was something to do with the Abbey, so he phoned the Abbess. She called the community together and said, 'We've got two people on their way from Leeds, so you'll all have to go to the talk, and I'll be there, too'.

When we finished our talk, a priest should have given the second talk, but the snow had prevented him from coming, and the session turned into an impromptu prayer meeting. We couldn't get back that day and stayed overnight in a nearby bungalow. After Mass on Sunday morning, many of the twenty sisters came to talk to us. Suddenly, one of them said, 'I am totally deaf, and for some time the Lord has been telling me in my prayer that he would send someone here to lay hands on me and pray with me, and I would be healed. I believe you are the people.' We placed our hands on her arm over the barrier of the enclosure, and we prayed. Some minutes later she burst out, 'I can hear you, I can hear you'. It was not a complete restoration of hearing, but was sufficient for her, subsequently, to have deaf-aids fitted.

We visited the Abbey again years later while staying with Bishop Langton Fox, to look after him for a few days, after his retirement due to strokes. The sisters told us of a clear attack of evil on the Abbey and neighbouring property. The bishop rang them to confirm the advice which we had given, as to how to pray against the attack. Our last contact, years later again, was to visit one of the sisters, who had stayed in contact by letter, when she was dying in hospital in Chester, to where the community had moved.

Whilst we were travelling around Ireland for two weeks, following the call of God to Ballybane (referred to elsewhere), we visited Kylemore Abbey in Connemara. One of the sisters from the community was showing us round. Suddenly, without our saying anything, she asked, 'Do you pray with people for healing?' When we said, 'Yes', she took us into an unoccupied room. There she spoke of her need and we prayed with her.

Within a short time of our move to Norton, the Provincial Superior of the Mercy Sisters came to our home, to ask us if we would give a day of recollection on the subject of praise of praise of God to all the sisters of all the convents under her jurisdiction, in the North East and the North West of England. A year or so later, she asked us to give another day of recollection, this time on healing. It turned out that the sisters at some of the convents had already arranged to be on retreat at that time, so were asked to repeat the day a few weeks later. At all three days of recollection, held at the Crossbeck Convent, which was then the provincial house, the Blessed Sacrament was exposed for a long time in the afternoon. They asked us to be in a separate small room beside the Chapel, in order to be available to any sister who felt she needed individual prayer ministry. A very high proportion of the sisters came to us. Also, sisters from a number of other orders have come to our home for prayer ministry.

On the Saturday evening of one of the six weekends of teaching on praying for inner healing which Betty and I gave at Minsteracres retreat centre, we thought by about eleven pm that we had come to the last person who was needing us to pray with them that evening. Betty had just gone to get herself a brandy, when there was a knock at the door. It was a sister who had been with her order for around thirty-five years. She gave me a letter to read, a letter that she was about to post to her Provincial. It poured out some of her hurt and anger and said that she was leaving the order. I brought Betty back and together we listened to the sister, and then prayed with her. At the end she gave us the letter to destroy. She is still with her order after well over fifty years with them and, despite much suffering with ill-health, she is happy and content. She prays for very many people and keeps in close touch by telephone.

Over a number of years, we prayed many times with one young man, not originally a Catholic. He was searching for God's will for him. Before he left the area he gave us prophetic words: 'You are to enlarge your tent.' These words were later confirmed from an entirely different source, but their meaning is still not completely clear, though they did lead on directly to our bishop supporting the twelve-week course mentioned in the following section. He is now a fully-professed Cistercian monk, very happy in his vocation. He prays a great deal for our ministry and he too keeps in touch by telephone.

In 1975 a priest asked me to accompany him to a Carmelite community. He had been requested by the Prioress to come in order to pray with every one of the community, that they might be baptised with the Holy Spirit. After the celebration of Mass, the grill was opened and each sister came in turn and knelt, with the Prioress placing a hand on her shoulder, while we all prayed.

About a month later, whilst in Rome, I was telling Cardinal Suenens about this over dinner, and he told me that his secretary, Canon Wilfred

Brieven, had similarly prayed with the whole Carmelite community in Mechelen. Then, travelling on a bus, the priest from the USA sitting next to me, out of the blue, asked me to pray for a Carmelite sister whom he had never met. She had written to say that she couldn't come to his ordination, but he had never heard of her; so she had not actually been invited. I found myself alone in the big arena at the catacombs of St Calixtus, apart from some musicians tuning up. Later that day, 10,000 people from about 120 countries, all involved in charismatic renewal, were due there to praise God together. The chairs were stacked in piles. I found a barrow and started taking them, opening them and setting them out in rows. Into this empty arena came two ladies who walked up to me. Again, out of the blue, they asked me to pray for a Carmelite sister.

A day or two before this had happened I had met an Austrian professor who had stopped working in a university in order to live in a community with his family and others in a castle. They would pray for five hours a day, yet he still had time to pursue his research, and worked for the United Nations. One day in prayer, his sixteen-year-old daughter felt that they were being asked to go to Graz, 120 miles away. They prayed for discernment and it seemed to be confirmed, so they drove to Graz, not knowing what to do next. However, they needed petrol. As the garage attendant filled the tank of the car, the professor asked him if he knew anyone in Graz with spiritual need. The man said, 'Please don't tell anyone, but I live next door to a Carmelite convent, and I believe they need spiritual help'.

They parked outside the convent and prayed. When they rang the bell a sister came, and the professor said, 'We don't want to trouble anyone, but we believe that Jesus Christ sent us here'. The sister brought the Prioress, who was in tears. She said, 'This is the ninth day of our Novena to the Holy Spirit for help'. Within a short time they were asked to go back to pray with every sister for baptism in the Holy Spirit. When I returned to the UK, I wrote to the Prioress to ask her to pray for all those Carmelites, and I seem to remember that there were others.

Some years ago Betty wrote to a Carmelite community, enclosing a cheque for a book which one of the sisters had written about the remarkable life of a now-deceased member of the community. On impulse she enclosed a list of our teaching tapes. Back came the book, together with a cheque for some of our tapes. When some of the community had listened to these, we were recommended by them to send information to a Poor Clare abbey. The sisters there ordered many of the tapes, and now members of both communities continue to pray for us and for the inner healing prayer ministry.

Urgent Need for Priests to Gain Understanding and Teaching

In 1997 a priest suggested we should give an all-day seminar to bring together people aware of Christ's power to heal alongside members of many secular groups who, through counselling, seek to bring healing to a great variety of people, in marriage problems, addiction and other areas. Invitations would go out to organisations from Newcastle-upon-Tyne to York. I wrote to our bishop to ask if we could say in the invitation letter that we had his blessing and support. He replied that not only could we say that, but also that he would be present at the beginning of that day. The day before the seminar, he telephoned me to say that he was now free all next day, and said, 'I'll stay all day if I'll be of any use'.

At the end of the seminar, the priest who had chaired it asked the bishop if he had anything to say. 'Yes', he said. 'As a result of today I now understand why it is necessary to pray specifically and in detail for inner healing'.

The bishop was delighted with a 12-week course of teaching which we gave in 1999, after he wrote to every priest in the six southern deaneries of the diocese recommending it. The course was attended by 97 people, of whom over 30 were recommended by nine priests. The bishop then asked us to give a similar course for the north of the diocese. In the letter which he wrote to all priests to guide them as to the kind of people to nominate, he wrote:

> I think it is important that attendance at the sessions should be by invitation only because those taking part will need to be well-balanced, with a real prayer life, and people who could be trusted never to break confidences, and who would be willing to listen and pray non-judgementally out of love and compassion, and not out of any wrong motives, such as curiosity or the desire to give advice or their own need of satisfaction.

Because he had this deep awareness of this ministry he shared our concerns that so few people were able to find others in the Church to whom they could go for ongoing listening and prayer. A few years later he decided to raise his concerns at a meeting with other bishops. Soon afterwards, following a Mass which he had concelebrated, he came over to my wife and myself to tell us he had done so. I asked what the response had been. He grinned and said, 'Moderate'.

We heard nothing more, for he was then retired. The other bishops will not have had his opportunities to discern at first-hand what is involved in various parts of the inner healing ministry. I have often wondered how reliable second-hand or third-hand discernment is when trying to judge whether or not some happenings are inspired and guided by the Holy Spirit. A number of priests have spoken to us about the lack of teaching on healing included deliverance in their seminary training. These grave omissions need to be remedied.

Pope Paul VI stressed that the Church 'has a constant need of being evangelised if she wishes to retain freshness, vigour and strength in order to proclaim the Gospel. The Second Vatican Council recalled, and the 1974 Synod vigorously took up again, this theme of the Church which is evangelised by constant conversion and renewal in order to evangelise the world with credibility'.[2]

In examining the means by which this may be done, he emphasised that 'the first means of evangelisation is the witness of an authentically Christian life given to God'. He continued: 'Modern man listens more willingly to witnesses than to teachers, and if he does listen to teachers, it is because they are witnesses'.[3]

As the Church seeks to follow the call of The New Evangelisation towards the re-Christianising of the Western world, it is surely important to reflect on the teaching of Pope Paul VI regarding the role of witnesses. Also, Vatican II emphasised that 'the witness of life is not the sole element in the Apostolate; the true apostle is on the look-out for occasions of announcing Christ by word'.[4] How often do seminarians have their expectant faith built up during their training by hearing direct witness accounts of what the Holy Spirit is doing today, not merely in the past, including how the Scriptures are playing a part in changing lives now? They do not learn to follow the example of the early Church, where a vital part of the witnessing was to pray for Jesus to go on healing people, just as He did when He walked the earth. His commands to do this (Lk 9:2; Lk 10:9; Mk 16:18) are being neglected. How often do lay people have the opportunity in a homily, or in other ways made available by their priests, to hear a 'living theology' of God doing amazing things in the lives of people within their own community in the present day? When our then parish priest invited such witness at the end of Mass, only three people came forward on different days with his prior agreement. There seemed to be no follow-up conversations from people in the congregation, perhaps because many Catholics do not expect to hear about God doing wonderful things today.

A sociologist, examining the decline in the Catholic Church, wrote of its theology: 'Generally speaking it seems that academic study reflects on beliefs rather than faith; on doctrine rather than practice; and on theological publications rather than individual and collective experiences. Some of the hallmarks of academic theology are knowledge rather than spiritual growth, along with structural change in the Church rather than individual conversion ... For ordinary parishioners, academic theology, like Mandarin, is a language difficult to master, while the languages of Scripture and pastoral sociology/theology are easier. Most pastoral strategies are blends of biblical and pastoral reflections.'[5]

For the ordinary Catholic, the search for gems buried in what seems like a mass of unfamiliar verbiage in Church documents can seem to bear comparison with the need for skills and experience required of various professionals in the search for veins of precious metals buried deep in the earth. In any case, as my wife and I realised 28 years ago when, at the request of the parish priest, we introduced the RCIA into the parish, it is transformation rather than information for which people are generally searching. It is to the challenge for the Church to foster this transformation, to which the final chapter is directed.

Notes

[1]   Vatican II, *Apostolicam Actuositatem*, 10.

[2]   Pope Paul VI, *Evangelii Nuntiandi*, 15.

[3]   *Ibid.*, 41.

[4]   Vatican II, *Apostolicam Actuositatem*, 6.

[5]   P. Hegy, *Wake Up, Lazarus—On Catholic Renewal* (Bloomington In: iUniverse, Inc, 2011), pp. 5–6.

9

THE CHALLENGE FOR THE CHURCH

Urgent Need for More Prayer Ministry—of the Right Kind

The ministry of inner healing is one which can only be accomplished by God's love and mercy. There needs to be discernment, preferably involving the parish priest of those who are called by God, and they need to be in obedience and accountable to him, or to some other priest(s). We were commissioned 28 years ago by our parish priest, and confirmed in it by our bishops. No one, unless specially prompted by the Holy Spirit, should pray with another unless asked to do so by the person concerned, so that there must be no pressure of any kind. The only motive out of which such ministry should flow is through the love which God Himself gives us for those who are burdened. Those praying with others need to have their lives and relationships in good order, and be in unity in the usual case where a pair of people minister together to someone in need. My wife and I would ask one another for forgiveness for any ways in which we might have hurt one another. We did this immediately before praying with someone else, and also prayed for unity so that God could guide and empower our prayers. Immediately after this person left our house, we asked the Holy Spirit to come afresh to us to cleanse and refresh us. Anyone in this ministry will need back-up prayer from others. Apart from people in our group and locality praying for us, there are, as mentioned in Chapter 8, two contemplative communities praying for the ministry in Norton. Prayers for protection are needed daily. There are many other aspects which can be helpful to those called forth for this work, and we have discussed these on various occasions, and recorded tapes and CDs, but it is not appropriate to go into them in more detail here, though a list of those resources is provided in Appendix 4.

Such things as pride, self-satisfaction and judgementalism in those who minister must be brought to die daily on the Cross. We found that we only used the counselling technique which we had learned for two or three out of over five hundred people, because each person is unique, and only the Lord knows the right timing and pace and approach, as each becomes more ready to open to Him. It is vital to depend entirely on the Holy Spirit for guidance. For the sake of confidentiality, the only record we have ever kept has been a diary appointment with name and time, so that we are not trying to record progress or make any plan, and we have to depend on the Holy Spirit at each new session. It is heartening that some have been very willing to give written testimony, which was made available by our parish priest without disclosing any identities, in the hope that this will lead to deeper expectant faith growing in those who read these accounts.[1] This booklet of twenty-nine testimonies contains a foreword by Bishop Ambrose Griffiths OSB.

One example showing that a listening prayerful ministry is necessary to complement the sacraments occurred recently when, at the end of 3 hours 45 minutes of listening one evening, on an occasion not planned as a ministry session, on a day in which I had already had two two-hour sessions, some remark of mine triggered the revealing of something never before told to anyone. This person said, ' I thought I was going to have to go to my grave without ever being able to tell anyone this'. Even before I was free to meet again for the first prayer session, a message came to me: 'I can't believe how much better I feel now that I have told someone' (see Ps 32:3–4). After a few sessions, God was being thanked and praised by this person because there was no longer any painful burden from past events. This lady had been receiving the sacraments for years, but had not felt able to reveal this matter in the sacrament of Reconciliation, though she was an innocent victim. A very experienced priest told me he was not surprised, and that many others keep silent out of such feelings as embarrassment. This is just one example of how a lay person, perhaps through long patient listening, or through one of the gifts of the Holy Spirit (eg a word of knowledge) (1 Co 12), may be used by God to work alongside the grace which the person receives from the sacraments.

Testimony 9A (p. 208) from a parishioner illustrates how God can pour out grace and change lives through prayer ministry, and bring people to a deeper appreciation of the sacraments. The lady who wrote testimony 9A also wrote 7E (p. 169) about praying for people in her hospital department. Her life has been so transformed that the Lord has been using her for many years in a great many prayerful ways to bless other people.

The working together of graces of two kinds, as happened in this lady's life, is brought out in the Catechism:

> Grace is first and foremost the gift of the Spirit who justifies and sanctifies us. But grace also includes the gifts that the Spirit grants us to associate us with His work, to enable us to collaborate in the salvation of others and in the growth of the Body of Christ, the Church. There are sacramental graces, gifts proper to the different sacraments. There are furthermore special graces, also called charisms, after the Greek term used by St Paul, and meaning 'favour', 'gratuitous gift', 'benefit'. Whatever their character—sometimes it is extraordinary, such as the gift of miracles or of tongues—charisms are oriented towards sanctifying grace and are intended for the common good of the Church. They are at the service of charity which builds up the Church.[2]

The point was made even more clear in *Lumen Gentium*:

> It is not only through the sacraments and the ministrations of the Church that the Holy Spirit makes holy the People, leads them and enriches them with His virtues. Allotting His gifts according as He wills (cf. 1 Co 12:11), He also distributes special graces among the faithful of every rank. By these gifts He makes them fit and ready to undertake various tasks and offices for the renewal and building up of the Church, as it is written, 'the manifestation of the Spirit is given to everyone for profit' (1 Co 12:7). Whether these charisms be very remarkable or more simple and widely diffused, they are to be received with thanksgiving and consolation since they are fitting and useful for the needs of the Church.[3]

It is particularly sad, so many years later, to hear some priests and lay people claiming or implying that the only source of grace lies in the sacraments alone. Of course there is always a need to monitor and discern the use of such gifts, and the same document continues with the caveat:

> Extraordinary gifts are not to be rashly desired, nor is it from them that the fruits of apostolic labours are to be presumptuously expected. Those who have charge over the Church should judge the genuineness and proper use of the gifts, through their office, not indeed to extinguish the Spirit, but to test all things and hold fast what is good' (cf. 1 Th 5:12, 19–21).

Pope Paul VI made it clear that real evangelisation results in total interior renewal, a radical conversion of mind and heart. We now have Pope

Benedict XVI initiating the New Evangelisation to evangelise the West, so that it is urgent for the Church to focus the graces of the sacraments and charisms towards bringing about this growing conversion in those who respond to the call of Christ with repentance and openness. As part of this we need to awaken deeper faith in all of the sacraments, as well as building up prayer ministry with a new openness to the charisms.

The Power of the Sacraments

If we had sufficient widespread expectant faith in the power available to us in the grace which we receive from the sacraments, there would be less need for the additional grace which can come from the right use of the charisms and prayer ministry, and people would be healed far more quickly. The Catechism describes the sacraments as 'the masterworks of God'.

Anyone who has listened to the testimony of Betty Brennan is likely to find their faith in Christ working through the sacraments not just revived, but very greatly enhanced. Through long ministry from a priest, she was completely set free from her involvement in the top echelons of satanism, so that she could work for an American archdiocese to stir up faith in the power of the sacraments. From first-hand experience she knows that a bona fide witch, shown 2000 hosts, only one of which has been consecrated, could always pick out the one which is truly the body, blood, soul and divinity of Christ. There is evidence in the Scriptures that evil spirits recognised who Jesus was, long before His own followers perceived His true nature when demons screamed, 'What do you want with us, you Son of God?' (Mt 8:29).

Fr McManus began his series of books on healing, where it should begin, with the sacraments.[4] There is particular power in the Holy Eucharist, the sacrament of Reconciliation and the sacrament of Anointing of the Sick, and some examples are given. Many priests could add stories from their own experience, but we should be seeing all around us, many more people being healed from receiving Christ at Holy Communion, and in prayers from a priest for absolution and for the sick. We do not always allow the reality of the indwelling of the Holy Spirit from our baptism to penetrate from 'our heads to our hearts' sufficiently to begin to transform our lives. When we run into inevitable problems of one kind or another in marriage, we do not frequently enough pray together and call upon the power in the sacrament of Matrimony. If many more couples did so, there would be far less heartbreak and damage to children, which then goes on to infect the next generation, and much less need for inner healing later on in their lives.

Vatican II tells us, 'The purpose of the sacraments is to sanctify men, to build up the Body of Christ and finally to give worship to God'.[5] Just as with prayer for inner healing, we are meant to receive grace to bring us into a more complete conversion of heart and mind to Christ.

Deeper Conversion

As discussed earlier, many people are not free because of binding of various kinds between them and other people, particularly those in close relationships, and they need to be helped with the authority of Christ for Him to cut them free of all unhelpful bonds, so that He can strengthen the bonds of His divine love between them all. They may also need to be freed from some bondage of evil spirits through deliverance prayers. If that ministry is needed because they have, willingly or unwillingly, had involvement or contact with some activity forbidden by God such as occult practices, then their willingness to repent and renounce further involvement is required. In many other cases they are entirely innocent. Some influence of evil may have entered them through some childhood experience, say of great fear, or may have 'rubbed off' on them through contact with others. St Alphonsus recommended that priests should be ready to pray silent prayers of deliverance when discernment indicated a possible need. It is often wiser to pray for this silently to avoid alarming the person, who may have become oppressed quite innocently, or where one is unsure whether or not deliverance prayers are needed. In that whole area, great wisdom and caution are particularly needed, and few are called into this. Advice from qualified priests is advisable, as is cooperation with health professionals as the occasion demands, especially if there are any signs of mental illness.

We can thank and praise God our Father that He longs for each one of us to repent and be set free to receive a deeper gift of faith in His Son, so that through the free gift of salvation and the power of the Holy Spirit, we may cooperate in growing obedience to His will, and after purgatory we may be welcomed into His life, restored to the image and likeness of God for which He created us. Inner healing is the part of this process occurring in this life to free us from all damage due to sin and evil, and progressively restore us to our real self. Thus the process of praying for inner healing, together with all the means of grace (sacraments and charisms), is part of the sanctifying work of the Holy Spirit which is needed together with purgatory, for us to be made holy and ready for God's presence. It is a vital part of the process of deeper and deeper conversion towards the goal of 'It is no longer I who live, but Christ who lives in me' (Ga 2:19–20). The more we allow God to do this work in us before we die, the more He can use us to do His will in serving others, and build up the Church.

Further confirmation that praying for inner healing can be a vital part of praying to the Holy Spirit to transform and sanctify us, came from a survey some years ago, which used the diary appointments of people who had come to our home. We did this survey because we were puzzled at a comment we had received in a letter from a sister. Writing of a group of people whom we had met one weekend, she claimed that they did not need any healing. We thought to ourselves: 'We meet people daily at Mass, and we don't know which ones need what amount and depth of healing'. As our now retired parish priest used to say, 'We all need healing'. Sometimes, when people we have seen regularly, perhaps daily, have chosen to come and share with us in depth, we have been amazed at what they have gone through and are still coping with, and surprised at just how much needs to be healed. Thus we thought, 'How can this sister make this statement about people she may be seeing once or perhaps twice a year?' Then we began to wonder if it was because most of them were fairly recently 'baptised in the Holy Spirit'. This sister is greatly gifted and used by God to help in this stage of people's lives.

Of all the people who by this time had come to our home, around half had only come once or a very few times, and were not yet committed to letting God make really deep changes in their lives. The other half, who did continue for a considerable time, and really wanted to change, were people who had already experienced, in a new way, a deep awareness of God's love for them and a growing relationship with Him, and would in most cases say that they had experienced the Holy Spirit working afresh in their lives, through what they would term 'baptism in the Holy Spirit'. Of these people, some 25% had 15–20 years of this new experience; 40% had 10–15 years; 32% had 5–10 years; and only 3% had less than 5 years. This indicated that the majority of those coming with a persevering desire to be changed and healed by God only realised their deep need of inner healing some 10–15 years after this new experience of the Holy Spirit.

The findings of this survey accord very closely with teaching by Fr Thomas Green SJ,[6] based on the writings of St John of the Cross and St Theresa of Avila, that it is only in the desert experience that the Holy Spirit begins His work of purifying and transforming us, as we learn to live by faith not feelings. In his follow-up book, he wrote: 'While we might spend two to three years in the getting-to-know stage, where knowledge of God and self is the primary focus and fruit of our prayer, and five to seven years in the honeymoon stage, where loving experience is the dominant characteristic, we can expect this third stage of dryness and darkness to last as long as we live—if, that is, we are courageous enough to respond to grace and persevere in the dryness'.[7] This teaching accorded extremely closely with the personal experience both of myself and of my late wife, and was confirmed many more times from the people coming to our home after we made that survey.

Testimony 9B (p. 211) was written by a man who did not seek prayer for inner healing until 27 years after he had experienced a turning point in his life in a new awareness of his relationship to God. Since then he has gone through fresh suffering, including losing his job, but that has led to God using him in an entirely new way in the Church, in which he is proving to be a great blessing to many people as he uses vital gifts which the Lord has given him.

Testimony 9C (p. 211) was written by another wonderful person in whose life I have been privileged for twenty-five years to see the Lord working more and more deeply in her need and openness. Again, she is being used tremendously to serve others. She refers to a passage of Scripture which has the power to bring new hope and encouragement to all who become ready to cry out to God: 'The desert will rejoice and flowers bloom in the wilderness. Give strength to hands that are tired and to knees that tremble with weakness. Tell everyone who is discouraged, "Be strong and don't be afraid. God is coming to your rescue". The blind will be able to see and the deaf will hear. The lame will leap and dance, and those who cannot speak will shout for joy. Streams of living water will flow through the desert. There will be a highway there called "the Road of Holiness"; no sinner will ever travel that road; no fools will mislead those who follow it. Those whom the Lord has rescued will travel home by that road. They will be happy forever, for ever free from sorrow and grief' (Is 35:1, 3–6, 8–10).

Praying with those who are ready at any stage of their spiritual journey to ask for inner healing and wholeness is a part of the ministry of the Church to remove the effects of sin, through the suffering and death of Christ, working particularly with grace from the sacraments of Confirmation, Reconciliation and the Eucharist, to bring us deeper into the outworking of our baptism. It is of the greatest importance to back up the grace of those sacraments by praying with one another. Thirty-nine years of this ministry has given clear evidence that great growth in faith in Christ can take place as a direct result, resulting in inner peace and in devotion to doing the will of God.

Healing as Wholeness

In some quarters, 'healing' has been taken only to refer only or mainly to physical healing. There is no doubt that remarkable physical healing can take place following prayer, and we have witnessed some of these healings directly. However, over-concentration on physical healing has sometimes obscured examination of the ministry of praying for the whole person, with the main emphasis on emotional and spiritual healing and wholeness. We do not generally know when or if God wants to bring about a particular physical healing, whether through prayer alone, or in combination with medical treatment. However, we can be absolutely certain that He wants to bring each one of His beloved children to spiritual and emotional wholeness, and to free us and restore us to the real self which He created us to be. Inner healing has an eternal dimension which physical healing does not have. If we pray for the whole person, body, soul and spirit, but with our main focus of attention being the person of Christ and His infinite love for this wounded person, then He can accomplish the will of the Father and free them of damage and obstacles within them. Physical healing may occur alongside the growing inner peace and faith. It is interesting to note that a study[8] states unequivocally that the two main ways in which Rome was converted to Christianity were healing and exorcism. When Jesus sent out the 12 and the 72, He did not merely command them to give the Good News but also to heal (Lk 9:2; 10:9), and repeated this after His Resurrection (Mk 16:15–18). This fullness of His commission to the Church is brought out in *Lumen Gentium*: 'Christ was sent by the Father 'to bring good news to the poor—to heal the contrite of heart' (Lk 4:18); "to seek and save what was lost". (Lk 19:10).'[9]

As I work on the final revision of this book, I have been made aware, just in the last few days, through people coming here for ministry or through telephone calls for prayer, or visiting, of a huge variety of suffering. This has included two friends needing visits while undergoing hospital treatment for mental illness, one quite protracted; several friends with life-threatening illness; the death of the mother of several young children; a sudden explosive flare-up in a family with a long history of deep and complicated suffering in which I have been involved for over twelve years; Christians turning to spiritualism for comfort following bereavement; another bereavement leading to the uncovering of deep pain, long-buried; severe stress in a working place; marriages under strain. These have mostly been in addition to around twenty appointments already in my diary. Even two of these appointments had to be cancelled in the morning and afternoon of a single day due to both people experiencing a serious flood. This is just a snapshot of needs brought to the attention of one person in a tiny corner of the country, and only involving fellow Christians, but it affords a glimpse of some of the deep problems in our society. There will always be suffering, but Jesus has come into that. He said, 'I have told you this so that you will have peace by being united to Me. The world will make you suffer, but be brave, I have defeated the world' (Jn16:33).

Lumen Gentium made clear that the Church recognised its responsibilities in the outworking of the mission to help suffering people given to it by the Lord.[10]

> Similarly, the Church encompasses with her love all those who are afflicted by human misery, and recognises the image of her poor and suffering founder in those who are poor and who suffer. She does all in her power to relieve their need, and in them she strives to serve Christ. Christ 'holy, innocent and undefiled' (Heb 7:26) knew nothing of sin (2 Co 5:21), 'but came only to expiate the sins of the people' (cf. Heb 2:17).[11]

The Church, the People of God, includes every member so that there is a call for every lay person to be involved in some way in this work of Christ, and this needs to be examined further.

Role of Laity—The Call of Baptism

Pope John Paul II, addressing the question 'What do you consider to be the most important tasks facing the Church in today's world?', wrote: 'Today an enormous amount of work is needed on the part of the Church.

In particular, the lay apostolate is needed, as the Second Vatican Council reminds us. It is absolutely essential to develop a strong sense of mission'.[12]

At the present time the Church in the West is losing more and more members. Just from my own limited experience, I have witnessed that those who leave are not just those whose faith was never strong or active, but that there are substantial numbers who had experienced a real deepening of their relationship with Christ, and had been greatly gifted by the Holy Spirit. In many cases they have now been given very active roles and important ministries in other churches. They have included a number of priests as well as lay people of various ages. Others have left because they were saddened and disappointed that they were not growing into any deep faith and personal experience of God's love and power within the Catholic Church.

I have listened to a great many people reflecting upon their early experiences and lasting memories of their Catholic homes, schools and parishes. It has been so very sad to hear all the negative messages which took root in them concerning God and themselves. I could write a long list of those which I have heard, none of which come from the true teaching of the Catholic Church. These people did not receive the life-giving truth about the constant omnipresent love of God for each of His children, from the behaviour and words at home, in school from teachers, including some nuns, and from priests and others in their parish. This has been yet more evidence of great discontinuities between the official teaching of the Church and the experiences of many Catholics. In many cases this has played a large part in their leaving the Church. Since virtually everyone who has come to my home for ministry has already become a Christian of some faith, these people are now attending a variety of evangelical or Pentecostal churches. In these, other people have helped them to come to a personal experience of God's love and power, and they have felt accepted, understood and loved, and they have found new life and freedom in Christ.

If the Church is really serious about following the call of Pope John Paul II and Pope Benedict XVI through the New Evangelisation, then it needs to have the humility to learn from mistakes and from experiences of the Holy Spirit working in the lives of Christians in other churches, and perhaps also from outside studies of the Church, as well as its own reflections. The Holy Spirit has many channels through which He may guide us as He seeks to lead us into His plans for renewal. We need to be humble and open enough not to impose our fixed ideas or to copy slavishly something which the Lord has done elsewhere, but instead to seek Him wholeheartedly in our need and in our desire to do His will.

One sociologist, for example, who first began to study the Catholic Church in the late 1960s, has examined its decline and looked at some possible ways in which renewal may occur.[13] He concludes that the evangelisation strategies published in 1992 by the Catholic Conference of American Bishops have made no significant dent in the ongoing decline. One might also want to ask what fruit came from the decade for evangelisation which received publicity in the UK. He went on to examine in some detail one Catholic parish with 3,800 registered families and just one priest, where all the ministries are carried out by the people. This non-geographical parish is said to have begun at the initiative of the diocesan bishop,[14] following the local growth of an evangelical church, which gained several thousand worshippers, 60–80% of whom were estimated to have left the Catholic Church in their search for a deeper experience of God. The new non-geographical Catholic parish, which grew as people flocked from neighbouring parishes was 'best described as a community of communities as it consists of scores of small Christian communities meeting weekly'.[15] Even this did not completely stop a fall of 500 in weekly Mass attendance between 2002 and 2008, because, as he concludes, 'This is a laity-driven parish where lay ministries develop within the pastor's grand vision. This is a vibrant parish to be emulated, yet it is not totally adequate to overcome the Catholic downturn, as it is, like most parishes, essentially looking inward. He notes that it is Christ-centredness rather than church-centredness that correlates with spiritual growth, and that it is important that a church looks outward to its neighbourhood, nation, the world, rather than inward. One is reminded here of the teaching of Pope Paul II, referred to in the next section, that the Church exists in order to evangelise, and of how the vast majority of Catholic parishes tend to focus on maintenance rather than mission, at least in the UK and perhaps much of the West.

Professor Hegy suggests that the basic principle of renewal is to help the faithful to move from passive to active participation in the liturgy, next from active participation to parish involvement and finally from involvement to commitment.[16] However, there are many Catholics, including my self and my late wife and many others that I know, whose spiritual journey did not follow this pattern. In many cases, some 'awakening' through a growing awareness of some emptiness, through disturbing events, needs or suffering may precede a deepening conversion experience, which then leads on to greater appreciation of the Mass and other sacraments, and then to more involvement and commitment through various ways in which the Holy Spirit works. In this process one is learning that true religion has far more to do with what God longs to do for us, in us and through us, than it has to do with what we might try to do for God. In fact it leads to new deepening peace and freedom, instead of striving to obey rules or being driven by inner habits or compulsions.

In all of this, God works sovereignly through the uniqueness of each individual and differences in local circumstances and availability of supportive, faith-filled Christians. Somehow we will be guided and empowered towards real and lasting renewal if through personal prayer, group intercession, witnessing and teaching we can encourage more people in our parishes as they become conscious of their weakness and needs, to open themselves to the powerful loving presence of God. Then they can begin to pray for their own spiritual growth and intercede for the Church as well as spreading the Good News to others. Each of us is needed to play our part in all the ways we find open, but it will finally be God who fulfils His plans to prune, cleanse and renew His Church. No matter what ways renewal may develop in our local church, the primary call for the individual Christian is always to grow in holiness, and thus in deepening surrender to being used by God in loving service to reach out to others.

In the words of St Paul: 'He did this to prepare all God's people for the work of Christian service, in order to build up the body of Christ. And so we shall all come together to that oneness in our faith and in our knowledge of the Son of God; we shall become mature people, reaching to the very height of Christ's full stature. Then we shall no longer be children, carried by the waves and blown about by every shifting wind of the teaching of deceitful men who lead others into error by the tricks they invent. Instead, by speaking the truth in a spirit of love, we must grow up in every way to Christ, who is the head. Under his control all the different parts of the body fit together, and the whole body is held together by every joint with which it is provided. So when each separate part works as it should, the whole body grows and builds itself up by love'. (Ep 4:12–16)

While we are on this ongoing journey, we should be prepared to take account of and reflect upon the Scriptures alongside Church documents, to some of which we will now make brief reference.

'Lumen Gentium' points out the role of the laity:

> The laity—no matter who they are—have, as living members, the vocation of applying to the building up of the Church and to its continual sanctification all the powers which they have received from the goodness of the Creator and from the grace of the Redeemer. The apostolate of the laity is a sharing in the salvific mission of the Church.[17]

That salvific mission of Christ, through His suffering, death and Resurrection, is not only to redeem us from our separation from the Father due to sin, but also to bring us into a greater and more complete wholeness, including health and well-being and safety, as the origins of the word 'saviour' reveal, so that we can work through Christ to bring this to others. Jesus said that He came that we might have 'life in all its fullness' (Jn 10:10). Through our baptism, we are all called to be ministers of health and well-being and peace to one another, and to help others towards what Pope Paul VI called 'a transcendent and eschatological salvation, which indeed has its beginning in this life, but which is fulfilled in eternity'.[18]

Evangelisation—Transformation Through and into Christ

This salvation involves the total interior change which is the aim of the inner healing prayer ministry. As Pope Paul VI wrote about the kingdom and salvation:

> Each individual gains them through a total interior renewal which the Church calls a metanoia: it is a radical conversion, a profound change of mind and heart.[19]

> For the Church, evangelising means bringing the Good News into all the strata of humanity and through its influence transforming humanity and making it new. The purpose of evangelisation is therefore precisely this interior change.[20]

> As the kernel and centre of His Good news, Christ proclaims salvation, this great gift of God which is liberation from sin and the Evil One, in the joy of knowing God and being known by Him, of seeing Him, and of being given over to Him.[21]

All of us, as members of the Church, are expected by God the Father to respond in whatever ways the Holy Spirit leads each of us to the call of Christ to help one another. Pope Paul VI made this clear:

> Evangelising is in fact the grace and vocation proper to the Church, its deepest identity. She exists in order to evangelise.[22]

> Moreover, the Good News which is coming and which has begun is meant for all people at all times. Those who have received the Good News, and who have been gathered by it into the community of salvation, can and must communicate and spread it.[23]

> All Christians are called to this witness and in this way they can be real evangelisers.[24]

Nevertheless this always remains insufficient, because even the finest witness will prove ineffective in the long run, if it is not explained, justified—what Peter called always having your answer ready for people who ask you the reason for the hope that you all have—and made explicit by a clear and unequivocal proclamation of the Lord Jesus.[25]

Attempts at evangelisation in the Western world in recent times have often failed to achieve appreciable ongoing changes in the lives of many people. Is this partly because the Church has largely neglected or truncated the healing part of the mission given by Christ, and because those involved have leaned towards the devising of programmes stemming more from human thinking and academic study, rather than spontaneously using opportunities and power given by the Holy Spirit, as was done by Jesus and the very early Christians? St Paul, having learnt a painful lesson in Athens (Ac 17:16–32), altered his approach when he went to Corinth: 'When I came to you, my brothers, to preach God's secret truth, I did not use big words and great learning. For while I was with you, I made up my mind to forget everything except Jesus Christ, and especially His death on the Cross. So when I came to you, I was weak, and trembled all over with fear, and my teaching and message were not delivered with skilful words of human wisdom, but with convincing proof of the power of God's Spirit' (1 Co 2:1–4). Our message needs to go beyond the 'head' to the 'heart', so that people have a real encounter with the living God. How often are we listening to where people are, and then revealing the loving, accepting, compassionate face of Christ to those in pain, and praying with real expectant faith for the Lord to ease their suffering? Are we working with the Holy Spirit to show them that Jesus Christ is the answer to every human need?

From this, and from all that has been discussed in this book about the inner healing prayer ministry, it follows that part of the mission which Christ gave to the Church is to pray for the total conversion (inner healing) of one another. It is not a choice for the Church to make as to whether or not to do it, and it cannot be relegated to consideration as one among a number of priorities. This is borne out in the Catechism:

Christ's call to conversion continues to resound in the lives of Christians. This second conversion is an uninterrupted task for the whole Church who, 'clasping sinners to her bosom [is] at once and always in need of purification [and] follows constantly the path of penance and renewal'. This endeavour of conversion is not just a human work. It is the movement of a 'contrite heart', drawn and moved to grace to respond to the merciful love of God who loved us first.[26]

Even those who are not called by God to play a direct personal role in the inner healing ministry of other individuals need to be helped to have the awareness and expectant faith in the desire of God to bring about inner healing in themselves and in everyone else, and so pray persistently for this and encourage others to seek this ministry. There is a great need for more people to come together in deep intercession.

A scripture passage which helps us to appreciate this need is: 'Upon your walls, O Jerusalem, I have set watchmen; all the day and all the night they shall never be silent. You who put the Lord in remembrance, take no rest, and give Him no rest until He establishes Jerusalem and makes it a praise in the earth.... Go through, go through the gates, prepare the way for the people; build up, build up the highway, clear it of stones, lift up an ensign over the peoples... And they shall be called the holy people, the redeemed of the Lord' (Is: 62 6–7, 10, 12).

This passage can help us to realise that when the Lord reveals His love and power to us and begins to make us more whole, we are needed by Him to look outward and constantly intercede for and help others to wake up to the urgency of our situation and the signs of the times. Using such prayers as those to destroy strongholds as a part of our personal intercession and healing work, we can play our part in clearing away stones of obstacles in ourselves and others. Isaiah 11:10 confirms that the ensign we lift up is Christ.

Called to Serve

In view of the clear teaching of Scripture and of the Magisterium of the call to all Christians, and the needs of many people who may have to travel long distances to seek ministry, the Church needs to pray for and work towards inner healing ministry becoming available in every deanery, if not, eventually, in every parish. The damage in our society is now so deep and pervasive that huge numbers will begin to reveal their needs, provided that they hear the Good News that Jesus has the power to heal them, and that there are Christians in the neighbourhood who will pray lovingly with them and help them on their journey towards peace and wholeness. For this to happen on any scale, there will need to be great changes in the training, teaching, awareness and attitude in the priesthood.

The responsibility of priests to identify the people particularly gifted by God, and then to help them obtain knowledge and experience of His ways and power, was identified in the Second Vatican Council:

> While trying the spirits if they be of God, they must discover with faith, recognise with joy and foster with diligence the many and charismatic gifts of the laity, whether these be of a humble or more exalted kind. Among the other gifts of God which are found abundantly among the faithful, special attention ought to be devoted to those graces by which a considerable number of people are attracted to greater heights of the spiritual life. Priests should also be confident in giving lay people charge of duties in the service of the Church, giving them freedom and opportunity for activity and even inviting them, when opportunity occurs, to take the initiative in undertaking projects of their own.[27]

Pope John Paul II joined Pope Paul VI in welcoming the right use of the charismatic gifts in the work of the Church: 'It is from this providential discovery of the Church's charismatic dimension that a remarkable pattern of growth has been established for eccelesial movements and new communities'.[28]

The guidance and leadership of bishops will be key to all of this work because:

> The bishops have been designated by the Holy Spirit to take the place of the apostles as pastors of souls ....For Christ commanded the apostles and their successors and gave them the power to teach all peoples, to sanctify men in the truth and to give them spiritual nourishment.[29]

Pope Benedict XVI was calling for deeper understanding and participation in this work of ongoing conversion leading towards sanctification when he wrote that:

> 'Alongside the commission to exorcise, Matthew adds the commission to heal. The twelve are sent "to heal every disease and every infirmity" (Mt 10:1). Healing is an essential dimension of the apostolic mission and of Christian faith in general... When understood at a sufficiently deep level, this expresses the entire content of redemption.... Whoever truly wishes to heal man must see him in his wholeness and must know that his ultimate healing can only be God's love.'[30]

Those called by God into this ministry need to ask God for total acceptance for each person who comes, and for more of God's unconditional love, compassion and gentleness, as well as expectant faith. At the present time the level of expectant faith in most of the Western world appears to be extremely low, and all possible means made available by God need to be employed with freshness and vigour.

The Way Forward

The fostering and development of networks of inner healing ministries is an urgent issue which needs to be pursued in every way offered by God, particularly in the light of Pope Benedict's recent initiative to establish a new Pontifical Council and to call a Synod of Bishops to meet in October 2012, to focus on the 'new evangelisation'. This new evangelisation recognises that our own families, parishes, communities need to be evangelised, so that we in turn can evangelise others. Pope Paul VI had written in 'Evangelii Nuntiandi' that 'the Church needs to be evangelised by constant conversion and renewal in order to evangelise the world with credibility'. The *Lineamenta* state that the Holy Father clearly places this topic at the top of the Church's agenda and speaks of 'the courage to forge new paths'.

There is already at least one new course on the new evangelisation at a seminary in the USA, leading to an STL degree for priests. Will there be many more, and will they include teaching on praying for inner healing in real openness to the Holy Spirit?

The new evangelisation is primarily a spiritual activity capable of recapturing in our times the courage and forcefulness of the first Christians... The goal of the transmission of faith is the realization of a personal encounter with Jesus Christ ... which allows individuals to share in the Son's relationship with His Father and to experience the power of the Holy Spirit.[31]

This is precisely what praying with people for inner healing - accompanied by their ongoing cooperation as they also seek grace through the sacraments, daily prayer and Scripture meditation - is bringing into increasing reality in the lives of people who are desperate for help. It is happening, not through new or complicated schemes or structures, but through God's love flowing between very ordinary people as they listen and pray. It is happening—but only in a few places.

Pope Benedict XVI, speaking in the context of the priority of The New Evangelisation, reflected upon his meeting with twenty thousand World Youth Day volunteers:

> These young people did good, even at a cost, even if it demanded sacrifice simply because it is a wonderful thing to do good, to be there for others. All it needs is the courage to make the leap. Prior to all this is the encounter with Jesus Christ, inflaming us with love for God and for others, and freeing us from seeking our own ego. Finally, I would like to speak to you of one last feature, not to be overlooked, of the spirituality of World Youth Days, namely, joy. Where does it come from? How is it to be explained? Certainly there are many factors at work here. But in my view, the crucial one is this certainty, based on faith: I am wanted; I have a task; I am accepted; I am loved ... Man can only accept himself if he is accepted by another. He needs the other's presence saying to him with more than words: it is good that you exist. Only from the 'you' can the 'I' come into itself. Only if it is accepted can it accept itself. Those who are unloved cannot even love themselves. This sense of being accepted comes in the first instance from other human beings.[32]

The challenge for the Church today is to seek ways in which bishops, priests and lay people can, as one united body, work together in the power of the Holy Spirit to bring Christ's healing and wholeness to people in their church and community through loving, accepting, personal ministry, so as to complete the whole mission given by Christ to give the Good News to all mankind. What channels can be used to enable the love of Christ, through prayer, to heal, restore and bring new freedom and joy? The ministry of Christ's healing has been and is still available to some degree in some churches but, by and large, tends not to be at the heart of the Church. It has more often than not been seen as an optional extra that attracts a certain personality type and is regarded with suspicion, fear or disinterest. The challenge offered to us by Pope Benedict is to find new ways of making this personal encounter with Jesus possible, and to bring prayer for healing and use of the gifts of the Spirit into mainstream church life.

There is a great need for people to come together and pray to discern ways of using what already exists to foster this ministry as well as the courage to try new things, the forging of new paths that the Holy Father describes. These ways are likely to vary appreciably from place to place.

In one city recently, a weekend of teaching which I gave was sufficient to encourage the immediate opening of city centre parish premises one weekday evening and one Saturday each month. People now meet to worship God together, and then pairs of selected people are available to listen to anyone in need and pray with them. Appreciable numbers are coming, but this fast response is likely to owe much to the active welcome by the parish priest and to over thirty years of faithful, persistent prayer by a very small number of people in the city.

In other places where there is ongoing prayer that 'we will be filled with the knowledge of His will and all the understanding the Spirit gives' (Col 1:10), those involved may be led to a variety of further prayerful preparations using various means. Some of the indirect and direct ways which may be considered in different places, as part of the process of helping those chosen by God to become available to offer deep ministry to others, are listed in Appendix 3, together with opportunities to provide actual ministry.

Our journey to know the Lord more intimately, to discover our true selves, to be healed of our brokenness and to help others do the same, is at once a privilege and a challenge. It is not a human work but the work of the Holy Spirit, the encourager and the comforter. He is also the disturber, always gifting us at the right time in the right way if only we are open and deeply committed to Him. May we be all thoroughly and healthily disturbed by Him as He brings us together on the journey into the peace and fullness of life for which Christ died to give us. There is a great need in the Church for what might be called 'holy disturbance'.

Pope Benedict XVI has been acknowledging and discussing the state of the Church and the disturbances and challenges faced by it, in a series of lengthy interviews with journalists beginning in 1985.[33] These challenges have been increasing in recent decades with the growth of secularism and moral relativism. I have recently become reminded of a conversation which I had years ago with a bishop. I remarked that I suspected that more and more of the time of the senior leaders of several churches was being spent reacting to an agenda arising mainly from pressures coming from the world and the devil. This was making it much harder for them to pray and listen together or alone to the Holy Spirit guiding them to respond to His agenda. The bishop agreed that this was true in his experience. In the case of the Catholic Church, these pressures have included, amongst others, changes in moral attitudes, behaviour and expectations in society leading in some cases to government legislation, the scandal of priestly abuse, loss of vocations, climate change and economic crisis.

It is not surprising therefore that in the latest of these interviews in 2010 with Pope Benedict XVI, Peter Seewald concentrated upon questions regarding those matters which have been aired most widely in the media around the world. It was only towards the end of his sixth hour with the Pope that he asked the vital question: 'Jesus does not merely bring a message, He is also the Saviour, the healer. Given this society of ours, which is so broken and unhealthy in so many ways, as we have so often said in this interview, isn't it an especially pressing task of the Church to take extra pains to highlight the offer of salvation contained in the Gospel? Jesus, at any rate, made His disciples strong enough, not just to preach but also to expel demons and to heal.'[34]

The Pope began his reply with 'Yes, that's key.' He went on: 'The really crucial thing is that the Church offers Him. That she opens wide the doors to God and so gives people what they are most waiting for and what can most help them. The Church does this mainly through the great miracle of love, which never stops happening afresh. When people— without earning any profit, without having to do it because it is their job—are motivated by Christ to stand by others and to help them.'[35]

This then is the main challenge for the Church, to pray and work for the power of the Holy Spirit to bring about deep and lasting conversion of more and more of its members, so that they fulfil this mission of loving service given by Christ to bring about true wholeness, freedom and peace to individuals, families and communities, especially in the Western world.

Epilogue

It seems to me that it will not be sufficient to rely upon any means such as:

1. prayerful new local and national initiatives in evangelisation and renewal,

2. learning from and attempting to follow even the most fruitful experiences of others,

3. synods of bishops,

4. meetings of the Pontifical Council for Promoting the New Evangelisation,

5. new Church theology and documents,

to bring about a profound and lasting true metanoia in the hearts and everyday lives of Catholics on any substantial scale in the West. They need far more than this in order to be awoken from their drowsiness so that they long to lead others outside the Church to Christ.

It is going to take a sovereign new outpouring of God's loving power and mercy, following deep and widespread repentance in humble recognition throughout the Church of our spiritual poverty, helplessness and desperate need, and that of all mankind. The dire situation of the whole world will get worse without this, and such a call will never come from elected politicians. The Church needs to accept that of itself it is powerless, in constant deep awareness of the awesome imminent presence of God, and of our total dependence upon the power of the Holy Spirit. It is then that God comes to our aid and makes possible what was previously impossible.

Such a full-hearted and sufficiently widespread repentance and crying out for mercy is only likely to come about if called for by the Holy Father and all the bishops. Perhaps this will happen if sufficient numbers of a faithful remnant, called to be the watchmen on behalf of those who are asleep (Is 62:6), recognise the urgency and intercede deeply and powerfully with humility and love, and with great praise and thanksgiving.

If we do not do this, could we hear Jesus say to us with great sadness, 'On Judgement Day, the people of Nineveh will stand up and accuse you, because they turned from their sins' (Mt 12:41)? The responsibility of the Church is not limited only to its members—'The Church is able, indeed it is obliged, if times and circumstances require it, to initiate action for the benefit of all men, especially of those in need, like works of mercy and similar undertakings'.[36]

Significant Points

- Inner healing prayer ministry is necessary to complement the sacraments.

- Both sacramental graces and charisms are needed to build up the Church.

- Evangelisation should bring about a radical conversion of heart and mind.

- The Church exists in order to evangelise.

- The laity have a vital role in sharing in the salvific mission of the Church.

- That mission involves their using their gifts in helping others in growing wholeness in Christ which leads towards holiness.

- Praying for inner healing is an essential and inescapable part of the mission of evangelisation given to the Church by Christ.

Scripture for Meditation

I ask the God of our Lord Jesus Christ, the glorious Father, to give me the Spirit who will make me wise and reveal God to me, so that I will know Him. I ask that my mind may be opened to see His light, so that I will know what is the hope to which He has called me, how rich are the wonderful blessings He promises His people, and how very great is His power in us who believe. This power working in us is the same as the mighty strength He used when he raised Christ from death and seated Him at His right side in the heavenly world. (Ep 1:17–20).

Testimonies

Testimony 9A

For years I was a Sunday Catholic. My mother was a daily Mass-goer and a very devout Catholic, and would go to 2/3 Masses every day, besides all the other services. She was very strict and very much the boss. My father was a quiet man and kept himself to himself. He was not a Catholic but over the years was constantly pressurised by the parish priest to convert, and it was for the sake of peace that he became a Catholic. I don't think he really understood the Catholic Church. He spent most of his time at the local pub just to keep out of the way. Unfortunately he died of cancer at the age of 56 years.

But God has a plan for each one of us. I was a very rebellious teenager. I never dreamt that the road ahead could ever change and that my concept of God would ever change. From a very early age my concept of God was a God of discipline and punishment. I was constantly in trouble, punished for being late for Church and many trivial reasons. I grew up in an atmosphere of strict discipline, daily Mass, the rosary on our knees every night, benediction, confession etc. I did not I thought have a very happy childhood.

The homilies I listened to applied only in Church, something you heard but did not know how it worked. My constant prayer was, 'O God, what is all this about? Please help me to understand, make me a better Catholic'. So for many years I was a nominal Catholic, a non-believer, one who had not experienced God's love.

So how did this change come about? It is only when you look back in hindsight that you realise the graces and the blessings you receive. I worked for many years and met my husband. I was married in Oxford and settled in a village forty miles from London. Looking back, it was never my intention to be married, but as my circumstances changed and I became pregnant my life took on a whole new meaning. I carried my baby in silence hoping and praying it would go away. After I gave birth to my son my whole attitude began to change. I saw life in an entirely new way. My husband was not a Catholic but he encouraged me to go to Mass. For me the church had no meaning, it was a matter of duty. Within the year my daughter was born and I was very happy with my life.

Every day I would go to the railway station with my children to pick up my husband travelling home from work in London. This particular day he was not on the train so I just thought that he would be on the next train, but I had a very strange feeling inside. I went back to the station a second time but there was still no sign of him. Where could he be, I thought.

An hour or so later there was a knock at the front door and in front of me stood a neighbour and a policeman. He told me my husband had been found dead at his place of work. So within three years my life was shattered; how on earth could I bring up two children on my own, they needed two parents, not one. I found I was making a lot of unrealistic decisions.

I was told by my mother not to tell anybody how my husband had died. In those days to take your own life was to bring shame on the family and was considered a disgrace, a stigma. I felt trapped and I felt I was living a lie. What could I do? I dreaded when somebody would ask, 'How did your husband die?' and I found it easier to say he had had a coronary or that he had had a works accident. For years I prayed, 'Lord, help me, please, Lord, help me'. I never thought God listened to me or heard my prayer.

I was angry with everyone. I was irritated and angry with the children even though I tried very hard not to make the same mistakes as my mother had made bringing us up. When I smiled at people my eyes never lit up. I was spiritually dead. I went to our local church every Sunday. I felt very inadequate. I remember sitting both children on my knee and praying, 'Lord, I cannot possibly bring these children up on my own—you will have to help me'. In my frustration I tried to talk my situation and hateful feelings over with the parish priest, but he told me I needed a psychiatrist, not a priest. I felt hurt and rejected by the Church and by the people.

As time went on both my children made their first Holy Communion and eventually the time came for their Confirmation. I heard the priest talk about a loving God, full of compassion and mercy for His people, spontaneous prayer. I thought I was in a different Church. My God had always punished me. He was a God of discipline. How could he have changed so much? My eyes were beginning to see, my ears were beginning to hear. People began to talk with me. I had been ten years in the parish, but nobody had spoken to me.

Then into the Parish came a group from Ireland. The priest had met them in the Holy Land and invited them to come to the parish to do A Life in the Spirit seminar. After the Confirmation talks this lady invited me to a healing Mass. Out of curiosity I went back the following evening, and it was the laying on of hands for the Holy Spirit to come afresh. People were holding their hands up in the air praising God and they seemed to be so happy. I suddenly felt I wanted to be like them. I prayed, 'Lord, why should I be so miserable and unhappy? Why can't I be like them?' I hadn't a clue about prayer meetings. When the time came to be prayed with I just shrugged my shoulders in agreement. Tears came in abundance, different from ordinary tears.

The following evening I went back to church again and once again this lady said I needed to be prayed with. I had seen people resting in the spirit but I thought that was not for me. Suddenly I was surrounded by a very bright light as I rested in the spirit. The words going round in my mind were, 'Prepare ye the way of the Lord'. It was a road to Damascus experience. I had no idea where the words came from but from that time I was filled with joy. I was happy and I had a great desire to read Scripture, I suddenly had a great desire to go to daily Mass, and I began to say the rosary. I felt a great love and devotion to Our Lady and I just could not explain it. But God was asking me to repent, to go to confession, to conversion. Like Saul, I too had been persecuting God in my way. I had not wanted to be like my mother, a religious fanatic. I had rebelled all my life about being a Catholic, it did not make sense. Now I too began to understand why my mother had a great love of the Mass, and where she received her inner peace.

I began to look forward to Mass, and everything took on a new meaning. I could hear the readings, the Gospels, the homilies. I could not get enough of hearing about God. People started to talk to me and I suddenly found a lot of new friends.

Testimony 9B

My wife and I were married in the early 70's and we have a family of five grown up children. I became a Catholic shortly before our marriage and thought that simply attending Sunday Mass was the expected 'norm' for my faith. By 1976 I had become discouraged and attending Mass became a chore rather than an inspiration.

In the autumn of '76 I experienced an amazing turning point in my life. Without going into too much detail of this astonishing moment of change, I prayed like I had never prayed before. I then realised just how far I was away from what I had professed to be and felt so hypocritical. 'Lord, if you really do exist, then I want to know you and from here on in I give my life to you,' I said in my despondency.

Then it was as if the whole air around me instantaneously solidified with love and acceptance. I felt completely flushed with love. I had never experienced anything like this before. Later that week I was introduced to a priest in the diocese who initially enquired about the experience and then encouraged me to grow in faith. Through his support and encouragement I became more dedicated in faith.

It is now 2005 and I have continued to try my best to grow in prayer, love and faith. For nearly two years now I have been fortunate to receive healing from the Lord through the patient ministry in St. Joseph's Parish, Norton.

Although I had previously been greatly blessed by the Lord, I had not realised or understood, until then, that my life had still been inhibited and restricted by many painful experiences that had scarred my memories, even from very early life. It has also transpired that some behaviours and attitudes could well have been passed down from my ancestors through the generational line and which appear to have caused me distress in other areas of my life. This is still ongoing.

Recently, I experienced a crisis which, through prayer, helped me to understand the origin and root cause of my reaction to the stress of this situation. It was as if the Lord had allowed me to relive these feelings of deep anxiety and relate them to an experience of perceived rejection by my father when I was at the age of about three years old. I fully understand that I am now placing an adult interpretation upon an infantile experience, yet through the careful prayer and discernment of those who listened to me and then prayed for the Lord to heal me, I do feel released from a bond which has been with me for about fifty years. I have also been able to forgive my deceased father (and myself), whereas I doubt whether I could have done this without this support.

I have been healed of the debilitating difficulties in my life through this loving ministry. This process of inner healing has brought me to appreciate and understand that each person's 'journey' is different and that the Lord desires to heal us more than we will ever know or understand. It is a mystery to me. I have been given freedom to be my true self even when I had no idea of how damaged I really was. I have so much to thank God for.

Testimony 9C

I had been married for four years when in 1979 the relationship was beginning to show signs of breaking down. There was little communication between us and many external pressures, including financial problems and the demands of stressful jobs. Although I had always believed in God, for the first time I prayed from my heart, crying out to Him. 'If you really do exist, then please help me, I need you so much'. In response to my heartfelt prayer, I felt the gentle breeze of the Holy Spirit caress my being. I experienced a deep peace and a strong sense that God would always be with me, no matter the difficulties I may encounter. I was elated and enjoyed this 'honeymoon period' with the Lord for a few years. Everything in my spiritual life seemed rosy. I hungered to know God and to love Him. My Catholic faith and my Christian friends became important to me. I was blessed with many consolations and seemed to exist in a 'faith bubble'.

Some years later this bubble burst, and I found myself in a painful and lonely place. I was in a spiritual desert. I felt discouraged, abandoned by God, and gradually many of the props I had relied upon were taken away. Past hurts resurfaced and my mind became flooded with painful memories. I had believed that in coming to know Jesus as my Saviour and Lord all my problems would just melt away and all my inner wounds would be healed. I needed these precious times in the desert to grow and to bear fruit in my spiritual life.

It has been almost thirty-five years since that first real encounter with the living God in 1979. I have sought help and healing from loving Christians who through listening, counselling and prayer ministry have opened the way for me to receive God's healing power in my heart, setting me free to help others. 'The desert will rejoice, and flowers will bloom in the wilderness' (Is 35:1).

Notes

1   *Jesus Is At Work Among Us* (booklet of twenty-nine testimonies, with a foreword by Bishop Ambrose Griffiths), available from the parishes of St Joseph's or English Martyrs and St Peter & Paul, Stockton-on-Tees).

2   *Catechism of the Catholic Church*, 2003.

3   Vatican II, *Lumen Gentium*, 12.

4   J. McManus, *The Healing Power of the Sacraments* (Chawton: Redemptorist Publications, 1984).

5   Vatican II, *Sacrosanctum concilium*, 59.

6   T. Green, *When The Well Runs Dry* (Notre Dame, Indiana: Ave Maria Press, 1979), pp. 78–96; Idem, *Drinking From A Dry Well* (Notre Dame, Indiana: Ave Maria Press, 1990), p. 23.

7   Green, *Drinking From A Dry Well*, p. 23.

8   R. MacMullen, *Christianising The Roman Empire: AD100—400* (New Haven & London: Yale University Press, 1984).

9   Vatican II, *Lumen Gentium*, 8.

10 *Ibid.*

11 *Ibid.*

12 Pope John Paul II, *Memory and Identity: Conversations at the Dawn of a Millenium* (London: Weidenfield and Nicolson, 2005), p. 131.

13 P. Hegy, *Wake Up, Lazarus—On Catholic Renewal* (Bloomington In: iUniverse, Inc, 2011), pp. 3–4, 113–164.

14 *Ibid.*

15 *Ibid.*

16 *Ibid.*

17 Vatican II, *Lumen Gentium*, 33.

18 Pope Paul VI, *Evangelii Nuntiandi*, 27.

19 *Ibid.*, 10.

20 *Ibid.*, 18.

21 *Ibid.*, 9.

22 *Ibid.*, 14.

23 *Ibid.*, 13.

24 *Ibid.*, 21.

25 *Ibid.*, 22.

26 *Catechism of the Catholic Church*, 1428.

27 Vatican II, *Presbyterorum Ordinis*, 9.

28 Pope John Paul II, *Address to the New Communities and Lay Movements* (30 May 1998).

29 Vatican II, *Christus Dominus*, 2.

30 Pope Benedict XVI, *Jesus of Nazareth—Part 1* (London: Bloomsbury Publishing, 2007), pp. 175–177.

31 *Lineamenta* of Synod of Bishops, XIII Ordinary General Assembly, The New Evangelisation for the Transmission of the Christian Faith, 2011.

32 Pope Benedict XVI, *Address to the Roman Curia* (22 December 2011).

33 J. Card. Ratzinger with Vittorio Messori, *The Ratzinger Report—an Exclusive Interview on the State of the Church* (San Francisco: Ignatius Press, 1985).

34 Pope Benedict XVI, *Light of the World—The Pope, the Church and the Signs of the Times* (London: Catholic Truth Society, 2010), pp. 175–176.

35 *Ibid.*

36 Vatican II, *Gaudium et Spes*, 42.

APPENDICES

Appendix 1: Aspects of Inner Healing

Areas of Healing

1. Physical

Inner Healing (these three inter-connect)

2. Psychological: healing of memories, emotions, attitudes and compulsions; becoming free to love and accept oneself.

3. Spiritual: healing of sinfulness through repentance, accepting and giving forgiveness, reconciliation with God and others.

4. Deliverance: being set free from some hold of Satan.

Roots Needing to be Healed

1. From birth to about the age of seven.

2. In the womb; from conception to birth.

3. In past generations of our family

Obstacles to Receiving Inner Healing

- not listening and surrendering to God
- lack of forgiveness (towards others, self, God)
- poor sense of self-worth (true identity in Christ)
- being unable to 'live in the creative house' (Jn 8:31–32) by speaking and thinking positively in the ways that God is doing
- fear of God who is not perceived as a loving Father
- un-repented sin
- unwillingness to face up to repressed or partially repressed feelings and hurts and thereby discover roots which need healing
- not letting go of strongholds and all damaged reactions to past hurts

- subconsciously not wanting to be healed because of challenges and responsibilities which would follow, and to face loss of the attention which present disabilities bring
- influence of Satan

Situations in which we have seen Jesus Heal People through On-going Prayers as they Co-operate with Him:

- marriage problems and breakdown
- depression and manic depression
- rejection: feeling unloved and unwanted
- sexual abuse, incest and rape
- abortion
- unease within homosexuality and lesbianism
- physical abuse, violence, bullying
- addictions
- guilt burdens and guilt complex
- obsessional neuroses and phobias
- anxieties and fears
- bereavements
- lack of unconditional love — performance orientation
- judgements and negative perceptions of parents and others
- distorted perception of God
- feelings repressed: family unable to face them in childhood
- effects of family or own involvement in spiritualism, reiki, fortune-telling, tarot cards or other occult practices
- Christian living with anti-Christian members of own family
- anxieties about our own children
- families with tragic deaths, e.g. suicide
- patterns coming from past generations of family

Appendix 2: Poisons and Scriptural Antidotes

Poison	Antidote
Alcohol Abuse	Ep 5:18; 1 Th 5:6–8; 1 Co 10:12, 13, 31
Anger	Ep 4:26–27; 4:31–32; Jm 1:19–20; Col 3:12–14
Anxiety	Phm 4:6–7; Ps 46
Apathy/Complacency	Jn 3:17, 18, 35, 36; Rev 3:15–16; Rm 3:22–24; 6:22–23
Bereavement	1 Th 4:13–18; Rm 8:38–39
Broken Heartedness	Ps 34:17–18; 147:3
Critical/Judgemental/Bitter	Mt 7:1–5; Heb 12:14–15; Ep 4:32; 1 Co 13:4–7
Despair	2 Co 1:8–11; Ps 55:22; 62:5–8
Distressed/Troubled/Discouraged /Depressed	2 Co 1:3–4, 4:8–9, 16–18; Ps 9:9–10; Rm 8:28–39; Jn 14:1–6
Doubt	Mk 9:17–24; Jn 4:50; 20:24–31; 1 Co 1:18–25
Drug Abuse	2 P 2:19; Rm 13:13–14
Envy/Jealousy	Ga 5:22–26; Jm 3:13–16; Phm 4:12–13
Failure	Heb 4:14–16; Ps 73:26; Jude 24–25
Far From God	Ps 145:17–20; Jm 4:7–10; Ac 17:22–28
Fear	1 Jn 4:18; 2 Tm 1:7
Fear of Circumstances	Mk 4:35–41; Rm 8:28; Ps 139:8–10
Fear of People	Ps 62:5–8; 27:1–3
Fear of the Future	Mt 6:25–34; Ps 23
Friends Fail Us	2 Tm 4:16–18; Lk 17:3–4; Ps 27:10–14
Guilt	Heb 10:17; Col 2:13–14; Jr 31:34; Mi 7:19; Is 43:25
Hatred	1 Jn 2:9–11
Hurt	1 P 5:7; Ps 27:13–14; Heb 12:2–3
Ill/In Pain	Jm 5:14–16; 2 Co 12:9–10; Ps 103:1–5
In Danger	Mk 4:37–41; Ps 91

Poison	Antidote
Inadequacy	1 Co:20–31; 2 Co 12:9–10; Phm 4:12–13
Judging Parents	Ep 6:2
Loneliness	Ps 23; Heb 13:5; Jn 14:15–21; Rev 3:20
Lost/Unwanted	Ps 107:4–9; Lk 15:11–24; 19:10; Heb 13:5–6
Lying	Ep 4:22–25; Rev 21:8
Needing Assurance	Is 40:1–11; 1 Jn 3:19–24
Needing Guidance	Jn 16:12–13; Is 30: 19–21
Needing to be in Control	2 Cor 12:9
Poor Self-Worth	Ps 139
Resentment	2 Tm 2:22–24
Revenge	Rm 12:17–19; 1 Th 5:15
Self-Righteousness	Lk 18:9–14; Ep 2:8–9; Rm 3:9–12, 21–24; Tt 3:3–7
Sexual Immorality	Ga 5:19–24; 1 Th 4:1–8; 1 Co 6:9–10
Shame	1 Jn 2:28
Sleeplessness	Mt 11:28–30; 1 P 5:6–7; Ps 4:8
Sorrowful	Is 61:1–3; Rev 21:1–5
Speaking Negatively	Jn 8:31–32
Stealing	Rm 13:8–10; Ep 4:28; Heb 13:5
Stress/Worry	Mt 6:25–27, 34; 1 P 5:7; Jn 14:1; Phm 4:6–7
Suicidal	1 Cor 10:13, 6:19–20; Ps 34:6; 31:9, 10, 14–16
Tempted	Mt 4:1–10; 1 Co 10:12–13
Unforgiveness	Mt 18:21–22; Mt 6:14–15
Unrepented Sins	Mt 26:28; Jn 8:7–11; Lk 5:32
Weariness	Mt 11:28–30; 2 Co 4:16–18; Phm 4:13; Is 40:28–31

Acknowledgements to the Gideon New Testament and Psalms for some of these.

Appendix 3: Opportunities for Prayers, Healing and Teaching

Liturgical Contexts

- Liturgies with a celebration of the sacrament of Anointing of the Sick
- Masses advertised as 'Healing Masses', followed by individual prayer ministry
- Masses advertised as celebrated for intergenerational healing in families, followed by individual prayer ministry
- Liturgies of the Word, followed by prayers for healing
- Prayer for the healing of the sick during exposition of the Blessed Sacrament
- Prayer for healing following the end of a liturgical service which is not directly related to healing

Non-Liturgical Contexts

- Special meetings for healing ministry, e.g. healing services at parish, deanery or ecumenical level
- Prayer groups meeting at parish, deanery or ecumenical level which include prayer for healing
- ad hoc responses to need, when Christians encounter people in need of prayer for healing
- setting up prayer chains and intercessory prayer for people in need

Opportunities to Share and Learn in Preparation for Possible Involvement

- Inviting speakers and those already involved in the healing ministry to give training workshops or retreats or courses, e.g. at parish or deanery level, or to groups
- teaching by priests in homilies focused on healing and wholeness through prayer
- formation of parish or deanery groups, meeting regularly for teaching, sharing, fellowship and prayer

- Alpha courses
- Life in the Spirit seminars
- Setting up a lending library with relevant books and CDs, etc.

Appendix 4: The Healing Power of Christ

CDs and Tapes by Alan and Betty Guile

1. Healing the whole person

   Praying for healing

   General principles of inner healing

2. Preparing to be channels of God's healing love

   Helping those in depression

3. Performance orientation

   How do we move forward?

4. Bitter root expectancy and judgement

   Marriage problems and their healing

   Healing of homosexual and lesbian persons

5. Healing victims and abusers in sexual abuse

   Deliverance from evil into Christ

6. Introduction

   Healing grief and connecting with Jesus and through Him with the deceased

   Healing of memories and feelings

   Praying by proxy or substitution

   Forgiveness: the choice between enslavement and freedom (Martha Freckleton)

7. Intergenerational healing

   Healing relationships with miscarried, aborted and stillborn babies

8. Healing the addictive personality

   Healing obsessional neurosis

   Prayers for intergenerational healing

9. Desert experience (Betty Guile and Elizabeth Flynn)

   Transformation into Christ

10. Eucharist; a covenant relationship (Fr. Luke Magee, C.P.)

    Scripture meditations

11. How can we work with Christ to bring more inner peace and wholeness to people?

12. The challenge and the need

    Guidelines on praying for inner healing

13. What do you want me to do for you? (Betty McGurk)

    Our call to intimate relationship with the Lord (Betty McGurk)

14. The healing of our soul (Alan and Betty Guile)

    God's loving call to us (Betty McGurk)

15. The offering of ourselves as a living sacrifice at the Eucharist

16. Forgiveness

   • Possible even after murder of a loved one

   • God offering grace to forgive

   • Our choice to be willing to receive the grace

   • Various stages in the process

1–10 and 12, 13 and 14 are talks given at Minsteracres Retreat Centre during six weekends, 1990–1994 and 2000; 11 is of a seminar at St. Joseph's, Norton in 1994 and 15 is three talks given there in 2008

Other CDs available

RETREAT OF THE AMPLEFORTH RENEWAL DAY COMMUNITY

The Briery, Ilkley : 28–30 August, 2009

CD 1   Healing of early roots of every hurt
CD 2   Becoming free to love and accept ourselves
CD 3   Receiving grace to forgive and being given God's love for others
CD 4   Healing our soul through bringing strongholds of damaged reactions to die on the Cross

Appendix 5: List of Some Important Daily Prayers

- Commit myself afresh to Jesus Christ and ask for a fresh infilling of the Holy Spirit so as to be empowered to do the will of God our Father.

- Pray for protection for myself and others dear to me—put on the armour of God (Ep 6).

- Pray for children and others dear to me as Jesus is praying to the Father 1) for repentance 2) that they come to know Jesus as Saviour and Lord 3) that they experience the power of the Holy Spirit in their lives 4) and any other way the Lord may reveal.

- Pray for the grace to forgive 1) others 2) myself 3) God. Ask for God's love for my 'enemies' and pray with God's longing that they may be with me in Heaven.

- Pray to bind myself to the will and truth of God and to the Cross and mind of Christ and to loose and destroy with the authority of Christ the strongholds of my soul. Pray this way also for others as recommended by Liberty Savard.[1]

- Pray for myself to receive God's gift of His infinite love and acceptance for me (Love your neighbour as yourself). Use three steps recommended by Fr Jim McManus in *Healing in the Spirit*[2] to heal lack of self-acceptance and to take away the power which others have had over me; viz: 1) Thank God for the wonder of myself and for the wonder of anyone causing me a problem. 2) Thank God for the good things He is doing in my life and in the life of these others. 3) Make allowance for my own failures asking God's pardon and make allowance for the failures of these others.

- Ask for the grace to live in the creative house (Jn 8:31–32, Jerusalem Bible) speaking and thinking in the way which the Bible shows that God speaks and thinks. Use the authority of Jesus to break the power of any negative words I have spoken or thought.

- Take the authority of Jesus to cut any emotional bonds or soul ties between myself and anyone else. God will not cut the bonds of His love between us but will strengthen them.

Appendix 6: Prayer for the Release of the Holy Spirit

> 'You will receive power when the Holy Spirit comes on you, and
> you will be my witnesses ... to the ends of the earth' (Ac 1:8)

Come Holy Spirit, and baptise me with the fire of your love. I have
surrendered to the best of my ability, and now I want to be filled with
your Spirit. I need your power in my life. Please come, and fill me now.
Lord, I believe that when I surrendered to you as Lord, we became one.
You are the vine, and I am a branch of the vine. All that you are is within
me. My life flows from you. I believe that as I yield and ask, you will
release your strength, wisdom, healing, etc. to meet the needs of the hour.
I yield now to receive your sanctification gifts of Isaiah 11:2: wisdom and
understanding, counsel and might, knowledge and fear of the Lord. I
need these gifts in my life to grow as a Christian. I yield and ask you to
release your manifestation of gifts of service, as listed in 1 Corinthians
12: wisdom, knowledge, faith, healing, miracles, prophecy, discernment,
tongues and interpretation of tongues. I need them to witness to a hurting
world. Only in your power, guided by your Spirit, can my life be fruitful.
Holy Spirit, come. Holy Spirit, come. I want it all, wrapped in the greatest
gift of all: love *'the greatest of these is love'* (1 Co 13:13). Melt me, mould
me, fill me, use me. Give me opportunities to use your gifts to reveal your
love and mercy. Stretch me, Lord. I will not limit your gifts by my
perceptions of what I can handle. Holy Spirit, expand my capacity. Work
in me in a powerful way. I want every purpose God has for my life to be
fulfilled, and I need you, mighty Spirit of God, to bring that purpose to
fulfilment. Come, Holy Spirit, come.

As you flow through me to minister to others, I know that you are
flowing within me to heal my life, too. Thank you for flooding the deep
places of my life with your love. Thank you for washing and cleansing
any wounds or scars from the past that still have the power to dominate
my thoughts and suppress my physical and emotional freedom. Thank
you for bringing light into the shadows and warmth to any cold, dark
rooms in my soul. Compassionate Holy Spirit, thank you for coming and
drawing out the un-cried tears, the unfinished grieving, the pain of loss,
the traumas, the fears, the emotional hurts so painful that they were
'buried alive'. Spirit of Wisdom, thank you for coming into the root cause
of any chronic failures. Gentle Holy Spirit, thank you for walking through
my early years and facing the past with me. Thank you for reminding me

that the love of Jesus was always there, filling in the gap between the love I needed and the love I received. [Thank the Holy Spirit for scanning your life and bringing to mind any hurtful memories that need to be healed. When they surface, say simply, 'Holy Spirit, I surrender that event to you for healing. Thank you for bringing your good out of the hurt (Rm 8:28). Praise you, Jesus'. Let this be an opportunity for a deeper release of the Holy Spirit as more of your emotional life becomes unbound.]

Thank you, Holy Spirit, for your presence with me, flowing freely in me and through me. Thank you for being my friend, my teacher, my comforter, my counsellor, my intercessor, and the giver of extravagant gifts. Thank you especially for *. [Continue thanking Him spontaneously.]

Appendix 7: The Need for Recognised Ministry and Information in the Local Church

The map on the following page shows how far people have travelled for ministry in our home, simply by hearing about it by word-of-mouth. They have come from places as far apart as Holy Island and Haywards Heath, Shrewsbury and Cambridge. There were many more from elsewhere in the UK including Scotland, Wales and Ireland, and even the USA, who came to us for ministry whilst we were away from home, in a retreat centre or on holiday. In some cases there may have been other people in their own locality with a reliable ministry of prayer for inner healing, whether within the Catholic Church or in some other Christian fellowship. However, those in need did not have this information or presumably they would not have travelled such long distances.

Since it has been shown in this book that the ministry of prayer for inner healing is an essential part of evangelisation, each diocese should provide readily available information about those with a recognised ministry in their area through any appropriate means, such as diocesan websites, diocesan directories, information provided to every priest, etc. It would also be helpful if everyone had ready access to all the sources of ministry anywhere in the country, because I have sometimes been asked if I could provide the names of others with a similar ministry in some other area, and I have generally been unable to do so.

Notes

1   L. Savard, *Shattering Your Strongholds* (North Brunswick NJ: Bridge—Logos Publishers, 1992), pp. 139–141.

2   J. McManus, *Healing in the Spirit* (London: Darton, Longman & Todd, 1994), pp. 92–94.

Lightning Source UK Ltd.
Milton Keynes UK
UKOW05f2207060814

236500UK00001B/143/P